James Doran

In the Depths of the First Degree

A Romance of the Battle of Bull Run

James Doran

In the Depths of the First Degree
A Romance of the Battle of Bull Run

ISBN/EAN: 9783744676311

Printed in Europe, USA, Canada, Australia, Japan

Cover: Foto ©Thomas Meinert / pixelio.de

More available books at **www.hansebooks.com**

In the Depths of the First Degree

A ROMANCE

OF

THE BATTLE OF BULL RUN

By James Doran

Author of
"Zanthon," "Our Brother," etc., etc.

The Peter Paul Book Company
Buffalo, New York
MDCCCXCVIII

CONTENTS.

In the Depths of the First Degree

In the Deaths of the First Degree

CHAPTER I.

AN ENEMY TO RECTITUDE.

N THE fourth year of the presidency of James Buchanan, while west winds were heard whispering strange love songs to autumn leaves and the glow of summer was giving place to tints of a darker hue in the heavens and on the earth, a man stood in the face of the morning on an upland north of Omaha, Nebraska, evidently intent on observing the changes in progress on the plain beneath. This man, although not distinguished by characteristics peculiar to eminent men nor endowed with the rectitude of an average citizen, was nevertheless no ordinary individual, although with proper precautions directed toward the adjustment of his dress, he could easily pass unnoticed in a crowd; but his conduct had been reprehensible and his line of life outside the pale of civilization for many years.

In figure he was about the medium height, with shoulders a little contracted and sloping, showing physical signs of age. The round head bent slightly forward on a thick neck must have been erect at an earlier date. The hair worn short, and originally dark, was now mixed with gray, while the diminutive eyes, dark and cunning, indicated in the man treacherous propensities, as well as that they possessed a wolfish cast capable of inspiring terror in a peacefully disposed person if suddenly encountered. Other parts in the facial expression were shaped in proportion to his thickset body: large pug nose, capacious mouth, and retreating chin.

The pallor on his countenance was remarkable, and his ears were flattened out above, making it probable they had, while off his guard, been pressed with a smoothing iron in the hands of an enemy. In addition to these suggestive signs he wore a scowling aspect, as if menaced by some impending danger or difficulty. The lower jaw would fall heavily at times, showing his senses were shocked by some fearful vision.

Sounds indicative of pain or distress broke through his lips like the whimpering of a lower animal or an insane person ; and he would walk at intervals on a line east and west, retracing his steps to the point from which he had started, in the manner of beasts in a menagerie.

It was only during the present year he had come up regularly to this elevated place from the base of the slope about two hundred yards distant where his rude cottage was situated, the better to make observations in accordance with his thoughts ; but people imagined his object might be speculation in land or business of some sort. No such idea, however, influenced his movements or touched the darkness of his soul.

However questionable it may appear, it was nevertheless true that he was in the presence of the beautiful in nature, yet knew it not. He did not note the sunshine of the morning nor the Missouri River winding southward like a serpentine thread of bullion flanked by patches of dark green wood or low brush. Neither did he observe the great plains to the right, nor the hills and valleys of Iowa to the left, nor the flickering light among the taller trees that invaded the deep shade in fantastic dances. He did not perceive the birds of bright plumage which shot arrows of light through the air as they whirled before the sun, nor the rich haze that enveloped the distant landscape in a splendor such as ideal minds associate with fairy tales.

His gaze was fixed on the transformations taking place in Omaha. He appeared to be terrorized at the approach of progress as witnessed in the fast growing city.

This circumstantial evidence in his case will indicate to some extent the true character of the man, even before the statement of his earlier history is perused by the reader. He was a criminal who had compromised with the law for his freedom, and became a resident of this place in early days so as to avoid society. As a matter of course, he lived under an assumed name, but the record of his birth showed he had been called Hamilton Hitch.

The Hitch family resided in one of the Eastern states in the suburbs of a large city, and were very respectable as well as wealthy people. Hamilton's aunts, three in number, were sterling ladies, leading members of good society and highly esteemed for their intelligence and genial manners, while the individuals of his own family stood, in public estimation, above reproach.

Up to the age of fourteen he attended school with fair educational results. At that time he was residing in the home of his uncle, having been encouraged to study for the ministry, the eminent profession of his friend and kinsman.

Suddenly it became known that the young student was afflicted with kleptomania, an unconquerable desire to steal. It may well be imagined what consternation this discovery created among his friends. It seemed inexplicable. His wants and requirements had been supplied in every conceivable manner. Luxury surrounded him. Companionship, friendship, and love were his in abundance. Even fame was about to be thrust upon him gratuitously. All these acquisitions, acquired or in perspective, he rejected for the low-bred propensity of theft. As far as known, his operations were first confined to the valuables of his uncle and aunts, but when this field gave out he turned in on their acquaintances.

When the case came up in the household of the Hitches for examination, and Hamilton was upbraided for his criminal propensities, he lied in answering the charges preferred against him, thus exhibiting another detestable habit. Of course, it was easy to find the truth and prove beyond a doubt that he was guilty, seeing the number of thefts he had committed as well as that much of the stolen goods was found in his bedroom or on his person.

When every suspicion or hope of his innocence had given place to the certainty of crime perpetrated with deliberation and premeditation on his part, the grief of his relations knew no bounds. They expostulated, prayed, threatened; they reminded him of his duties in life as well as what he owed themselves. Then they promised him extraordinary gifts if he would only reform: all his former deeds would be forgiven and they would love him with a greater display of feeling than ever before. This was not all.

He was kept on trial or probation for six months, his friends hoping for reformation. It did not come. Nothing appeared capable of moving him towards goodness. He made no effort whatever to control his criminal disposition, but practiced it as heretofore. It appeared to be a fascination from which he could not be separated — a link in a chain binding him to a course of evil forever.

The liability of his conduct to entail disgrace on innocent individuals of high social standing in his family became more menacing to them in its attitude than the appearance of a cyclone or a plague. With them there was grief on the one hand but prudence in the interests of honor on the other. After mature deliberation it was determined to protect themselves by heroic methods, regardless of personal feelings.

Hamilton Hitch was invited one evening by a friend of the family to accompany him to Boston on the night train, and upon their arrival there was given in charge to the captain of a ship bound for a long voyage, with instructions to have the young man work before the mast until he became an able seaman.

The boy understood the movement thoroughly and the causes leading to its enactment. He made no complaint of any kind. It was characteristic of him to be reticent, to continue in a mood called by some people "a dogged silence," so as to avoid giving a clue to his inner thoughts. This was the only wisdom he seemed to possess. So tenaciously did he adhere to it that his favorite school companions knew nothing of his evil inclination during the whole period of their association with him, and when told the rumors of his fate they would not give them credence, like generous little men.

At home, all traces of the boy's existence were carefully removed, his books, clothing, and playthings burned, and his name forbidden to be mentioned among his friends. ·

Thus were created two items as sources of human sorrow — the criminal abroad and the memory of him at home — one bringing chastisement to the body, the other misery to the soul.

Hamilton Hitch adapted himself to his new position as best he could, working in the rigging among ropes and clip hooks or aloft in the shrouds, sometimes in the slush of the sea on deck, filling his allotted time of two hours on and four off through all kinds of weather, day and night. There were no means of shirking his duty, or utility in opposing the will of the skipper, his commander. He soon learned to avoid the blow of chastisement from a rope's end or the butt of a belaying pin. What he suffered no one noticed, what he felt no one knew.

Whether the recollection of his fond mother's solicitude for his welfare haunted his thoughts or that he yearned to be again in the fields and woods of his boyhood days, there appeared no evidence either in his words or deeds. It was only known that, when his ship returned, he left her and sought in the slums of great cities the indulgence of his ruling passion, theft. His identity became lost in the darkness of crime and the oblivion which encompasses degradation.

He fled before civilization like the shadow of the earth before the sun, as something that would interrupt the course of his existence and destroy the fascination on which his mind eternally feasted.

His tussle with the law which then confronted him became terrific. The struggle for supremacy or immunity from punishment while pursuing criminal practices was great and persistent. He fought like a desperate man imbued with the idea that the battle, being for his own interests, should be maintained to the end with all the power available.

The instinct of evil in him, gifted with subtle energy and strategic devices, stood up before justice only to fall in ignominy at its feet. In his ignorance of truth, he felt like one stricken with lightning. The petty schemes concocted by his false reasoning vanished when he was most in need of help, like icicles in the rays of the sun.

To the excitement of his habits there were added hardship and punishment as well as defeat. He became familiar with wretched clothing and scanty fare, the scowls of an unrelenting public, the stubborn watchfulness and opposition of the police, the vitiated atmosphere prevailing in places where criminals sought concealment, the loathsomeness of prison cells and the harsh, uncompromising shock of hard labor. Shame, regret, honor, and decency deserted him. No peace, no moiety of happiness or contentment or sunshine of the heart ever was his. If he were not afflicted with the dread of being captured, he felt the shackles on his arms, or the hustling of the officers running him to jail, or the stare of the people while he stood in the criminals' dock, or the dreadful society of the chain gang !

To him, the bright world, fashioned to be beautiful by the eternal powers and supported by an invisible counterpoise, was dark. His thoughts regarded humanity as an enemy to be attacked on sight and pilfered without remorse.

Notwithstanding successive periods of imprisonment, he still held on in his course, believing there was as much merit or glory in his profession as that of him who betrays his trust in society and escapes the consequences. Besides, he desired to graduate through all the degrees of it from petty thief to highwayman where murder is associated with robbery. It may be said that he went through his curriculum as contemplated ; but, after a practice of twenty years as a professional thief, he found his health very much impaired and himself behind prison bars with the prospect of paying the penalty of his crimes on the gallows.

In the last act, he had aimed too high. The glory he anticipated had come, but with it a certainty of untimely death. In company with a chosen band of robbers, he had attacked the traveling equipage of a rich merchant who was conveying his family to his country home. What fol- lowed was atrocious in the extreme. The good people were murdered, and the perpetrators of the crime, except- ing Hamilton Hitch, escaped.

The case attracted widespread attention and commotion. Large rewards were offered for the apprehension of the other criminals. As there appeared some fear that they might escape, a detective suggested to the prisoner that he could save his neck by revealing the names of the members of the gang with whom he had been identified in this last murderous transaction.

It was a tempting offer, and, when duly considered, Ham- ilton Hitch, yielding to the importunities of the prompter, gave such information as brought his associates to execu- tion, thus satisfying the law and the people. The com- promise, however, while granting him liberty, imposed cer- tain conditions which he must strictly observe.

The place of his sojourn would be recorded and com- municated to the local police or other authorities in his vicinity so as to establish a kind of guarantee that he was living out of mischief. He must leave the state and on no

account commit crime in future, as he was merely a criminal enjoying leave of absence on good behavior; otherwise
he would be prosecuted and his former career exposed so
as to militate against his case and secure his condemnation.

This important turning point in his life convinced him
conclusively that his game against the law had been played
with a losing hand; but at the same time it did not induce
him to espouse rectitude. Oh, no! His own reflections
on the subject decided that although beaten he was not
conquered to such extent as to be forced to renounce his
principles, whatever their character. If the muzzling
process prevented him from biting, he might bark with
impunity. Deprived of the rights and privileges of a
robber, he could be a cynic. If he could no longer
appropriate the coin of other people for his own use, it
would be possible to reach out and assail character without
interruption or fear of civil statute. Like Lucifer, he could
design evil over and above the constituted powers.

Hence when he crossed the Missouri to seek a hiding
place among the paths of the beasts and the homes of the
birds in the beautiful territory of Nebraska, his record was
filed in the breast pocket of the sheriff and his heart
charged with malice against the human race.

It was thought he possessed some wealth; and the supposition seemed well founded, for he followed no regular
trade or business, yet possessed ample means of support.

As land was cheap in those days, he purchased five acres
for a trifling sum of money and erected on the margin of
it a cabin for a home. It was not that he desired to be the
owner of real estate even to the extent here named, but
there was nothing less for sale in the market at the time.
Then he took a wife whose history need not be written on

these pages. She became the mother of one chiid, a boy whom she called Danderton, and tended to his wants until he was ten years of age, when she died. From this time forward, father and son lived with the inconveniences and rough habits of backwoodsmen.

In view of their house there grew up a village with its main street of tunnel-like stores, its roadway disfigured by gulleys and ruts, its sidewalks dilapidated, and the signs above the doors capable of oscillating on rusty hinges in the wind. While this primitive evidence of man's ability for design remained a trading post, it was tolerable to Hamilton Hitch; but when, in the course of time, it acquired new strength and began to assume metropolitan airs in pushing its limits far beyond the last outposts of his boundary fence, he became visibly distressed. Then labor and capital rolled in and set industry in motion. Every improvement troubled him.

At the time of his introduction here, when his age must have been about fifty-eight or fifty-nine years, his dissatisfaction exceeded all bounds. Not only was the evidence of human progress displayed before him in the opening of new streets, the construction of large brick buildings, and the influx of strangers, but wild rumors were afloat that a transcontinental railroad would actually pass through the place and Omaha become a great city!

It was singular that what contributed unbounded pleasure to every other citizen in the community should inflict punishment on him. The invisible power struck him with a golden rod, causing as deep a wound as if it had been iron. Nor did it appear that the increase in the value of his own property served to mitigate his mental hardship. His vitiated imagination conjured up a strange supposition that the eternal powers connected with the affairs of mankind were operating against him purposely with the view of effecting his utter extirpation, and had stimulated the present work in Omaha in order to deprive him of his resting place.

Habitual reference to such thoughts made him despondent even while the sunshine shed its glory on the spot where he stood, as if some fiend from the illimitable depths of darkness maliciously touched his spirit with concentrated fright. It was evident he was tortured by irrepressible anguish such as admits of little or no relief.

The savage retreat he had instituted for himself would soon be wholly obliterated and its obscurity illuminated by the light of progressive industry. This would necessitate a transfer of his record further west—into mountain caves or the society of rocks, perhaps.

If he were to remain in Omaha, many newcomers, ignorant of his true character, would invade his residence and intrude on his attention with their undesirable presence. He would hear again the platitude of the fool and the boasting of the vainglorious clown. He would be called pioneer, trapper, squire, or mossback, according to the temper of the crowd. The daily routine of society would again surround him with its hypocritical show of virtue to cover the deformity of vice, its pretense of friendship exercised in behalf of self-interest, and its false love fleeing like a meteor that appears for an instant and is gone.

Must he reverse the instincts which guided him heretofore to follow such examples of rectitude? Oh, no, no! not by the most minute sign imaginable! He would show the true color of what was in him by adhering fast to his preferences, and war—mentally, at least—against the industrial and moral efforts of the human race.

In this attitude he was not alone. If his fate was to exist in the shadow of civilization, it must be admitted there was a large number of persons coming under the same category in civilized countries. They opposed law, and in their ignorance advocated measures which, if carried out, would overturn justice and all good principles as known to man. There was a sprinkling of them everywhere, from the halls of legislation to the inner circle of secret conclaves where the restoration of chaos was contemplated.

If he relaxed any of his intentions, it must be in favor of his son's advancement, whose career would probably be directed into different ways from that of his own. Perhaps it might be possible to live within society and yet be the thing he always was! Others did likewise! The smile passing over his features at these thoughts seemed cast in a mold of the bottomless pit. He drew in the air through the side of his mouth with a whistling noise as he descended the upland to his home intent on a conference with his son on their future situation and prospects, a subject discussed on several previous occasions.

CHAPTER II.

FOUR CARDINAL POINTS.

DANDERTON HITCH, the son of Hamilton, was bred with evil influences. As a boy, he sought to emulate his father in those characteristics which had made the latter notorious in the records of criminal proceedings heretofore noticed, but was energetically and persistently restrained from pursuing this course as if his moral training had been committed into the hands of the most exemplary character in the township.

This action on the part of his parent proved the variety of motives that may be adduced in support of any particular case as well as the resources of circumstances. It was not that Hamilton Hitch loved right and hated wrong like his own parents, but that he had resolved, if possible, his son Danderton should not suffer the severity of prison discipline which had given such a deep and lasting impression to his own mind. Hence every aspiration of the father for his son, mental and physical, resolved itself into this single admonition, 'Keep him out of jail.'

It is true some of Danderton's petty thefts from emigrant trains were unknown to the authorities or his father; but whenever the boy was found disturbing the peace of the village or doing any mischief liable to bring him under the notice of the constable, the man invariably came forward and offered restitution or compensation for the injury, trespass, or offense complained of, so as to keep public opinion in a favorable mood towards his son.

As the boy grew, the desire for criminal practice ceased to a minimum under the nature of his surroundings, showing he possessed no taint of kleptomania and that hereditary transmission did not hold good in his case. Therefore when he reached maturity he was not hopelessly and absolutely committed to the perpetration of wrong-doing.

His struggle to imitate the conduct of other men as factors of everyday life proved fairly successful, and many persons, newcomers, thought him a good fellow. Besides his efforts at appearances, there was an internal monitor urging him to adopt good principles on their own account; and there were moments when his young head and heart turned suddenly in that direction, as if he yearned to espouse them or were in search of other channels of self-gratification than the pursuit of perversity alone.

On such occasions, gleams of delight that startled him into mute wonder flitted across his mind. These promptings grew up side by side with his other propensities and strengthened with his years until he began to make suggestions that alarmed the father, relating to a position in good society. While his education had been neglected, the aptitude he displayed for the retention of knowledge impelled him to seek information of value from every person he met, and in this way increased considerably the amount collected at the day school in the village, which he had attended some time. His language, too, was carefully studied by imitation, so that, hearing him discourse on the questions of the day, one would imagine he was a professor of metaphysics endowed with the ability of deducing new facts from chaos that would revolutionize the world !

The power most wanting in him appeared to be an incapacity for discriminating between good and evil. He did not know, and it seemed he did not care to know, one from the other so long as he committed no overt act whose effect would place him in jeopardy with the law.

During his schooldays, he was taught technicalities for the most part, to the exclusion of principles, and therefore was not, perhaps, solely responsible for the deficiencies referred to here.

As the father entered the house on the memorable occasion mentioned at the close of the last chapter, Danderton's look of recognition was clear and intellectual, with a certain amount of proud self-confidence in it that persons usually exhibit when conscious of possessing individual power.

He was now a man above the average in strength, with broad features and large limbs. His height reached six feet two, and the massiveness of his chest appeared conspicuous. There were some minor deformities in his person : one of the shoulders seemed higher than its fellow ; while his eyes, when poising to observe an object, trembled in their sockets, on account of a permanent nervous disorder or defect connected with the orbital attachments. The countenance was not prepossessing, but the figure might be accounted straight. A dark color displayed itself on his appearance. The hair glossy black like an Indian's, the skin tawny, the eyes brown, and the eyebrows heavy and black. His dress was neat, and altogether Danderton Hitch looked like a young man of the times.

The elder man's harsh, complaining voice was first heard, although at certain periods he insinuated a modulating roll into it that sounded strangely musical. He said :

" Those Eastern people mean to settle down here, it seems to me."

" What of it, old man ? " returned Danderton, good-humoredly.

" We'll be disturbed. I don't want so many fools near me, I can tell you. The idea that this western country will ever be filled or amount to shucks is all buncombe. There's nothing on the earth here or in it that I can see. If they hunt antelope, they will find it a poor paying job."

" They ain't going to hunt antelope."

" No. I suppose they'll pry open other people's business and nose around to find something wrong with old settlers."

"I think," replied Danderton seriously, "we have no reason to fear either disturbance or misfortune, no matter how many come into the place. I rather believe it will be better for us, as real estate is booming, and your property is sure to fetch you a tidy sum."

"Aye, but the old record is there," said the man with bitterness. "Money is good enough in its way, but—"

He stopped suddenly, not knowing how to qualify his words or what he was about to say. After a little reflection he proceeded :

"I never paid any attention to the prospect of gaining money here. I believed there was nothing in it. The amount secured formerly proved enough for our wants, with a trifle left to keep the wolf from the door. It would be strange if my investment in this piece of land should prove as successful as that of other men—*I*, the hound that was hunted !—*I*, the black sheep that had no rest until chained in solitude, and then nothing better than reflection that pierced my heart like a lance ! I hated society in former times and I hate it yet for its meddlesome ways and foolish aspirations after superiority that cannot exist. We'll be run out of here to make room for low trash coming in to try their hands at progress. Such humbug ! They cannot induce me to take that in if I know myself — not much."

"We shall stay right here all the same," remarked Danderton quietly.

"I want no law, or church, or society, or neighbors around me," said the father in a voice filled with the bitter sarcasm of malignity and despair.

"You are amusing this morning," returned Danderton with a smile, "but you may change the program when I explain the situation as I see it. If we put on appearances like half the world, we can get along as right as a fiddle without the least notice. While you act inside the law, you may be as good as the next man. The people who have come to look for homes or employment will never hunt up your past history. That you may rely on."

"Do you mean we ought to make a show of being religious, charitable, and just, loving the law, and all that?"

"No, not to the extent you mention. Let us be plain citizens, join the crowd in city affairs, and take our chances with them. There's policy in it, if nothing else."

The scowl on the face of the father darkened, and his eyes emitted the fire of a villainous look as he answered the suggestions of his son.

"I never will. I'll be the thing I am, straight. I have taken my choice of sides, boy, long ago. It is too late to turn back."

Still unmoved by the acrimony of the man, Danderton . pleaded for the predominance of his plans with the deliberation of a skilled diplomatist. He resumed:

"Something must be done to meet the changes in the times. We cannot remain stationary as heretofore. I must go into business, sure, or travel. No more delay is admissible in our case. I have been studying for quite a while on certain things which I shall reveal to you now, because the time for doing so has come."

"What things?"

"I may call them four cardinal points, as they relate to you and me individually and collectively, or are designed to meet our wants at present and in the future."

"Ah! but the record is still there that nothing can erase," said Hamilton Hitch.

"Hang the record! What's the matter with it, anyway?
Now hear me.

"The first point is all under the head of appearances.
We must build a house with modern improvements, furnish
it according to the ideas held by people in good society,
dress ourselves in broadcloth, pull on dandy boots and silk
hats, and show ourselves on the streets either as business
men or speculators anxious to advance the prosperity or
well-being of the city. Your property is now as valuable as
any here, and therefore we can command as much money
as we may require by the sale of a small portion of it.
Why, dad, some of us may be selected to run for the
mayoralty!"

The semblance of a smile flitted across the father's face
at the hopeful tenor of the young man's views. Danderton
continued:

"You need not be troubled much, because I shall do the
working part. All in the world I want is the assistance of
your approval, and I promise you will be satisfied."

"I ain't in it, boy. Any acquaintance with the people
must end in trouble. I'll keep out of danger as long as I
can. If I saw a lady carrying her purse in her hand as a
kind of show-card, I would be tempted to touch her
forcibly on the elbow so as to make her hand powerless,
when she would drop the valuable receptacle; and in the
confusion I could, of course, make it mine. My plan is
best: where there is trouble, steer clear of it."

Danderton straightened himself for a new effort. The
shadow of a malicious thought passed over his features.
He looked at his father for an instant, calculating, no
doubt, the effect of his words, as he said:

"You hanker too much after the one thing. Why not

take something new for a change? For instance, you might operate against the people in other ways than robbery. If you hate 'em, I shall place you in a position where you may strike to your heart's content and yet be accounted guiltless. It is possible to live on the borders of crime and get the support of a large part of public opinion. There are thousands at the game.''

The man started. He opened his mouth — not to speak, but in wonder that such a condition mentioned by the son could possibly exist. The strange prospect smote the center of his intelligence with peculiar force, bringing out of it a gleam of his favorite ambition. Nothing would suit him better than a place where he could work injury to his fellow man with impunity. He glanced at his son as if inviting a continuation of the subject. Danderton continued:

"On the pretense of being right, advise the people to do wrong. There are many who do not know how to judge for themselves. Manufacture the worst lies imaginable, but maintain they are your opinions, and claim the right to express them where you please. They cannot be worse than what other fools say, even on public questions. Be a little careful not to go too far on this line, unless you are attached to a party, when it will be understood that money or place is your real object and not a desire to reach the truth, and your associates will back you under the obligation of by-laws or political fellowship. Encourage workingmen to acts of violence on the grounds that you are their friend and that they have been deprived of their rights, which they should recover in the way prescribed. The disturbance will cripple industry, and bring poverty to the doors of honest men. Suppress the truth or misrepresent it; afterwards it can only be said you did the best you could under the circumstances. Distort the news until it becomes sensational; in the meantime it may cause widespread failure or calamity. Defend criminals and defame virtue whenever possible without stirring up public censure. Advocate the impossible, so that men and women may pursue it and fail, catching in their struggles at the belief that there is no good at all in human life. Malign the character of men in public offices, by insinuation if not directly; it will be supposed you are endeavoring to purify the political atmosphere and restore good government. Do all this on the grounds of being a magnanimous person wholly interested in the elevation of the human race, and you will not only be admired, but have a large following whose members will swear you are a true representative of the people's rights!''

The eyes of the father kindled with enthusiasm. The harsh lines of obstinacy worn heretofore on his features became softer as he gazed in astonishment at his son, admiring evidently the indication presented in the foregoing speech of his talent for crime such as might make him in time the counterpart of himself.

After further reflection he said:

"Danderton, that beats me. I reckoned an expert thief ahead of everybody; but I guess I'm away back.''

Seeing the success gained over his father's stubbornness, the young man resumed his discourse with the dictatorial voice of a master.

"You stopped the law against yourself and thought it a great feat, but I can use worse implements than yours under cover of its wings and make it work with me. The trouble in your past life was this: you did not know enough to

be thoroughly bad. You were too honest — mere greenhorn. Hypocrisy should have been added to the desire
for robbery and murder, and smooth-faced sycophancy
that deludes the unsuspecting and smothers golden-haired
judgment. You should have denounced goodness wherever
it appeared, and vilified innocence until public opinion, so
far as possible, reckoned it on a par with infamy. Why,
dad, you were a noble fellow compared with men I
have met who held society by the ears at their pleasure.
Now, in order to comply with my program, we
must join one of the parties contending for power in the
United States. There is a demand for outspoken words,
whether right or wrong, that should be turned to our
advantage. We might talk back, for instance, to the men
who want slavery abolished, and get pay as well as protection for it. To do this and be on the safe side, there
is but one way of working that I can see. It is the second
undertaking I wish you to approve."

"What is it, Danderton?"

"Start a newspaper. There is money and money's
worth in it, besides what I mentioned. The discontented
classes will follow us to a man if we be sure and pander to
their prejudices. Society is so much disturbed — that is, all
classes of people — we may recommend the most extravagant
schemes and get plenty of backing for them. I tell you, dad,
our times are coming. Give growlers lots of rope. Instead
of leading, we shall follow. Play with men's ideas until
they imagine they are capable of overturning the world.
They will believe everything you tell them while under the
influence of flattery, and will spend the last dollar in their
possession to help the business and never think we were to
blame, whatever happens."

The smile on the father's face gradually disappeared, and the lower jaw fell with a snap, as if his feelings were engrossed by the marvelous in an unusual manner, like one looking into a pit where wild beasts were making preparation to fight.   He glanced furtively around, searching for something which his son understood to signify ability sufficient to maintain the journal contemplated.

Danderton continued :

"I'll manage things.   If we need talent, there is lots of it coming in here that can be employed for trifling pay. The job office in connection with the paper will cover expenses and give the people an idea that we own a large and important establishment. As for ourselves individually, I shall write editorials, while you will be the literary editor, confining your duties principally to review notes on new books and rehashing other men's opinions on the subject."

Hamilton Hitch made no reply to these extraordinary propositions of his son, but he laughed like one tickled by a combination of pain and pleasure, the echoes being so unnatural as to startle even Danderton by their peculiarity.

"You will have to deal with a class of people that are easily duped," said the son.   "As a rule, none of them will strike back if you say disparaging things of their works, and you will be sustained by the law guaranteeing the freedom of the press."

"Ah! that is substantial," said the father eagerly, and he continued :

"We may squeeze the writers of books at our pleasure, damn their works in the eyes of the public, terrorize them into bribery, goad them to commit breaches of the peace or suicide, and yet be reckoned in line with one of the great institutions of the country. For me, this is a glorious prospect."

" It is a mere item in the case," remarked Danderton.

" There is inequality in it," returned the father. "Nothing could suit me better than the control of power over persons who have not the means or the ways of retaliating except they brave the stern arm of the law, under which we shall be sheltered."

"The privileges, moreover, will bring you many other benefits," resumed Danderton. "Good writers will make it a point, on this account, to praise you as one capable of leading in literature and of promulgating ideas tending to secure the prosperity of the state and nation. You shall have eulogies of your genius, real or imaginary, published in the state magazine, embellished with your portrait, side by side with the best people in the West."

" Danderton ! Danderton !" exclaimed the father, trembling with excitement, "don't go too far, boy ; remember the record."

"You make me tired," said the young man hastily. "Some people don't know what's good for them. Wait until I finish. We require neither a certificate of qualification nor permit, license, or any document guaranteeing honest services to the public on our part. Even recommendations from qualified persons will be out of place, because, in a country where it is held that all men are equal, our claim to equality cannot be questioned to any effect. Buy the outfit and cut away at everything in sight. Time will bring you fame. People shall talk of your cleverness as something above the average. Under the spell imposed by terror, you can creep along until even you yourself will come to believe that you know something.

Attend public meetings, walk across the platform like a person making the first movements of a dance, smile at the audience, keep your mouth shut so as to hide your deficiencies. It will then be believed for sure you are brilliant, and everything in politics will be opened to your advances."

With this forecast of a great future, Hamilton Hitch was not yet satisfied. There appeared to be an unsurmountable obstacle lying directly in the way, which his mind's eye clearly discerned. Over his pale features a faint smile flitted, and his voice became melancholy in tone as he said :

" You are a good boy, Danderton. The hopes you have inspired in me are great and good, considering my circumstances, but there is one thing, my boy, you have forgotten. I cannot write. I could not compose or dictate a review to save my life."

" Is that all ? " queried the son, laughing loudly so as to emphasize his merriment. " Why, dad, you need not write or read anything. Get somebody else to do it for you until your hand is in. Give your own opinions ; no matter how extravagant they be, they will pass. You can string a few sentences together so indefinite in meaning that the latter part may contradict the first, and still be accounted wise ! The notes will be anonymous. Become a compiler. Take up the history of men and rewrite them in your own way ; it will make you imagine you are an author."

Hamilton Hitch was silent. He sighed as he reflected on some incidents of his career which had been enacted under a false conception of the world and the methods employed in human life to delude the great, struggling, paying public. Then he asked :

" Is that the way they manage, Danderton ? "

"Never you mind what other people do. It will be our way when we come to it," replied the son.

The preliminary discourse on prospective journalism having terminated in a satisfactory manner to both men, Danderton introduced another cardinal subject, equally interesting, if not far more dangerous, than the one just quitted. In doing so, he lowered his voice and glanced around to see that no strangers were in sight.

."Now, we must get heeled better than we have been heretofore." This referred to weapons of defense. "You must not suppose I'll scare up danger without preparing to meet it, for one never knows how the temper of these Western people may be turned against you, whether good or bad. That ain't like me, I can tell you. I have been feeling my way carefully in regard to our method of defense in case of attack, and there is this about it, revolvers ain't enough, nor shotguns."

"Daggers?" suggested the father.

"Pshaw!" responded Danderton, "these may be good enough on occasions when your enemy is near and off his guard, but what I have in view is far above any of the old methods or means of taking life, and the beauty of it is this, it's sure."

At this juncture the father became eagerly attentive. He bent forward, assuming a listening attitude, lest a word even of the discourse should escape him.

Danderton continued:

"With a little more information, which I can easily obtain, we shall be in a position to meet all persons showing us a hostile front. Listen! Take it into your head. We'll blow 'em up."

"Blow 'em up, Danderton!"

" Aye."

" How, my good boy?"

" Some new explosive recently discovered.   It is said to be at least a hundred times more powerful than gunpowder. Of course, we could do great things with it ; we might terrorize a whole community."

The father rubbed his hands with intense delight, while his laugh became sharp like the whine of an animal, so much did his personality submit to the anticipation of controlling a great power.

Danderton resumed :

" Speaking for myself, I know nothing outside of gunpowder, but there is a man living on the other side of the river who gets the credit of being able to post me.   I'll try him, although not acquainted, but I'll pay for what I get if nothing else will do."

" Be cautious, my son; remember we are not as free as others."

" Now, pap," said Danderton, as, rising from his seat, he began pacing the floor of the apartment like one suffering from some intense feeling, " the last question to be discussed is the greatest.   I may fall in your estimation according to the way you reckon things when you hear the case, but don't be hard on me.   I want to get married when our new house is completed."

The elder man bent his gaze to the floor with the gravity peculiar to *good* men as he answered :

" No objection, Danderton, but you need not be told twice it is hard to choose a wife.   I'm prejudiced against women in general ; I own up to it like a little man.   If you fall in with a handsome one, mind what I say, it will lay you out as flat as a flounder."

"Lay me out!"

"Yes. Bung you up. Scotch you. Drive your manly spirit out of your body and bring the balance to blue ruin."

"Then I assure you, old man, there is a poor prospect in front of me."

"You have located the game already!" returned the father, with a forced laugh.

"I don't deny it, nor would you under similar circumstances. The lady I dream of is without doubt the handsomest woman in the territory."

The father groaned, on hearing this declaration, like a person stricken by lightning. His pale face became white, and his hands trembled while clutching at his knees — an effort made to relieve the nervous attack by which he was evidently afflicted. He said, with resignation in his words and deportment:

"Go on."

"She is there," continued Danderton, pointing with his finger towards a residence in the neighborhood of the cottage.

"Here!" said the father, raising his hand in the same direction. Danderton nodded, signifying his assent.

"The daughter of our neighbor?" inquired the father.

"Yes, dad, the same, and don't you forget it."

"Have you been speaking to her?"

"No. I went it blind so far."

"Is it gone the length that you love the woman, Danderton?"

"I plead guilty to the charge, pap."

"Has she encouraged you?"

"Not much; not at all."

" You love her as if she lived in the clouds. Have not even heard her tongue or know whether it is mild or clattering."

" That is about the lay of it."

" My poor boy, you are lost !"

" Ah, shucks !" he exclaimed. " What has got into you? Won't things be changed when they're changed ?"

Without noticing the force or incongruity of this sentence, the father resumed :

" She is reckoned the best lady in this section, while you are the worst scalawag."

" I guess I knew it years ago."

" She is handsome, but you are out of plumb."

" The defects of my body will only add interest to my suit. Some people like the spice of ugliness mixed up with their ideas of beauty. Perhaps she may turn out to be one of that class. Men are not always rejected on account of ill looks."

" Her daddy is rich, and you have nothing except you get it from me."

" I can earn my own living, if I like; besides, if I get her, I'll come in for her money, anyway."

" The people would cry out against the marriage."

" By what right, sir ?"

" Meddlesomeness, perhaps."

" They won't dare to, if they know what's good for them."

" What makes you think she would have you? Are you crazy ?"

" I'll take my chances, like anybody else. I'll tell you one thing — if she consented to be my wife, I would become good. Mark that. I'll follow her to the ends of the earth, no matter where located. If she desires it, I'll pray, throw money into the poor box, help to make collections for the minister, and believe every word he says whether true or false."

"Ah!" exclaimed Hamilton Hitch, with a long drawl, speaking to vacancy. "How well I knew of the curse that follows a nice face on a woman! I could swear to it any time without help. This misfortune will discount all our projects, if there was a million of them."

"My sakes!" remarked Danderton, excitedly. "I see nothing in it to call for such opposition from you. I imagined it would not be wise to marry a character like myself."

"Wouldn't it, though? What else is good for you? Like should have like. It don't need learning to know that much. I am as much in favor of your marrying as the newspaper business, but I swear I hate to see you go and make a fool of yourself on account of a handsome face. Don't you see you'll get fooled?"

Danderton, whose pride was wounded by this language, went into a towering passion. He stormed through the apartment in a manner that precludes the possibility of recording his words in these pages, so terrible and obnoxious were their significance. On the other hand, the father endeavored to temper his own fury by advice tending to avert the threatened danger. Like an angry sea under the hurricane, his sarcastic bitterness of expression arose or fell according to the intensity of feeling embodied in his son's remarks. Indignant protestations of the son clashed with fiery repartee from the father. The air became charged with evil specters, emanating from the deathlike pallor of the men's faces, the fierce glances, the distorted laugh, and the tempestuous repetition of blasphemous words. The walls reverberated with the horror of infamous affirmation and negation. It was a struggle between two giant spirits whose souls had previously been saturated with iniquity, until they were qualified to be reckoned the followers of the Prince of Darkness. The contention ended in favor of Danderton, who positively held the position that he was competent to judge for himself, and unless conceded this privilege would quit his home and the society of his father forever.

CHAPTER III.

IN THE TOILS OF LOVE.

THE feelings held by Danderton Hitch for his neighbor's daughter, Grace Finnestare, resembled platonic love in some features only. The intensity of admiration and fascination was there without the desire of self-sacrifice for the loved object peculiar to the condition when genuine. He loved her for *himself*, not for *herself*. This kind of affection becomes dangerous under disappointment. Although living outside the society in which she moved, yet he believed it possible to win her, favored by circumstances, perhaps, and time, two items that so frequently and forcibly induce women to accept companionship otherwise distasteful to them.

Besides these considerations, however, he nurtured her image in his mind until he began to be troubled with unrest day and night. A mysterious power seemed to have entered his person, which controlled his heart, his will, and intellect without opposition, as if his faculties had been suppressed or were incapable any longer of independent action. Still, during his reasoning moments, while cogitating on the question of his mental condition, he made no effort to institute a change favoring relief. This indicated he was spellbound.

In the past he only caught a sight of her at long intervals, but now the routine of his life favored the sustenance of his daydream, for his father had conceded the utility of his propositions and granted him full power to launch into public business with all the appearances and auxiliary forces which he could possibly employ. While superintending the construction of their new residence, Finnestare's place was constantly in view. His glances at the external appearance of the domicile had a soothing effect on his troubled imagination and brought a kind of happy humor to the surface of his thoughts, like men who smile at their own faces in a mirror, believing them to be the most perfect on earth.

Finnestare's residence was only a few hundred feet south of his own, on the opposite, or west, side of the street. It was a portly house, surrounded by rare shrubs and fruit trees where humming birds sometimes flitted in summer; and the verdure within the boundary picket fence, contrasted with the ancient appearance of the dwelling, made the scene exceedingly attractive. The space occupied in the manner here mentioned was only a block, but to Danderton it appeared more valuable than the whole of Omaha. Here in this abode lived Grace Finnestare, whose beauty had inspired him, not alone with love; but ambition to be great, and for whose sake he had threatened to espouse righteousness in opposition to the will of his father. It seemed odd that the old-fashioned roof and faded walls assisted to deepen his passion whenever he gazed lovingly at them, yet it was true. The smoke from the chimney stack, as it ascended skyward on calm evenings, or bent to the breeze, possessed peculiar charms for his heart that contributed to make up the sum of his affection or affliction. If he could have seen the atmosphere even which encompassed the situation, he would have loved it.

All the details respecting the construction of the Finnestare dwelling were familiar to his memory, as far as could be gleaned from early settlers — how Finnestare offered no opposition to the builder respecting the quaint gables of his design or the plain windows and overlapping weatherboarding instead of rustic, so long as the walls would be well braced, the studding of unusual strength, and the spaces large so as to provide an ample amount of air for the occupants.

Under the joint management of these two improvised architects the domicile grew to completion — a two-story structure of twelve apartments, angular and barn-like; and when the material of which it was composed had suffered deterioration through climatic exposure, it looked far older to the mind's eye and the physical eye than the actual years of its existence would determine.

The fulness of Danderton's ecstasy, however, appeared when occasionally he beheld the object of his love at an upper window or among the flowers near the house in all the glory of youth and beauty.

At the time to which reference is here made, Grace Finnestare was twenty. Sensible and sedate, her refinement sparkled with the vigor of a crystal fountain. The light-colored hair, done up in the fashion of the American

girl of the period, seemed to have been burnished by a
sunbeam in Nature's own hands. The face was classically
regular, of the old Grecian type of comeliness, with the
cheeks tinted vermillion color and the brown eyes lumin-
ous with luster. Her eyelashes were long and dark, while
the coloring of the eyebrows harmonized with that of her
silky tresses. In stature she was tall and graceful, the lines
bounding the head, shoulders, and arms forming exquisite
curves, which, taken in connection with the proportions
observable in the entire figure, made them exponents of
fascination far-reaching in their influence over susceptible
hearts.

The father, known to the community as Judge Finnestare,
was one of the early settlers on the Nebraska side of the
Missouri River, who became wealthy as a consequence of
careful management and wise investments. He was of
French extraction and related to Laramie, a trapper who at
an early date penetrated to the foot of the Rocky Mountains and slew buffalo without assistance from his people or
permit from the red man, but was himself slain by Arapahoe
Indians on the head waters of the river bearing his name.
Finnestare knew other celebrated men of the plains —
Sublette, Campbell, Bridger, Kiplin, and Sabille.

Incidentally it may be mentioned that he was not an
adept in law, nor did he hold any position during his life
justifying a claim to the title of judge. In fact, this honorable appellation was given him gratuitously by the people
to mark their appreciation of his wisdom and general conduct as a good citizen. As seen now, at his introduction,
he appeared to be at least seventy years of age. The white
hair and beard carefully tended were impressively remark-

able above his blue clothes, which fitted his figure comfortably and admirably.

He was not a large man, but activity had made his body firm and healthy. The erect position assumed in former years had disappeared, and in its place there came the curved vertebral column, attenuated hands, and the lessening of energy peculiar to old age. No one could turn away from him, however, without noticing the pleasing expression overspreading his countenance, or fail to recognize the bright gleam of penetrating intelligence in his eyes.

There was hope for the world at large while this good man and his daughter lived in innocence, and industriously untainted by the example of their neighbors, and indeed, almost wholly ignorant of their character. Standing on this ground, the one family adjoining the other, like day and night or the calm appearance of a rock-bound coast before the angry waves, the universal law above and the common law on earth kept them separated and distinctive.

Besides dealing in real estate, Judge Finnestare transacted a banking business. Originally a small concern in a downtown store, established as much for the accomodation of his friends of the village as an institution from which large personal gains might be realized, it had recently become so important as a depository and exchange that the profits derived from it were considerable.

Finnestare's wife had been dead many years, but father and daughter, clinging closely to the observances of sociability, good breeding, and respectable citizenship, entertained the best people in Omaha. Their set included a large number of pioneer families, with many of the newcomers, good, honest folk, having plenty of means,

fully alive to the necessities of the times and the obligation of preserving straight, wholesome law among them.

In times past, when Danderton Hitch sought low resorts
for entertainment, society at the Finnestares' never troubled
him; but when wealth crowded in upon his life, bringing
with it dreams of love, conquest, and future happiness, he
turned his attention to the assemblies of this upper
stratum of humanity with a longing desire to be in their
midst.   Then the keen pangs of disappointment smote him
to the heart, and he felt how terrible it was to be ostracised
by public opinion.   He saw the visitors enter the Finnestare home, heard the laughter and the music surging
through the windows day after day and night after night,
while he prowled around the angles of the fence in the
darkness, like a wolf disturbed by some voracious fancy.

Still, his hopes grew with time and the new era, which
had produced such abundant resources for him and his
father.   He became bold occasionally while viewing the
scene where his love resided, and asserted within himself
that, if necessary, he would shatter or destroy anything or
everything that intervened between him and her.   Yet he
made no attempt to gain a formal introduction or procure
access to the house on any pretense, calculating, no doubt,
that the auspicious moment had not arrived.

He saw the old-fashioned make-up of the Finnestare
residence become like a dear friend in his thoughts, but he
deferred approaching nearer to it than the fence, guided
by some mysterious agent in league with the powers controlling the destinies of man.

How absolute would be his satisfaction had he beheld
the interior, with its cleanliness and decorative append-
ages, the cosy corners and easy-chairs, the sweet-scented

bedrooms, the olive and buff-colored walls, the dining room with roses peeping in at the windows, the pictures of Western landscapes, and the large living room on the ground floor where society was entertained. Further, if he had seen Grace Finnestare at the piano, and heard her voice in the song, "Find me a heart that truly loves," he would have slept over it with such ecstacy as pervades the individuality of a lion when at rest among the fragrant shrubs of the deep wood.

Besides the persons and items mentioned in connection with the history of the Finnestares, a few others came under the notice of Danderton, whose influence went to make up the sum of his distress.

As Grace was an only child, her father, with paternal solicitude for her welfare, employed a lady capable of acting in the double capacity of cicerone and domestic, or housekeeper. This person proved to be very efficient, trustworthy, and honest in all her dealings. She was small in figure, with a pert-looking face, well shaped, neatly dressed in black, being a widow about forty years of age, and was known by the name of Madam Gloriana. She had lived with the Finnestares for years, and was content. Quick in her movements, gifted with rare discernment, full of exquisite designs in the management of the household affairs, she exercised much influence over all persons of her acquaintance. In places where she appeared, consistent with her duties, order prevailed. The family breakfast table, with its white cloth and glistening furniture, was delightful to behold. The perfume of flowers and fragrant leaves which pervaded the place around it made up a kind of relish that created a new zest for the morning meal. Her superintendence of the culinary department gave complete satisfaction. Nothing escaped her critical eye. Every nook, corner, and apartment in the house also gave evidence of her care and watchfulness. The glass in the old windows resembled crystal, the carpets appeared new, and the woodwork sent forth a glow as if it had just come from the hands of the polisher.

Madam Gloriana seemed to possess the power of ubiquity. Hearing her voice in the kitchen, you turned in the opposite direction, and, lo, she was in view. Enter the parlor, and the rustling of a skirt indicated she was near at hand. Raise a window on the outside and look into the interior of the house, her little lace cap and white apron blocked a part of the perspective. Try to gain access to the boudoir of Grace Finnestare, and her cicerone, with her bright smile and penetrating glance, was encountered face to face. Her voice, too, sharp but musical, was frequently heard directing the work of the colored woman, the servant, whose answers came in deep, guttural tones not unpleasantly to the ear, bringing with them her version of the housekeeper's name, "Mis' Goleyann."

Danderton soon recognized the importance of the position held by Madam Gloriana. She was mixed up in his thoughts to such extent that his glances at her, when they met in the street, or now while he was busy passing and repassing to his new house, indicated deep feeling, if not love.

She imagined she read his heart aright through the corner of her eye, and wondered how it was that her plain face and black dress could engage the attention of this young sport, whose instincts were supposed to be directed to louder colors. Madam Gloriana, with all her acuteness of penetration, failed to solve the mystery. Danderton's love was merely reflected on her like the manner of its solicitude for the old fence around the residence of Grace Finnestare or the quaint chimney stack. There was an index of sentiment and love visible in his countenance, surely, but they were of a secondary kind and did not contemplate fulfillment with her.

In like manner he felt a growing interest in the movements of the colored woman above mentioned, whose name was Felice. Although opposed to the freedom of slaves, he did not regard this woman's liberty in an unfavorable light, nor her color even, which approached ebony, for the matter of that. This was one of the good things wrought by the charm under which he labored, besides magnifying the focus of his senses. What could be more surprising than that the faded handkerchief, worn as a turban around her head, and the straight skirt, colorless, without flounce or frill, should excite his admiration as much, perhaps, as if they were select paintings from the great masters? When Felice, who was over fifty years of age, and dumpy-shaped, toddled on the road to market, Danderton viewed the display of dust raised by such action with greater pleasure than if it contained gold; and when she disappeared within the house at her return, some valuable item of satisfaction seemed to have deserted him.

He could not fathom the design of nature in this case. It appeared cruelly intent on foisting irrational or meaningless factors into the foreground of his imagination, where he had calculated on seeing only one loved object. Why could it not stop at that instead of contriving to collect a host of things, each of which endeavored to make common cause against his heart? It was evident the bur-

den of his cares grew heavy in proportion to the amount
of thought bestowed upon it and must soon become insupportable, unless made light by some subtle means of relief.

On reflection, he determined to arrange for a consultation with the man beyond the river, who had been already
booked for an interview on explosives. This person, reputed
to be an adept in the knowledge of fulminates, must know
how to cure a shattered heart, or at least devise means of
preserving it from total disintegration. In modern times
it was not unreasonable to connect the uncertain issue of
love in any particular case with powder, dormant or active.
It would be useless, he imagined, to refer the matter to
his father, whose sneering answers would do nothing but
aggravate his sufferings. He knew young men sometimes
sought information on love affairs, and in any case consultation had been the method by which he had obtained
most of the knowledge in his possession. Hence he would
lay his heart open to this man on the same terms as those
contemplated for his other scheme.

Grace Finnestare knew little or nothing of Danderton's
pretenses or passion for her. She had seen him scrutinizing the premises and the inmates of it, herself included,
but, like the others, was unable to determine his real
object. From all that could be gathered as evidence from
physical signs, she imagined Madam Gloriana might be
the person desired, and from the conversation that ensued
one evening in front of the living room at Finnestare's,
it would be fair to conclude that the little housekeeper
believed this also, although not favoring it.

It was the half hour before the arrival of visitors, when
Felice, having completed the labor of dish-washing in the
kitchen, came through the reception room to the front

door for the purpose of inhaling the evening air, always fragrant at that point, and, seeing Miss Grace and Madam Gloriana seated in a rustic chair in the vicinity, folded her arms crosswise on her breast and tilted her head a little to one side as preparatory measures to her taking part in the conversation conducted by the two ladies aforesaid — a privilege accorded her on all such occasions.

Madam Gloriana was saying :

" Oh, Mees Grace, he looks at me so," referring to Danderton.

" No doubt he admires your petite form and oval face," responded the lady.

" Ah ! but why, Mees Grace, why should he ? My good husband that is dead would never believe I marry again. Don't I show the sign ? My dress is black, and I mind my own affair."

" It is hard to understand men's likes and dislikes. It seems reasonably certain you are the object of his admiration. You might begin to wear second mourning as a reminder to him that you appreciate his taste," said Grace Finnestare, with a merry twinkle in her eye.

" Never, Mees Grace, never."

" He is building a fine home for somebody, and the prospect of wealth and distinction before him is favorable."

" Ah, ma dear child, you are too young yet to know men. Riches don't do all, nor fine houses. I fear him, Mees Grace, and I would not have you think of him either, on any account. I fear him. He has a wicked look in his eye, and his shoulder is too threatening."

Whatever ideas Grace Finnestare entertained of the

variety of Danderton's fancies, she made no attempt to dis-
close them at the present discussion.

Madam Gloriana continued, turning to the Negro
woman :

"Does Meester Danderton Hitch, that's building the
new house out there, ever look at *you*, Felice?"

"I's, Mis' Goleyann! dis nigger, dis ol' porpus?"

"Yes, Felice."

"Lor' bless yo' heart, no. Nebber seed me, nohow
more nor a dead possum in de canebrake."

"Who is he looking after, Felice, when he looks at the
house?"

"Golly! seed nobody with the house in front of him.
But now dat I's tinkin', I notis' de odder day dat he tuk a
mighty long look at dat big basket I was totin' along, but
I jes' walked 'long an' 'peared like I nebber seed him, foh
our folks don't notis no sich po' white trash."

Madam Gloriana looked at Grace significantly, and
said :

"You see, ma dear, even Felice understands the kind of
genteelman he is. I do not know the word you call it in
Eenglish."

"Intuitiveness, perhaps?"

"Ah, yes, ma dear, intuiteevness. She know it by her
feelings. See, I will ask her. How do you know, Felice,
he is not a ver' fine genteelman?"

"How dis ol' F'lice know *dat*, Mis Goleyann? Fink I
don' know quality when I sees 'em? Bin too long in
Massa Finnestare's fam'ly not to see de dif'rence 'tween
quality and po' white trash. Don't like de way he blinks
his eyes, nohow. Who you s'pose he's buildin' dat big
house foh, Miss Grace?"

"Why, for himself and his father, I suppose, Felice, and perhaps he intends to get married."

"Can't get no lady round dese parts. Nebber seed him keep comp'ny, nohow. Wha's dere manners an' bringin' up, when dey sta'es at pussons like dey nebber seed high-tone folks afore? Don' you tink dey shows what dey is, Mis' Goleyann?"

"Ah, yes, Felice, you have the right deescernmen'. I have remark before, ma dear Mees Grace, that they have not quite the proper way, though, of course, we may mak' a meestake about it, because they are not like our own many friend and acquaintance."

At this time some visitors were seen approaching, and the conversation ceased.

CHAPTER IV.

THE UTILITY OF PREVARICATION.

THE man beyond the river, referred to by Danderton Hitch as a person well qualified to render him assistance in overcoming his present difficulties, was named Crow Whifton, a dealer in trifles. His residence and place of business occupied an angle of two crossroads where Council Bluffs is now situated, about four miles northeast of Omaha. The roads in question came in directions from the southeast and northeast respectively, having several tributary highways joining them in their courses, and, after crossing at the point here indicated, stretched obliquely towards Nebraska, seeking the great westerly routes on that territory.

In selecting the situation Whifton entertained a keen perception of the profits to be derived from a traffic with the people engaged in moving to the West, usually distracted from their habitual caution by the soothing influences of new scenes or effervescent enthusiasm. As a matter of course, he did not calculate on the realization of a fortune or even large profits; but, apart from the amount that might be considered sufficient gain, he entertained an insatiable desire for that kind of trade — a peddling and swapping propensity which he could never overcome. With narrow views, his ambition had been proportionately stunted, nature, no doubt, having molded both attachments within a diminutive compass in order to bring them into conformity with his physical structure, which was decidedly dwarfish and effeminate. On this account, perhaps, he avoided the principal overland highway located further south, fearing his utter extirpation should he be found anywhere near its gigantic lines. Where twenty thousand people, including Russians, Mormons, Jews, and other foreign and native tribes of white men, as well as hostile Indians frequently in pursuit of them, and inferior animals to correspond, passed in one day, it was a wise policy to give such public road a wide berth. If the dust raised by Ali Baba and his forty thieves, thought Whifton, appeared terrible when seen in the distance, what must be the magnitude of the earthy commotion kicked up by these motley crowds eager to breathe the invigorating breezes of the Pacific Ocean? Hence, after a full investigation of the subject, he had determined when leaving his native state in New England to content himself with the prospect on an unpretentious tributary road, where thieves would find little to sustain their occupation and party strife be the least possible feature of the situation.

Nor did he neglect to secure other means of safety afforded by the laws of the state, after his arrival in Council Bluffs. He made the acquaintance of the sheriff of the county, the justice of the peace, the night watchman in Omaha, and the constable at that place, who carried neither badge nor baton to distinguish him from an ordinary civilian. This was considerable backing for a frail, single man against the possibility of Indian raids or marauders of the white species; and, being one of the class of odd characters who pass through great dangers unknowingly and are often found in places where brave men fear to tread, he seemed to think, in the present case, that this spot was as safe as the shadow of the police headquarters in his native town.

As previously mentioned, Crow Whifton was a little man. Lean in body, pigeon-breasted, with dark hair and complexion, the conformation of the ridge-like protuberance in front being also observable on the upper part of his mouth, where the two incisor teeth formed an angle having the apex outward, as if it had been intended by the powers concerned in his creation to run a small mountain range over the entire median line of the body. The fashion of the times gave tacit recognition to the cut of his coat, a black frock with long tails, pants and vest to match; but carelessness and frontier life left them sadly bespattered with grease spots and dust without disturbing the serenity of the wearer's mind. Above these disfigured habiliments he wore an uncommonly large hat, hard in the grain, round topped, and broad leaved, but fitting his head comfortably on account of extra material placed inside the lining band so as to narrow the aperture to the required size. His dainty feet were incased in boots with thin soles, the beveled edges resembling those on dancing shoes or turned pumps; but in consequence of their legs being nearly as wide as the lower parts of his pantaloons, he was obliged to shake each of them in turn after rising from a seat, in order to force the latter garment into proper position. This he did generally with a good-humored smile on his features, which made people who saw him imagine he had suddenly heard the sounds of distant music and was preparing to start off on a Highland fling.

It was pleasant to meet him in conversation, on account of his agreeable manner and the quaint appearance of his long, earnest face, ready at all times to exhibit a humorous expression. Though appearing solemn ordinarily, his bursts of tittering laughter were quite frequent, showing the light nature of his thoughts and the aptitude in him for sudden transitions from the meditative to the mirthful mood. His manner was also distinguished by another peculiarity worthy of notice. If, from any want of power, his jovial nature failed to assert itself at the proper moment, he manufactured for the occasion what people call a *forced* laugh, taking the usual risks as to whether his action proved satisfactory or otherwise. It is doubtful in which of the two characters he appeared more interesting — the one while showing the gravity of a rook, or the other the gayety of a sparrow. His power of mimicry was uncommonly high, and only needed cultivation to make him a stage light in the absence of stars.

The store in which the speculative ingenuity of this interesting specimen of humanity found vent was of primitive design and construction, built of rough lumber, the dimensions being about twelve by fifteen feet with an apartment in the rear utilized as a dwelling place. This inner circle, or rectangular space, of domestic accommodation was no great model of exquisite taste in regard to furniture or art decorations, although something of the kind was attempted by the occupant with the articles in his possession.

A rudely constructed bed stood in one corner, covered by a patchwork comforter, a rare design showing in detail the flags of all nations in their regular colors. A bolster, round and capacious, with ends protruding on each side, resembled the nosebag commonly used in feeding horses, as if the head accustomed to roll upon it during the slumbers of the night was as large as that of the Cardiff giant instead of Whifton's little cranium. In the center of the room appeared a small table, two and a half by four feet, flanked by a couple of hard-bottomed chairs; and near the head of it was a stove calculated to accommodate, in flush times, a frying pan and teakettle, as well as afford heat to the entire establishment during the cold season, while the door between the business and living apartments remained open. The walls were covered with clippings from newspapers, exhibiting descriptions of political discussions, scientific lectures, humorous anecdotes, accounts of executions, and pictures of famous men or noted criminals; but a miniature bust of Washington had been placed on a shelf in a conspicuous position so as to convince the incidental visitor, or, indeed, the world at large, of Whifton's patriotism and love for the truly great American household god whom it represented.

Egress from the room was attainable either by a door

leading into the store or by one on the west side, and light by means of a four-paned window opposite, which had coiled above it a blue blind with a yellow tassel. On an upper shelf near the ceiling there had been deposited a collection of miscellaneous articles for safe keeping, whose identity became known only when the owner took down each in turn to examine its character and take comfort from the memories thereby awakened.

Like two other houses in the vicinity, the gable of the Whifton establishment could be readily seen from the public highway, with a sign bearing the legend "Hardware and Notions," a phrase difficult to interpret, especially by the foreign immigrant, who had no notion whatever of its far-reaching significance. It must have appeared strange, also, why this man did not offer his wares for sale in Omaha, but they knew not of Whifton's intention of taking the trade before reaching competition at that point.

Besides an assortment of minor articles of the character indicated by his signboard, he carried a stock of goods manufactured by the Indians, such as purses decorated with colored beads, slippers, workbaskets, pouches, and other trifles, which travelers readily purchased as souvenirs of their journey. He had also society badges, cards, dominoes, prayer books, watch charms, oraculums, and almanacs.

Living here a few years content with his small profits, the current of his sober thoughts was suddenly changed on hearing in Omaha how it was contemplated sending a line of railroad across the continent through that village and that the great western highway would be discontinued for the more expeditious one trodden by the iron horse. Although fearing notoriety and the inconveniences generally encountered in a crowd, he gradually became reconciled to the prospect of this inevitable change and resolved to await its coming with all the consequences following its advance.

When the evidence of progress, or prosperity, began to appear on every side, and the influx of strangers made business lively, so that even the small coffers of the wayside store became periodically full of coin, his ideas underwent still further modifications, threatening to make him altogether a different man from the individual· known some years before as Whifton. From being purse-proud he began to entertain thoughts of future greatness. Ambition was developed in him simultaneously with avarice, which clutched at his soul.

It was noticed at this time that he stood more erect than formerly, puffed out his breast in an elaborate curve that even surprised himself, and shook his boots with the pride of one destined to reach a great future. Down in the depths of his mind aspirations nourished by a vivid imagination took root and began to grow. He had never held a public office ; but now, in this new country, where the light of success had so signally brightened his way, he would move upward in the social scale of society and make position a stepping-stone to permanent preferment and perhaps to distinction. Gads! how he laughed at the idea! In the first place, he would speculate on becoming a deputy sheriff, and, after acquiring fame in that capacity, go forward for county clerk or inspector of Indian reservations. He could inspect anything well enough, he thought.

Reflections on these important phases of his future

career, however, were insignificant compared to one standing nearer his heart. Whenever he thought of it, his eyes twinkled with peculiar luster, a tinge of bloom came into his cheeks, and he felt himself rise on the tops of his boots, as if nature through forcible circumstances was persuading him to assume a taller attitude. Oh! how secretly did he revolve that golden hallucination in his mind during long, dreary hours alone, while the night came over the bluffs of Iowa and bent its ear to the western sea across the great plains of Nebraska! He was not young, having passed the meridian of thirty-five; but many a man began the real enjoyment of life at a much later date, and the hope of his future acquisitions strengthened him in the belief of acquiring what he desired. No one would suspect him of folly or improvidence, but, above all, nobody imagined him in love, and yet this was his condition. He loved Judge Finnestare's daughter, of Omaha, on sight, without calculating the chances or the consequences! This was his daydream.

It was singular the possibility of a refusal never entered his mind; and, what was still more surprising, he formed no definite plan for the accomplishment or realization of his wishes in this respect. He was mentally active, but passive in action. Like Danderton, he loved the lady in secret, but postponed the time of declaring his passion, through cowardice or some unaccountable fascination peculiar to cases of this nature. In his loneliness he had been comforted by the bright vision the thoughts of her invoked, like a bankrupt merchant who hopes to rectify his financial embarrassment sometime, when his ship comes in, although having none at sea. The ideal proved so exquisitely endearing that it almost filled the whole measure

of his expectations. It is certain if the reality was presented to him, if Grace Finnestare came to his door with
a notification that the minister was awaiting their presence
in church with the view of uniting them in the holy bonds
of matrimony, he, Crow Whifton, would beat a precipitate retreat through the back door and abandon the country
altogether, so strange are the vagaries of nature in her
sweet moods on minds too weak to carry the burden of
her favors.

One night after closing the store, as Whifton sat in his
antique apartment meditating on the several gradations of
opulence through which he was destined to pass in the
future, some person knocked on the side door for admission. Believing it to be an acquaintance who frequently
came to converse with him at that hour, he promptly invited the visitor to come in. Responding to this invitation,
there stood in the doorway not the neighborly form of his
friend, however, but the tall figure of a man whose face
was concealed by the collar of his overcoat and the leaf of
a slouched hat drawn closely over his brow, and who
entered and seated himself without being asked, with as
much deliberation as if the place were his own.

In an instant Whifton concluded that the stranger's
object, calling in such guise, was robbery, and began to
sum up, with the rapidity peculiar to distressed minds in
such cases, the several methods and means of defense at
his command. To begin with, his revolver was just then
under the counter of the store and could not be reached
without exciting suspicion of his intention; the cane
sword brought from the East lay snugly confined in the
bottom of his trunk under the bed; the butcher knife
which served for all kinds of carving had been lent that

afternoon to a neighbor who needed the implement for the purpose of dressing a hog ; and his razor was on the high shelf and could not be made available without the aid of a stepladder.   Hence, to all intents and purposes, he was at the mercy of this intruder, whose mien betokened uncommon strength of will, and who doubtless carried concealed weapons for forcing obedience to his desires.

The newcomer, observing the expression of fear on Whifton's face, hastened to explain the nature of his business.

"I want a little information on a few subjects," he said. "People tell me you are as well posted in many ways as a scholar, and I thought I would drop in and hear what you could do for me."

This fair speech almost disarmed Whifton of evil thoughts regarding the stranger.   He felt flattered on account of the confidence reposed in him as a man of knowledge, which coincided exactly with his own estimate of himself, yet the man's muffled face and sinister aspect drove him back into the first position held respecting his character; namely, that there was danger associated with his presence then and there.   He answered:

"It is nice of you to think so.   I can assure you the people in the East felt that my coming in here was a dead loss to them.   However, by the bye, I thought I saw you pass my place a few days ago; so many are on the move now that we cannot place them."

The stranger paid no attention to this hint to reveal himself.   He merely resumed the delivery of what he intended saying in the first place.

"I shall pay you for your advice as I would a doctor or a lawyer.   Now, the first question is of a delicate nature. It is this: how can a man approach the lady he loves so as to make her understand the feelings he entertains for her?"

Whifton's heart began to palpitate violently on hearing this unexpected announcement, for it called up in his own mind exactly what he desired most to know. However, instead of making reply, he allowed the gravity of his countenance to assert itself thoroughly, and, assuming a listening attitude, waited the stranger's further interrogatories.

"Would it be wise to send her a deputy?" asked the stranger.

"No, sir; that would give the matter away," said Whifton. "Besides, in ninety-nine cases out of a hundred the deputy would make love to her himself."

"Do you recommend saluting her in public or winking an eye at her as she passes, so as to have her understand you were up to something?"

"By no means; the boldness of such acting might give her the impression you were a mere bummer without means or character."

"How do you regard walking in front of her with a manly swagger?"

"In a favorable light; although, if the swagger is very much put on, she might believe you were a fool. Now tell me," continued Whifton, "are you the man in love?"

"Yes."

"Does the lady of your affection reside anywhere in the neighborhood?"

The stranger raised the forefinger of his left hand and pointed in the direction of Omaha.

"Ah! I understand," said Whifton, while an unusual pallor overspread his countenance as if he had been seized by a death sickness. "It is the banker's daughter, no doubt?"

"You are correct," replied the stranger promptly, although no name had been mentioned. Whifton resumed in a weak voice:

"The Judge?"— to which the other replied:

"The same."

"Do you meet her in society?"

"No."

"You are not even acquaintances?"

"No."

"You love her in secret, but hope to get her somehow?"

"That is it."

Whifton said something to himself in an undertone, but presently straightened up in a cheerful manner before asking the next question. Then, as he spoke, he bent forward towards his companion.

"Have you a rival?" he inquired.

"I guess not," answered the man gruffly, and he added: "I would not tolerate one."

"You'd make it hot for him?"

"You bet."

After some reflection Whifton said:

"If I were you, I would not be afraid of the rival, but of a third man."

"There ain't no rival or third man, I tell you," answered the stranger in an angry voice.

Whifton raised his hand impressively as if counseling peace, while he resumed:

"Don't be deceived; there is always a third man in such cases, a kind of dark horse that gets in between the other two. It is really so."

"But where is the second man?" inquired the stranger boldly.

"Ah! I suppose — I believe — I think you are right — where is he?" stammered Whifton, unable to make out a clear sentence with his mind engaged in connecting his own personality with the second man.

"Hearing the case as I have stated it," said the stranger, "what would you advise?"

Whifton, assuming an air of importance, as if already on the bench, answered:

"Wait, be patient, do nothing to disturb the object of your love, and keep a sharp lookout for the coming of the third man. Mark my words, it never fails."

The stranger seemed inclined to regard this decision as a joke, for he laughed incredulously, like one making a virtue of necessity, and then began the introduction of his second subject.

"You understand how to mix substances in order to produce a combination that will explode?"

"I *did* know something of the kind," said Whifton evasively, "but I don't think I do now."

On hearing this, the mirth of the strange guest acquired a mocking tone such as smote his companion's heart with dread; and Whifton, following, executed some sounds of forced merriment that were palpably at variance with the genuine article.

"I have heard of your pleasant manner, too," continued the man. "It is handy, somehow, when a fellow ain't in a hurry; but take a friend's advice—don't trifle with *me*. When I want a thing, I want it sure."

This language changed the aspect of the subject under discussion at once. Whifton saw he must give the information desired or suffer the consequences of refusal, and he thought an instant on all that such knowledge involved. His reflections astounded him; for if Grace Finnestare refused the man, as, of course, she would, he might be driven to commit some fearful act of violence. In the dilemma here presented, Whifton called to mind an advice given by his grandfather in early life which was worthy of trial. " My boy," said he, " whenever you find yourself in a tight place, prevaricate, and never mind what people say to the contrary." With this purpose in view the little storekeeper answered, assuming a serious countenance:

" Oh! of course, we'll talk it over among ourselves. Isn't gunpowder lively enough for you?"

The last sentence finished with a laugh, but the stranger did not seem to have been moved in a similar manner; he replied:

" It ain't strong enough. People know it on sight. It's hard to carry around, and to blow it off requires a lighted fuse, or, if in a weapon, a percussion cap. I'm in search of something a small quantity of which would rip a brick or stone building from garret to cellar in an instant."

As if this had been the most pleasing announcement imaginable, Whifton tittered in his usual style ; then suddenly turning grave, answered:

" You're in the business?"

" If I am, it's no business of yours."

" Quite right. It is really so; but such an article as you describe is not on the market."

" Is not the method of making it, known?"

" Yes — no," replied Whifton hesitatingly. " I don't understand what you want or have reference to."

"Look here," said the stranger, "I'll give fifty dollars for the way to manage the best kind of stuff there is. Now be quick."

"It is the easiest thing in the world to tell you how to prepare gun cotton," answered the other, " but you would find it unsatisfactory. The same ingredients, two acids mixed, with glycerin added, give us a powerful agent such as you need, named nitroglycerin. Mind you, this fact is known only to a few persons outside the discoverer, an Italian of Turin. It would not be safe for you to attempt making it, even if you knew how; you would be blown sky-high in no time, because the least irregularity would cause the explosion to take place. There is another preparation made from the one just mentioned, the greatest of all, called dynamite. That's the daisy! The only chance of getting it would be this: I might send to the discoverer for a small quantity and offer him large pay with the prospect of being refused — or, by the bye, how would a mixture of a bursting character prepared from druggists' chemicals suit you?"

"I'm in for it," answered the stranger with alacrity.

"It is innocent-looking, a white powder no one would suspect dangerous."

The unwelcome visitor drew a notebook from his coat pocket and made preparation to write down the items of the important mixture.

"I shall take that one," he said hurriedly and decisively.

Whifton now felt he had gone a little too far in permitting the stranger to determine on selecting a definite article or compound. He parried the thrust with as much adroitness as possible by saying:

"I did not intend mentioning I knew the parts of it; and the truth is, I forget all about them."

The stranger moved uneasily in his seat like one whose mind is suddenly disturbed. Opening the notebook and touching a page with the pencil, he continued:

"Go on, my little man. Let me not try to assist your memory by force, for if I do you will think there are sparks of fire flying around the room in short order. No more fooling."

"What I said is the best that can be done at present," returned Whifton.

Then the stranger grew wrathful. Striking the table with his closed hand, he shouted rather than said:

"Go on, I say."

Whifton turned pale. He began trembling, and for an instant directed his thoughts to his weapons of defense; but was obliged to conclude that, even if they were available, it would be useless to contend against so powerful an antagonist as this mysterious man. Hence, although determined to resist the disclosure to the last and doubtful how he could evade it, he began the enumeration of the items of the secret mixture.

"Take yellow prussiate of potash, dried in iron ladle and powdered carefully in a mortar, thirty-seven parts; chlorate of potash, finely pulverized, forty-one parts. Now," he continued, placing the forefinger of his right hand against the side of his head as if desirous of conjuring up lucidity of mind in the case before him, "let me see, what is the third chemical? Aye, there's the stickler. Who would think I could forget so soon? It is really so; I have forgotten it."

The stranger, who had written in his notebook the

ingredients mentioned by Whifton, arose to his feet, and, seizing his companion by the shoulder, shook him until his little head oscillated like the pendulum of a clock. After being released from the iron grasp of the stranger, Whifton managed to say:

"You will pay dearly for this outrage; see if you don't."

"Make no threats to me, my little man; the business must be completed now, or I ain't nobody."

"I am not a professor," resumed Whifton in desperation. "The people who make out that I know all about explosives have no grounds for their belief. It is mere hearsay. I may tell *you* in confidence that I got the whole thing, such as it is, from a crank, one of those so-called revolutionary spirits who calculate on reducing the world to ashes just for fun. Accidentally some of his notes fell into my hands. While he was in prison, his trunk was held by my folks in part payment for his board bill. On opening it, ma found a few old clothes, a number of newspapers, and a manuscript. Disappointed in her expectations, she dumped the whole collection into the ash barrel, from which I extracted the last-named article, being curious to understand what such a man had collected or written."

"Have you that document now?" inquired the stranger, eagerly.

"Well," answered Whifton, "I had it then."

"Ah! my little trickster?" returned the unknown, "you're very smart, ain't you? I'll bet a nickel I could find it if I tried hard enough. Now, get that document for me, and we'll call it square. I'll pay for it. Moreover, I may say the crank, as you call him, is the kind of man I wish to follow. I'll take up his work and push it through for all it's worth; so be lively."

"I cannot say actually that I have it," said Whifton, "but I'll tell you what can be done: wait until tomorrow, and in the meantime I'll try and find it among my papers."

The man laughed in derision at this proposition. The acknowledgment made in his presence that there was secret information of great value in the house, of the kind for which his soul had yearned for years, roused up the latent ferocity of his nature and urged him to the commission of a desperate deed. With his left hand he caught Whifton by the throat, and, drawing a keen-pointed dagger from his waist belt, held it high above him, saying as he did so:

"Now or never. I cannot trust you. Give up the papers or your life!"

Then the little man felt that the end was near. He breathed hard, rolled his eyes upward and muttered something that might be mistaken for a prayer, if it had not been for the word prevaricate, which was quite audible and of doubtful orthodoxy. Before the dagger descended, the arm of the man who held it was clutched by a strange hand, and pushed violently backward. Then a dark figure insinuated itself between the assailant and assailed, while a low, guttural voice exclaimed:

"Ah! what foolhardy trick is this? Didn't I tell you never attempt injury to the helpless? There ain't no good in my rules, anyhow. Now, don't tempt me too far. Get out of here."

As Whifton's disagreeable customer stepped through the door, his companion, the new arrival, who was also disguised, turning to the storekeeper, said:

"Don't take any notice of him; he has a shingle off.

We have to keep him out of mischief, but he would not harm anybody.''

Whifton raised a finger and shook it in a threatening manner, which was understood to mean that he would prosecute the offender to the full extent of the law.

'' We can compromise here, now,'' returned the man, at the same time throwing off his disguise and revealing the pale face of Hamilton Hitch to Whifton.

''As there has been no injury done to you or your property, the affair may be kept secret. He is my son. Now, here is twenty dollars as compensation for intruding on your premises, with the understanding that the case is settled. Do you consent ?''

Whifton, who was gifted with good business talent, readily caught the gist of the proposition made by the father, that the attempted outrage by the son should be kept secret for the consideration of twenty dollars. Hence his answer was promptly given :

'' Never you mind. There will be nothing said of the encounter. You're a gentleman, and a bargain is a bargain,'' said he.

Then Hamilton Hitch turned and fled into the night.

When the noise of the retreating footsteps ceased, Whifton arose, and, carefully bolting all the doors and windows, drew his couch out some distance from the wall, lest any sharp instrument should be designedly pushed through it with an evil intention ; and prepared to rest under the clothing, and, if possible, under the circumstances. For hours he slept not. The peculiar expression on the features he had last seen haunted his mental vision Distressed resignation, mingled with ferocity and far-reaching knowledge of unlawful designs, were there, besides the traces of time's unrelenting decadence tinctured by melancholy. He had seen the man frequently in Omaha, but had heard nothing of his history or calling. Even now he believed him a citizen trying to do good under adverse marks and incidents of nature for which he was not responsible. Shortly after reaching this conclusion, Whifton slept.

CHAPTER V.

A PREDICTION VERIFIED.

LEST the visitors of the previous night should return and demand the money given him on the occasion mentioned in the last chapter, Whifton determined on adding it to his cash deposit in the bank at Omaha without delay. The business principle represented by savings was wisely observed by him, whatever might be said of his want of judgment in other respects. In connection with this frugal practice he made it a rule to remove the money in the house or on his person to a place of greater safety when the sum of his gains went over twenty dollars. The amount reserved for exchange purposes, some fractional currency, if seized forcibly, or stolen, could not be regarded as much loss. Under these arrangements he often surprised people by his fearless light-heartedness. With his money safe, his spirit was enabled to float above the common circumstances of life, like a cork on the surface of water or a bird seeking extra delight in the brightness of the morning air. It was a little method, but its results were incalculable for good to the individual practicing it.

The facilities available for reaching the commercial center of the district were ample, several stages passing his place daily, besides other vehicles at longer intervals driven by men of his acquaintance who would gladly give him a ride for the sake of his good company. Hence, after a light breakfast of crushed maize, coffee, and pancakes, he posted the ambiguous sign on the door, " Will be back," and rode off to Omaha on the first up stage.

While his face exhibited traces of excitement, no one heard him utter a word during the journey, for he avoided the box seat and merely nodded to a few passengers in front of him. The debate with himself on the pending question carried forward from last night was too absorbing personally to admit of rehearsal before any audience, however sympathetic it might prove to be. The little man with his inflated breast and grandiloquent estimate of himself had a huge subject to deal with, and he felt its importance. The ground broken in the case, metaphorically speaking, was too ticklish, he thought, for ordinary banter, but required the most careful analysis on his own part before being carried under the attention of strangers or acquaintances. It was evident if his side of the compact were not honestly observed by absolute silence the dark strangers could retaliate at any time, when it was certain he would fare worse than before. The vindication of the law might be a good thing, but the saving of his life seemed to him better. Hence, whatever resolutions he had previously formed of consulting the sheriff in that part of Iowa or the authorities in Omaha, in view of the dangerous tendency of the times were now set aside so as to keep within the bounds of prudence and agreement.

Besides, he was a winner. The gold piece in his pocket was testimony of that fact, as well as that the secrets concerning explosives were still unrevealed. Furthermore, he

had discovered an admirer of Grace Finnestare—a dangerous character, no doubt, seeing the nature of his designs—
and he had scored a great point in recommending that the
stranger should not do anything tending to interfere with
her freedom or prosperity. Instead of being cold in his
coffin, as any other man would be in similar circumstances,
he, Whifton, had received a handsome compensation and
was guaranteed immunity from further assault. Menaced
on the one hand, he was raised to the height of exultation
on the other. To what power or condition might he
ascribe such fortune? Plainly to no other than the golden
rule of his grandfather in regard to the utility of prevarica-
tion. When Whifton reached this conclusion, he chuckled
so violently that his hat was almost shaken off his head;
but, owing to the lurching of the stage, the phenomenon
passed unnoticed.

Arriving in Omaha, he directed his steps to the bank, a
one-story wooden structure in the northern part of the
principal street, conducted, as before remarked, by Judge
Finnestare. In a·pleasant manner he stepped daintily on
the threshold and looked in. He stopped. He opened
his mouth in wonder at what he beheld. The two large
safes were there as formerly, the polished counter, the plain
walls, and the low ceiling; but in the apartment adjoining
the bank and opening into it as if intending to be an
inner sanctum, he saw a young man of comely appearance
chatting gaily if not lovingly to Grace Finnestare.

This appearance, meeting him without premeditation,
smote his heart like a concussion of atmospheric air after
an explosion. Whifton seemed chained to the spot on
which he stood. In his earnest gaze at the lady he secretly
loved, there was a troubled aspect. It appeared as if he

saw death incarnate, instead of beauty. His prediction of yesterday was verified today. The third man was here. He had come even precipitately, like a sudden squall that drives ships to refuge, or a cyclone which buries towns in the dust. Oh! why did he not consider this phase of the case for his poor heart, or why did he foolishly imagine that Grace Finnestare would remain isolated from the companionship of gentlemen on his account and she ignorant of his feelings or his love?

Seated near the window, where her smiles fell upon him simultaneously with the sunlight, was the person whose presence aroused all the grief and the surprise in Whifton's mind. Judged without prejudice, he was a noble-looking man, the equal of Grace Finnestare in appearance and education. To say that he was handsome would merely record the fact without explicitly defining the circumstances. There was a look of sterling worth in the clearness of his eyes and the broad, manly features of his face, as well as a firmness of purpose in the poise of the head that could not be misapprehended. The thorax, or breast, was fully developed, showing muscular power and force in action. The lower limbs tapered gracefully downward, and the extremities, upper and lower, were exquisitely proportioned to the size of the man. In his slippers he must have stood over six feet. His hair was black, but the complexion appeared remarkably fair, illuminated as it was with lustrous brown eyes and occasionally a genial smile. He was dressed in plain clothes, whose neatness and cut gave ample opportunity to exhibit his admirable developments of person to advantage without being in the least degree obtrusive.

In all that Whifton saw, he read the death knell of his

plans and hopes. If there were further evidence necessary, their animated conversation in his hearing was sufficient proof. How glibly they spoke and laughed ! — as if
there were no world outside the apartment where they
met, or an individual with a consciousness half paralyzed
with pain, whose aspirations, after a blissful state, had gone
down forever.

Advancing mechanically to the interior of the bank,
Whifton, while placing his twenty dollars on the counter,
was greeted in a kindly manner by Judge Finnestare, questioned about his health (for he looked poorly), and encouraged to prosecute his business operations further, as
wealth was sure to come with the growth of enterprise.

"I often wondered," said the Judge, "why you did not
come to Omaha and bring your business with you, imagin-
ing you could do better here than at the crossroads on the
other side; but as often have I desisted from mentioning
the matter, on account of noticing how well you do in your
present location. Now, for instance, your deposit today,
coming so soon after the one at the close of last month,
shows conclusively that my opinions on the subject of removal were not well founded; or else that credit is due to
your superior management in a situation where few men
would be able to make money."

As a matter of course, Judge Finnestare had not the
least suspicion or idea how Whifton came by the last
twenty dollars; and, in any case, our little trader heard
but a moiety of the speech. The sounds of voices were in
his ears that smote his spirit like a two-edged sword. His
mind wandered to other scenes, endeavoring, no doubt, to
find one that might afford him some relief in the present
distress. The vision of his strange visitors also came up

as if to direct the character of his answer, and with it the word prevaricate; yet, rousing himself by an effort, he merely said: "It is really so, Judge, it is really so." Then he turned and left the place.

Whifton was desirous of meeting his friend Flanks Honeybone, the night watchman, so as to glean from him the truth regarding the new acquaintance of Grace Finnestare, whose presence gave him so much uneasiness and proved to be a most disquieting indication of future trouble. Turning suddenly to the right, he noticed a man standing near the door, who, though busied with a note-book and pencil, could have heard what he, Whifton, had said in the bank without being suspected of listening. As his secret was as secure as the money, he rather felt a pride in saluting this man, who was no other than the notorious Hamilton Hitch.

Seeing Whifton enter the town, he had pursued him to ascertain if he would or would not betray him and his son while placing the bribe in a place of safety. As the conduct of Whifton proved satisfactory, Hamilton Hitch returned his salute and added the usual compliments of the season in appropriate language. Whifton said to himself as he directed his steps downtown: "Somehow I have a liking for that man. I think him very honorable, and feel sure he would make a reliable commissioner or superior judge. He is very considerate."

Although obliged to witness vast improvements in Omaha, some little attention was paid to them on this occasion, until the meeting with Honeybone, which took place about two o'clock in the afternoon. At that hour the night watchman was accustomed to step jauntily from the door of a cheap boarding house, where he roomed and boarded, in the southern end of town, and, seeking the main thoroughfare, parade its entire length in holiday attire for the purpose of showing his patrons what a live man he was at that time of day. This movement in view of an appreciative public he called "taking a spin."

Honeybone was a man over thirty, tall and muscular; fond of rich food, and, in consequence, possessed a fair-sized paunch; good-natured to a fault, and jolly; ready and willing to give and take a glass of liquor from a friend as exchange blows with an enemy; and spending his money with a lavish hand to the extent of his earnings. When you saw him on exhibition in the afternoon of a pleasant day, the most of all his possessions were also in view. His clothing was of the finest material and latest style; the Derby hat was tilted a little on one side of his head; his boots were highly polished; he wore a seven-dollar ring on the little finger of his left hand, and a brace of pistols in his hip pockets, comfortably and carefully adjusted. One could see in his mien self-gratification and glorification such as has rarely been detected associated with the man of wealth. Some of his peculiarities seemed suited to his independent character. He would step across the street, for instance, before reaching the regular crossing, and abbreviate words in his speech for the purpose of making it agreeable, believing in each case that the shortest way was generally the straightest.

The greeting extended to Whifton on the present occasion was a genuine outburst of pleasure on Honeybone's part.

"Whif, my old friend," he said, "glad to meet you. How is biz? Hain't seen you in a dog's age. Guess you've been skylarking with the girls at the crossroads. Ain't you spliced yet?"

Whifton did not attempt to answer these questions categorically or otherwise. Raising his forefinger to the middle of Honeybone's breast, and crooking it a little as if about to seize one of the buttons of his coat, he said :

"I want to have a talk with you."

This sentence was uttered with such a serious air, unaccompanied by the spasmodic mirth characteristic of the speaker, that his friend readily conceived the necessity of infusing a more ardent spirit into the originator of it, so as to bring him on a par with himself, equality of sentiment on current questions being one of his favorite rules. Hence he suggested :

"S'pose we take in Cuffins's. Cozy hole that there. Cuff's a daisy at doin' things, you bet. There ain't no small fry on his spread."

Cuffins's was a saloon a few rods off from where they stood, to which the men repaired: It was famous, according to the testimony of the night watchman, as a resort for men of small means, or, indeed, of all means, who, while paying for drink, were accommodated with something to eat, gratis, called a lunch. This lunch was eaten off a common dish either by selecting a bit or bite with the fingers or the use of a fork kept near it for indiscriminate use. Whifton would drink nothing stronger than lemonade, nor Honeybone other than cocktail.

It was off the bar where they entered in a small reception room decorated with cheap prints of pugilists and some of the sporting fraternity of a lower order, whose exhibition seemed as necessary to the imbibers of potations as flavor to the drinks. Honeybone's face presented a smile of

great sweetness, vulgarized, however, by the red color of
his nose, as, taking his glass, he said, "Here's fortune,"
while his companion seemed wholly intent on studying the
phraseology by which he was to open the interview. After
some delay he said:

"You know everybody in Omaha, Flanks?"

"I guess so, purty much, 'cept strangers."

"The bank is one of the places you have to watch?"

"There ain't no crook livin' as could pull that there pen
while I'm round, an' don't you forget it."

"It would not surprise me to hear of Judge Finnestare
selling out his interest in the concern. What makes me
think so is this: I saw a man in there today who appeared
to be very intimate with the family. It is really so."

Honeybone burst into a loud laugh at Whifton's method
of characterizing the acquaintance of the Finnestares.

"Oh, *him!*" he answered. "A youngish sort of
feller?"

"Exactly."

"Good-lookin' from his boots up."

"There is no denying it. It is really so."

"W'y, he's sweet on the daughter, dead stuck on her,
an' solid for sure. He ain't goin' to be on the left side.
They'll be married."

Honeybone's glance was directed through the window of
the apartment while uttering these terse sentences, and for
sounds he had his ear bent to the tinkling of glasses in the
bar, where a second cocktail was being prepared for his
use. He had not the least idea of the effect of his words
on the mind of his friend; but they touched Whifton's
heart like sharp-pointed daggers. What that little dreamer
had anticipated was true. This newcomer referred to by

Honeybone and seen by himself was the lover of Grace Finnestare. The possibility of maintaining a rivalship with him must not be entertained for a moment. It would be preposterous, utterly ridiculous. He made a rapid survey of his exterior appearance, as if to prove the truth of this conclusion. He saw the little boots, the tiny legs, and the miniature breast, which, though prominent, was as frail as a mere eggshell compared with the pronounced manliness and strength of the person seen in the bank; and his hopes went out from his understanding like a light that is suddenly extinguished in the darkness of night! Furtively he glanced at Honeybone to ascertain if there was any trace in his countenance of love for Grace Finnestare, for he supposed that every man seeing her must have been captivated instantaneously, but the scrutiny proved ineffective. The man seemed indifferent to the influence of the rosy god.

"How wise he is compared with me!" thought Whifton. "He loves to flash his ring in the eyes of people, to be admired on the street for outside polish worth about five cents a yard, and guzzle the cheap meals of sixth-rate boarding houses until he groans with delight, while I have nothing but a sore heart from the foolishness of loving a beauty I could never get. I must live through it."

This honest resolution of making an effort to retrieve his mental equanimity seemed to give him some strength, so that he resumed his inquiries after the bartender had furnished the other round, as each order of drinks was called, and left the apartment.

"Flanks, where has this man in Finnestare's come from?"

" Pooh ! the Yeast. Hain't they all from it ? Noo Yark."

" Do you suppose I can learn what brought him here, or, rather, what his business is ? "

" He's up to snuff, you bet. Full of biz as an alligator. I guess he knows what he's after."

" But his business, Flanks ? "

" He dassent tell, himself. The talk is, politics shoved him out here on spec', to navigate somethin' about the border war they're havin' down in Kansas. There ain't no flies on him, nohow."

" Do you think we will have war, Flanks ? "

" Naw. How can we ? Where'll it come from ? No soldiers, no nothin'."

Thrusting his hands into the pockets of his overcoat as if his extremities were cold, Whifton rose to depart, but at the bar, on the way out, stopped to pay the reckoning as well as to order another cocktail for his friend, taking a cigar for himself in lieu of lemonade. Then as Honeybone toasted the prosperity of trade at the crossroads and accompanied him to the street, Whifton, presenting the cigar, inquired finally and impressively :

" What is the name of this strange man, Flanks, in Finnestare's ? "

" They calls him Herondeen, or Herondine, which is purty much the same," answered his companion, seizing the proffered root, nipped the point on one end off with his front teeth, and lighting a match, began to smoke.

As this new pleasure seemed to produce the motion necessary to separate from his friend, the two men exchanged adieus, Honeybone to proceed further on his spin through the city, while Whifton mounted the first stage-

coach passing to his home.   In the morning he had come
into Omaha charged with splendid hopes in a visionary
future that even magnified the beauty of the landscape
through which he passed ;   now he was going out feeling
that all these sources of ecstasy were lost to him forever,
as if blasted by the fury of a mysterious storm beyond the
confines of his thoughts.   The verdure of the trees of his
planting had been stricken by fire from the clouds when
their bloom promised to decorate the pathway in his last
years on earth.   He saw nothing but the diminution of
glory in the physical aspect of inanimate objects where
formerly he had been entranced by their effulgence.   The
sunshine appeared to have grown darker than usual ; the
distant prospect devoid of interest ; and his own home
drooped apparently in an insignificant manner as if conscious of the misery to which its owner had been reduced.

Entering the house in a half-crazed manner, he threw
himself into a seat exclaiming: " Oh, God ! how desolate
I am !   It is really so.   Spare me a little.''

CHAPTER VI.

WHERE TWO CURRENTS MEET.

DANDERTON HITCH was surprised in the midst of
his industrious calculations by the presence of the
stranger in Omaha whom the night watchman had called
Herondine.   This was his first experience with the profound unknown where immaterial circumstance struck him
like a material body.   The incident did not seem to war-
rant uneasiness, for Danderton was then ignorant of Herondine's acquaintance with Grace Finnestare and knew

nothing whatever of his business antecedents. Intuition gave him the cue. It was when Herodine first entered the city and Danderton seemed on the eve of possessing almost everything the world could afford.

In compliance with the custom of business men in America, Herondine proceeded to the best hotel to register, so as to announce his arrival, although having other living accommodations in the place, to which he would immediately repair. Danderton was sitting in the office as Herondine stepped up to the counter when the accommodating clerk wheeled the book on its pivoted support in order to receive his name. When it was written, Alton B. Herondine, with his late residence, New York, the recent arrival turned and encountered the glances of the son of Hamilton Hitch. As with bodies that repel each other, there was antagonism between these two men at first sight. The fine finish shown on the person of Herondine seemed to excite contempt in the mind of Danderton. This feeling caused a contraction of his features, which roused the manhood of the person against whom it was directed; and Danderton, on the other hand, was slowly but systematically scrutinized by the stranger.

For no reason that anybody could discern, the two men grew wrathful. Danderton arose and walked hurriedly around Herondine, viewing his signature and conducting himself in a manner that would appear as if he meant to intimidate him, but was met with such cool determination and self-confident power that he kept himself at a safe distance.

It was instructive to see two opposing currents of human thought meet like the tide of the ocean and the flowing of a river. Both men were fine specimens of manhood, physically, but in all other respects the contrast between them was remarkable. Herondine might be selected to represent the beauty of morning, while Danderton would be assigned to the gloomy night.

Danderton's intuition gave the warning note. "If this man meets Grace Finnestare, all is lost," it said. Danderton saw this plainly of his own accord. It struck him like a sword point. Every movement of Herondine showed the truth of it, and there seemed no doubt there was a rival before him who would cancel all his chances and annihilate all his hopes. It was a dreadful prospect, especially as it resulted from a careful communion with himself whose conviction he could not deny. He even remembered what Whifton had told him about the coming of the third man. "By h—!" he thought, "that little necromancer knows a thing or two."

It was strange he permitted disturbance of this kind to distress him without sufficient evidence as to its reality. The beauty of a man's person ought not to be an incentive to give an insult. Perhaps the incoming stranger, the immigrant, as he might be called, was married or had left some loved one in the East to whom he would return.

"Oh! no, no, no," Danderton's heart answered in the negative.

The mysterious sensation crowding upon him seemed to possess the property of removing all doubts on the question. Out of the darkness of the unknown the light of truth in this case came to him like a vision or as if it had been flashed by an internal monitor. Nature, that heretofore had favored him like a pet boy, now struck him as if he were an adder! When he trembled as if stricken by palsy, he knew some operator other than error was at work, whose mandate should be obeyed because outside the domain of fiction. Stepping up to Herondine he whispered, so as not to be overheard by others:

"Who the d— are you?"

The response was equally explicit and emphatic:

"Don't be in a hurry, young man; you can learn that soon enough."

Danderton seemed to get furious. Exclamations of hostility in single words or half-formed sentences escaped him as he wheeled and counterwheeled around his antagonist, but made no further effort to strike, as Herondine's manly form and conduct appeared equal to the occasion and fully qualified to repel an attack. Some of Danderton's acquaintances who came upon the scene at the time, observing his trepidation and fearing trouble, hustled him out of the hotel, while Herondine went quietly about his business.

It was a period in the history of America when the least indication of a quarrel, if not promptly suppressed, might induce a serious riot. Opposition and bad feeling were in the air like the germs of an epidemic, and people everywhere were actually listening for the first sound of war.

As has been hinted at, Danderton's speculations up to this date seemed sound and encouraging. A large party espoused his journalistic project. He was informed that on such issue he would get all the backing necessary. Some of the people were tired of sermons and wanted anything new, no matter what. On this account he would call his paper "The Western Gasconader," and through it spread broadcast all the scandal that could be collected. His residence, too, had been completed and was occupied. The old home at the foothills had been removed, and he and his father were frequently seen on the streets or in public places conversing with business men on questions of the times. In a few weeks, perhaps days, he was promised an introduction to Grace Finnestare. In the mental perspective which these incidents created he could discern happiness ; but while viewing its glittering aspect, some unseen hand thrust Herondine between him and it, thus shutting the fascinating vision out.

Explanations followed their first encounter. Herondine received two accounts of Danderton, one intimating that he was a rising young capitalist whose thoroughness and live ideas might be relied on to advance the interests of the city. The other description traced his history back to his boyhood and questioned the integrity of his character, classifying him also as a sport or a person to be feared.

On the other hand, Danderton was informed that Herondine was an agent of a powerful political party organizing throughout the entire country to give freedom to the slaves and otherwise infringe on the private rights of citizens. As such it was his bounden duty to oppose him.

Danderton's father became vigorous in sustaining the cause of his son on the above grounds. No one knew his secret motive any more than they were acquainted with the young man's thoughts regarding Grace Finnestare ; but he promised all the support at his command. Danderton would forgive everything in his rival but acquaintanceship with the lady of his love. He had not long to wait for the verification of his fears.

That evening, as he stood inside the curtains of one of the front windows looking westward, he saw two persons walking leisurely a few hundred feet beyond the street in the direction of the low hills heretofore noticed. The sunshine was dying out slowly, but the atmosphere was calm and the fragrance coming in from the great prairie enchanting. The couple proceeded until they reached a prominent point where the distant landscape would appear pleasantly to the sight. Then they remained stationary. It seemed evident from their movements they enjoyed each other's society and were happy. They were good people whose confidence each knew how to value and respect. There was no mistaking their identity. At a glance it could be seen they were Herondine and Grace Finnestare!

When first observed, Danderton's gaze became fixed and he felt as if a thunderbolt had fallen upon him. The interior of his heart was stricken by acute pain, as well as that his life or spirit became agitated as if threatened with death. Perspiration stood out on his forehead, while respiration seemed so difficult that he imagined it about to cease altogether.

The evil in his nature, however, soon came to his assistance. Withdrawing suddenly from the window, he sought a room looking toward the northwest, threw up the sash, rushed to a cupboard, and, picking up a rifle which lay against the wall, began loading it with round shot. One would imagine he beheld a lion whose life he proposed taking before it succeeded in its efforts to cross the bluff. The train of ideas started by his passion hurried him forward towards the brink of crime, without the lessons taught by his father being of any avail. He seemed maddened into a condition beyond the control of his powers. When the rifle was loaded and made ready, he raised it to his shoulder. He aimed!

"Ah! What is this?" he cried, with an oath.

Grace Finnestare was standing between him and Herondine! If he fired, she would fall and his rival probably
escape. Would he kill the two? "Not yet," he answered mentally, while he lowered the weapon to an
order arms. At this instant his father entered the apartment and became acquainted with the situation and the
causes leading to it. Placing his hand on the young
man's shoulder, he said:

"Danderton, I have guarded your safety for many years,
but if you did what I think you were going to do I could
not save you."

"I am willing to suffer for this business," replied the
son.

"No. We cannot afford to think so," continued the
elder man. "It ought to be fitting for me as a means of
reaching a tragic end; but quite unprofitable for you.
There is nothing in it."

"Can you give me some remedy to satisfy my revengeful
disposition — a panacea, as they call it — and at the same
time relieve the fearful pain of my head and heart?"

After some reflection the father answered:

"The time and place must be more suitable than these,
and the means of a darker kind. Come."

Danderton followed his father into an apartment which
had been set apart as a day room for his accommodation.
It was gloomy and secure from all intrusion. Standing
a few feet inside the door of this infernal sanctum, the
old man spoke in whispers, lest by any possibility his words
might be heard outside.

"When chance favors us, use your own method."

"How? What?"

"Dynamite."

"Ha! you have tumbled to it. I told you it was first-class."

"Have the two fall together. On the day of their marriage, for instance, when they are happiest!"

"The woman too?"

"Yes; and, for the matter of that, the old man her father. It is a great bill — a full hand — a game worth playing. It must be done so much on the quiet, however, that there will be no chance of discovery, and in the night, when consternation may be added to sensation."

These words of Hamilton Hitch were delivered rapidly, while traces of foam appeared on his lips and his pale face grew ghastly from excessive feeling. His head moved from side to side like one proud of some remarkable achievement. Danderton did not quail before the terrors awakened by the details of the fiendish plot. Once he trembled while meditating a little on the individuals concerned, but by an effort assumed a calm aspect when he said :

"It is a pity to slay the woman."

"Chicken!" remarked the father, contemptuously.

"You mistake me," resumed Danderton. "I am concerned for myself in this case much more than on her account. If the woman is killed, the memory of her will stay with me for sure. I would prefer to be free from such burden; whereas, if she lives and this man Herondine, her husband that is to be, dies, I may succeed —"

"Don't," said the father, interrupting him. "Let us have no more silly expectation. She would treat you then as she does now with contempt. Who, let me ask you, laughed at your well-meant aspirations and ridiculed your wishes — was it not the woman? Well, then, cut her image from your mind and hate her if nothing else."

"I could not live," said Danderton slowly, as if by explanation, "if she dies in the manner suggested. This remedy would only make matters worse. I might be forced like others to die by my own hand."

"Think of your prosperity, can't you? The fame awaiting your business enterprise and the popularity following our literary efforts in ' The Gasconader.' "

"They won't do worth a continental, pap. I'm tortured out of all patience."

The father, grasping his son by the arm so as to be felt, resumed: "Wait. Fight the trouble. Let the woman pass unhurt if you want to, but pursue the man until the opportunity arrives; then strike and take what chances there may be afterwards. Will that satisfy your appetite?"

"What am I to do in the meantime?"

"Work. Rustle. Go into politics, oppose Herondine in all his speculations, and set your mind on marrying an ugly woman. Nothing will cure you if that don't."

While the young man reflected on the terms of relief as dictated in the foregoing advice, the father proposed the provision of new solace. He resumed:

"I have something else to tell you, which, after all, is the principal thing. The little man beyond the river, and I, are acquainted. He suspects nothing. It appears certain he will be faithful to the conditions laid down for him. He will supply the dynamite and relieve us of the responsibility, don't you see, should anybody make a fuss over it."

"Pap, there's no denying the wrinkle. I acknowledge

the corn; you're smart. That's what's the matter, and don't you forget it," said Danderton' joyfully.

The father continued:

"When the article is received, place it under the house where Herondine is sleeping. Set the fuse at such length that you may have time to get out of danger before the explosion and return home immediately. In the morning we can join the citizens in offering a reward for the apprehension of the perpetrators of the outrage! This will cover our tracks."

There was a smile on Danderton's face as he returned to the apartment from which he had seen Herondine in company with Grace Finnestare. The hope inspired by his father expanded through the medium of reflection until he was full of his enemy's premature downfall and the glory of ridding the world of him by the new process so little known. On this account, he was not disturbed on seeing Herondine and his companion retrace their steps homeward as the twilight came over the plains and lovingly folded them in its embrace, as if they needed protection, and finally shut them up in Finnestare's while it deepened into night and disappeared.

About a week after the events here related there was a large procession in the streets of Omaha. One of its esteemed citizens had naturally gone to his account. Besides the friends and acquaintances of the deceased in carriages, many persons fell into line afoot, attracted by the solemnity of the occasion. Among the crowd thus situated was Crow Whifton, from the crossroads at Council Bluffs. He was alone, so to speak, as it was in the forenoon and the nightwatchman had not yet appeared. The old cemetery in the neighborhood of the city being still available, the procession soon reached its destination, and the minister begán the reading of the beautiful service of the Episcopal Church amid profound silence and the deep reverence of the spectators. Just as he recited, "I heard a voice from heaven saying —"

"Whifton, my dear pal, I'm with you," interrupted a whispered voice at the little man's elbow, and turning he saw Hamilton Hitch bent forward as if in prayer and with an unctuous appearance on his countenance.

Again the minister's voice prevailed, saying, "From henceforth now and forever."

"Amen!" responded Whifton, as if he had been forced into some declaration of the heart through the nature of his surroundings, and could no longer resist the impulse to be pious like his companion.

When the services were concluded, the men thus strangely brought together walked into the principal street, where the crowd broke up and dispersed into the ordinary business community. Hamilton Hitch, concluding a dissertation on the subject of his love for the company of successful men like Whifton, invited him into a popular restaurant, where he treated him to a sumptuous lunch. While discussing the menu, which had been flanked by a couple of bottles of dry claret, Hitch remarked in an affable manner:

"The joke of it is, my dear Whifton, that my son wanted a little dynamite to use in his scientific experiments, but, fearing public comment, applied to you in the manner we all remember until such time as his investigations were successfully completed. I told him a few days ago I would get it from you or have you send for as much as he required. Its manufacture is known only to a few."

"Why, certainly," answered Whifton, "I shall be happy to accommodate you, now that we know each other. It is really so."

"Remember," continued the elder man, "mum's the word. Let nothing tempt you to give the matter away, because, as you know, science has no relationship with worldly people."

"Never you mind," returned Whifton, with a friendly nod of his head. "They won't get anything out of me if I know myself." Then, after a little reflection, he continued: "I'll send for it. I have the address of the inventor."

"How long, my dear Whifton, will we have to wait before it comes?"

"Let me see; three and three are six, and twenty-one, twenty-seven, three — about two months. If not unavoidably detained, we may have it here close on to Christmas, say December twentieth."

"It will be the season for slaughtering ducks and geese," said Hamilton Hitch carelessly.

"Quite right," returned Whifton, evidently attaching no significance to the words other than their literal meaning.

The repast ended, Whifton was about to rise so as to depart homeward, when his companion made a motion with his hand to detain him.

"There is one thing more," he said. "Take this token of my esteem in consideration of your faithfulness. Keep it, and if you are ever in a difficulty that I can relieve it will serve you."

Whifton, glancing at the gift, saw it was a watch charm of triangular shape with some mystic signs on each side.

It seemed a mixture of precious metals and had an attachment to connect it with a chain or ring.

"I'll wear it," returned Whifton. "Thank you." Then,
as the friends separated, Whifton remarked to himself, "I
declare! that new friend of mine is the most agreeable
person I ever met. He is liberal, too—in fact, open-
handed and generous to a turn — a real gentleman. It is
really so."

CHAPTER VII.

AN UNGODLY HEIRLOOM.

ALTON B. HERONDINE, whose appearance in Omaha
had created some speculation in regard to the
character of his business and future operations, was a New
York gentleman of means, legitimately acquired through
the industry and economy of his progenitors. His property for the most part consisted of improved real estate in
the neighborhood of Abingdon Square, New York, which,
by the way, is a triangular enclosure not far from the
junction of West Twelfth Street and Eighth Avenue,
showing conclusively that the magnanimous person who
undertook to give the place a name was not well versed in
the elements of Euclid.

His father belonged to the Herondines of Hillville, a
maritime suburb of a large city on the eastern coast, and
claimed direct descent from a celebrated Herondine who,
a century before, swam three miles into the open sea for
the purpose of recovering his fishpole, accidentally carried
out by the tide, and returned safely to land with the
precious implement. So far from exhibiting a desire to

transmit this part of the family record to future ages, Alton B. repudiated it altogether, asserting that it was a mere travesty on the incapacity of his ancestor, who could not swim at all.

The Herondine of our day needed no fame of this kind, while his honesty of purpose and generous disposition towards mankind led him to seek the solution of intricate problems associated with the destinies of his country during his youth. For a long time he wavered between right and wrong, on account of his surroundings; but, persisting in his search, he came to know the truth at last.

It is necessary to present him to the reader struggling for a knowledge of political science in his New York home. The disintegration, or breaking-up process, which takes place in all families sooner or later, whereby the members are scattered by death, emigration, or marriage, or separated on account of other causes, set in with the Herondines while Alton B. was quite young. At the age of sixteen, when beginning his collegiate course, it was found that there remained to him from his family and relatives but two old aunts, one being the sister of his good father, and the other bearing a similar relationship to his honored mother.

These ladies possessed estates in their own right; so that their introduction into the Herondine household was not designed to be a means or an end of support as poor relations, but to enable them to form a home circle for the young heir, and endeavor to relieve his anxieties and attend to his individual wants. So well and assiduously did they bend to the labor assigned them in this case that the neighbors frequently called Herondine "the young man with the two mothers."

It was one of the curiosities of the times to witness
Alton B. stroll up Bleecker Street into Broadway with an
aunt on each arm, now listening to the suggestions of the
one, then turning suddenly to hear the opinions of the
other. As he was tall for his age and the ladies who
accompanied him very much the same height, gaunt, positive, and demonstrative while expatiating on familiar subjects, the spectacle presented by the group was amusing.
In like manner they were encountered in several public
places in and around the city — in Union Square, at the
City Hall, along the wharf, near the Battery or Castle
Garden, in the old Washington Market, at the Fifth
Avenue Hotel, on the Bowery, in Central Park, or beyond
the Hudson on the heights at Hoboken.

Mrs. Winling, the aunt on the Herondine side of the
house, had been gray-haired for years, but was now white ;
yet she still retained great vitality, clear perception, and a
volubility of language quite remarkable. Her laughter
resembled in some respects the clear sound of a bell. It
was customary to call her "Aunt Frill"— an abbreviation
of Frilistine, which was her Christian name. She was a
widow whose husband and children were long since dead ;
and on this account, perhaps, she sought earthly solace in
her attachment for Herondine, whose comfort she endeavored on all occasions to promote.

On the other hand, there was the mother's sister, Emma
Funton, whom Herondine familiarly called "Aunt Em."
Mrs. Funton was also a widow ; but her children, three in
number, had been well married and settled comfortably in
life, leaving her to select the method of living best suited
to herself. Seeing the hardship wrought by death in the
Herondine family, Aunt Em offered her services as com-

forter and joint guardian with Aunt Frill; and thus it came
to pass they were associated in a benevolent work that the
people at large heartily approved: but they had their
peculiarities.

Aunt Frill was an indefatigable searcher after news
relating to the pedigree of other people, more especially to
the phase of it known as family jars, and even going so
far as to find comfort in sensational scandal as noised
around by neighboring gossips. At meals Herondine
heard all the secret operations of society through Aunt
Frill with a great deal more accuracy than was related
in the daily papers, besides hundreds of choice items that
never reached publication at all. He was delighted with
it, which made his aunt say on one occasion that she
"believed its efficacy made him fat." Whether true or
false, this assertion need not be questioned in face of the
fact that the young man enjoyed the society of Aunt Frill
with keen discernment, and imagined he could not eat a
satisfactory meal if not listening to the force and eloquence
of her tongue on such subjects as appeared to captivate
her choice.

Mrs. Funton, however, held these characteristic traits of
her companion in some contempt. Her precise and
methodical manner was opposed naturally to frivolous
language, although she did not object to the circulation of
scandal if couched in appropriate terms. She was a good
speaker, and the modulating tones of her voice added
interest as well as a pleasurable character to her discourse.
As a rule, if not debating with Aunt Frill, she was expatiating on the nature of a physical trouble which had followed herself for years; namely, weakness of the stomach.
No one exactly knew whether the complaint had ceased

progressing or otherwise; her own testimony was all that could be relied on in the case, and that was explicit enough.

"My dear Frill," she would say, "you know my weakness. My stomach is gone — totally gone. I could no more hope for its return to the normal state than expect to meet Washington on Broadway. I am resigned to my fate absolutely. You can see for yourself how cheerfully I bear up against such tremendous odds. The doctor asserts there is no remedy for weakness equal to strength. Something strong should be applied to the weakness. Of course, that is quite reasonable, and based, evidently, on sound scientific principle; therefore, my dear, I shall take for breakfast on this occasion a beefsteak and fried onions with scrambled eggs on the side."

Divided in tastes and sentiments, the aunts stood apart also on the political issues of the period. Mrs. Winling espoused the teachings of the Northern wing of the Democratic Party, afterwards led by Stephen A. Douglas, of Illinois, while Mrs. Funton believed all hope of future prosperity for the nation lay with the Constitutional Union Party, previously known as the Know-nothing Party. In seeking information on the question of slavery, therefore, Herondine encountered a great deal of uncertainty.

While Aunt Frill went the length of recommending that the people of the territories should be permitted to solve the difficulties of the situation to suit themselves or appeal to the wisdom of the Supreme Court, no argument was advanced by her against the prevalence of slavery in the states as then existing, because the Constitution permitted it and she and her party imagined they could not assume powers sufficient to overturn that which their forefathers had so firmly established. This conclusion came so near being right that it presented the semblance of greatness to the world, which characterizes the conduct of strict adherents of civil law, and left Herondine at a loss to know how or where the whole truth could be acquired, if anything further remained to be discovered relating to the problem.

Mrs. Funton could not supply him with the desired knowledge, because he found of his own accord that the crude rules of her political belief were practically set aside by the intellectual spirit of the times, and must be repudiated by every young aspirant for public distinction or be reckoned an illiberal citizen.

When Aunt Frill found that her dear nephew remained for years disturbed in his political faith like a scornful irreconcilable, she marveled much on the character of a remedy for his case. Public opinion appeared so much divided on great questions that she considered it useless to apply to any one of the prominent statesmen in the country for enlightenment, because his sayings today would be controverted tomorrow by somebody else equally gifted; and how could she, a widow without children, determine who was right? Hence she observed to Mrs. Funton:

"We'll wait. It will be set right some day."

To which the lady addressed emphatically replied:

"Never, except through cause and effect, if not by means of Constitutional Union."

"My impression is," continued Aunt Frill, "things of this kind come of their own accord, even if not allied to genuine democracy—like a man deserting his wife, for instance, or an elopement in high life, that no one ever expected would occur."

"My dear Frill," responded Mrs. Funton, "these are accidents, mere everyday happenings, that bear no relation to Alton one way or another. I may reiterate, however, the assertion so plainly made before, that all endeavors to find some visionary benefit from a party or principle that has no existence — mark you, no *de facto* existence — may be pronounced waste of energy and distress of spirit."

Aunt Frill was silenced. Whenever her opponent in debate found it necessary to quote from the Latin or French, she felt her case hopeless, believing that the presence of these foreign languages, or any one of them, in the discourse indicated complete victory for the other side. Mrs. Funton's reasonings, however, did not bring conviction to her mind; and for a long time she kept her thoughts to herself, expecting some revelation. Strange as it may appear, her hope was at length satisfied, and the mysterious knowledge revealed as if to gladden her old heart in return for the solicitude so lavishly bestowed on Herondine.

One day, in passing through Union Square, while Herondine was listening to Mrs. Funton's description of the celebrated persons in her party who loved baked beans for Sunday morning breakfast, Aunt Frill espied a young man seated on one of the rustic benches near the central fountain, whose appearance seemed to revive in her some ambitious idea, if not the curiosity for which she was re-·markable.

The young man was comfortably dressed, slender in form, had a clear, pale face and brown hair, and appeared a little above the medium height. A book lay beside him, and as the party of the first part passed he bent forward and traced lines on the margin of the walk with the end of a twig.

Aunt Frill was charmed by such novel conduct, although unnoticed by her companions; and, as her nature demanded the solution of the mysterious sayings and doings of all persons within the limits of her acquaintance, as well as those without them whom she could in any way reach, she imagined she had discovered in the present case a fair subject for investigation. Besides, she became suddenly animated with the belief that this young man was an oracle whose words would break down the barrier of uncertainty, and clear all doubts away. In her enthusiasm she laughed like one brimful of pleasant memories.

"I declare," she said to Herondine, "we must retrace our steps and question that young man."

"Why, aunt, would it not be rude to accost a stranger without a formal introduction?"

"No, my dear, not a stranger if the design be good, such as the necessity existing of knowing as much as you can about his affairs. We must keep posted, Alton, or be nowhere. Besides, he may be able to prescribe a remedy for Aunt Em's complaint, which is defying all our care and watchfulness."

"I doubt it very much," replied Mrs. Funton testily, although evidently flattered by the kindness of Aunt Frill in remembering her at that time.

"But you will permit me to question him, Aunt," continued Herondine, as, wheeling round with his companions, he perceived they were committed to the undertaking.

"No, Alton, no," responded Aunt Frill. "You might frighten him, my dear, whereas my questions will only mollify his temper and draw him out."

Thus assuming the entire control of the prospective interview, Aunt Frill approached her object with the

cautious air of an uninformed person in order to excite the
ready acquiescence of the stranger.

"Excuse a woman's curiosity," she said, addressing the
young man, "but my friends — my nephew, Mr. Herondine, and Aunt Funton — were in doubt as to your object
of drawing lines in the sand; and to relieve their embarrassment I thought it only right to ask you, seeing you
looked like a young person that would be very obliging."

"Well," replied the stranger somewhat tardily, "I
imagine my work of little interest to you or your friends,
although you are quite welcome to know as much about it
as I do myself. I am endeavoring to establish a general
formula for the trisection of an angle."

"How strange that is!" said Aunt Frill learnedly.
"And may I ask, kind sir," she continued, "what sort of
an angle you propose to trisect?"

As the stranger seemed puzzled how to answer, Herondine said:

"A geometrical angle, aunt, to be sure."

"I suppose," resumed Aunt Frill, "you know pretty
much about everything. To what party do you belong?"

"To no party, madam,' replied the young man, with
spirit.

"No party!" reiterated Aunt Frill in amazement.
"How can you be so foolish?"

"The knowledge I seek is given by science," returned
the stranger. "To belong to a political party signifies
that you are bound hand and foot to its requirements and
conditions. I prefer freedom."

"Now that you mention it, that reminds me," said
Aunt Frill, "I intended to speak about slavery. What is
your opinion on the question? Do you think the people

of the territories should be permitted to have slaves like those of the states?"

"There should be no slavery in the states or territories," replied the young man. "It is a relic of barbaric ages, a disgrace to a nation claiming any affiliation with justice."

"But the Constitution? How can you reconcile its provisions with men's opinion?"

"We do not learn law from the Constitution. The American citizens who framed it found slavery prevail as a condition of things which they were unable to rectify. It was introduced into this country and fostered under the care of a foreign power until it grew to such vast proportions that it would be suicidal to the success of the American patriots to ignore it. Hence it remained as part of our country's obligations when the transfer of power was made. The foreigner was driven out, but he left after him something to be remembered, an ungodly heirloom, like a skeleton in the cellar, capable of harrowing the feelings of every individual in the household when its true nature became known."

"Isn't that cute?" said Aunt Frill, looking with some surprise not devoid of admiration at the young enthusiast.

At this point, Herondine, extending his card to the young man, expressed a desire to see him at his home near Abingdon Square when time permitted. The invitation was accepted, and while excusing himself for his carelessness in not carrying cards he wrote his name on a slip of paper and presented it to Herondine. It was handed round to the ladies as a means of reintroduction, Aunt Frill reading it aloud, "Rob Riddleton, of Belview."

"There is one more question I wish to ask, until we meet again," said Aunt Frill. "Mrs. Funton is troubled with weakness of the stomach. Indeed, as she herself expresses it, her stomach is gone — totally collapsed, apparently. Now, is there anything in science that would restore her to perfect health, or must she suffer all her life from this unfortunate trouble?''

"Let me hear a history of the case," replied Riddleton, "the symptoms, for instance — and you, Mrs. Funton," he said while glancing at her rotund figure, "please state all you know of the complaint. Speak at the same time, ladies, to expedite matters. I can analyze both accounts together.''

Then he bent his gaze on the ground and listened while Aunt Frill and Aunt Funton dilated with rare circumlocution on the eccentricity and persistence of the disease under consideration. When the ladies concluded their account, Rob Riddleton said with a smile:

" Whenever you are attacked by weakness such as here described, if it be at mealtimes — and I have no doubt it will — eat everything in sight."

"And you think she may be cured?" queried Aunt Frill.

" Unquestionably," replied Rob with emphasis.

"Ah!" said Mrs. Funton, "how wonderful is science! This assurance of the young man is equivalent to the doctor's diagnosis word for word. The weakness is not denied nor the condition doubted; therefore, my dear Frill, we shall continue the beefsteaks in the morning, to which may be added some boiled brook trout, with a variable diet for lunch and dinner, until the cure is well established.''

Herondine and Riddleton became intimate friends, visiting each other frequently and discussing the difficulties of the times for the purpose of extending their knowledge.

Alton B. soon understood the method by which he could arrive at the truth of things ; namely, to examine each case on its merits, and judge logically, discarding prejudice and opinion. For this purpose he read text books on the reasoning process, guided by Rob, until he felt the self-conscious independence of a scholar. He learned, too, the secret of Aunt Funton's complaint. The weakness complained of was merely hunger promoted by a sharp appetite, a healthy indication if promptly met by wholesome diet.

Besides this success of Herondine, which must be credited to Aunt Frill's remarkable watchfulness, there was another item of happiness acquired through the same means ; namely, acquaintance with Grace Finnestare. Some years before the opening of our story, Judge Finnestare and his daughter were visiting in New York, and encountered the young man with the two mothers at the residence of mutual friends. They appeared so nearly alike in superior attainments as well as physical aspect that an attachment grew up between them which culminated in love. Later Herondine proposed an engagement to Miss Finnestare, which was received favorably and accepted.

Hence, when the rumors of war brought him into activity as an advocate of freedom to the slaves, his obligations to his country stood heavily on the one hand, while his engagement to marry encumbered the other. In either case he could not escape from honorable duty. The men of his party saw he was a competent agent to send west, and delegated him to spread the new doctrine on the border, in order, if possible, to counteract the vicious teachings of their enemies. It was a sore trial to Aunt Frill and Aunt Funton when Herondine appeared ready, with a gripsack in his hand, to depart on his mission ; but they were reconciled when assured of his speedy return.

This was the condition of his affairs when he appeared in Omaha, little suspecting the existence of Danderton Hitch's enmity or the danger that menaced him on account of his faithfulness to his early love. He began at once to enlist public sentiment in favor of his party, whose representatives in convention at Chicago, May eighteenth, had nominated Abraham Lincoln for the presidency, and whose platform contained a plank recommending the prohibition of slavery in the territories as a preliminary provision of further legislation on the subject.

In conjunction with thousands of exemplary Americans, he was anxious to remove the base stigma of cruelty from the land of his birth, foisted on it by an unscrupulous enemy. For years the voices and aspirations of the humane people to whom he belonged were suppressed by the influence of the slave markets and the arrogant cry of "individual rights" from those whose selfishness demanded the bonded body and soul of a human being to satisfy their thirst for gain. Now the cruelty of war would meet the cruelty of slavery, and render an accounting of the issue at the expense of many a valuable life. Darkness would encounter darkness on the margin of the abyss dividing truth from ignorance; and, when the mists and smoke should roll away, the light of reason and of justice would appear in their stead to direct this part of mankind still further into the unknown future.

CHAPTER VIII.

VIEWING THE GATHERING CLOUDS.

THE crowd at Judge Finnestare's, which heretofore assembled in that hospitable household for sociability and good-fellowship, now sat closer together and grew less gay daily on account of the serious condition of the political situation throughout the country. Like the gathering of the clouds before a storm, whose movements are silently performed, as if conscious of impending rupture, so the people on the western border of the United States, as well as those in other places, began to divide or concentrate on the issues of civil war, which the signs of the period foretold to a certainty.

Since Herondine's arrival, many persons besides regular visitors availed themselves of invitations and came to hear him speak. He seemed ready to answer all questions, and denied no one the information in his possession on the approaching crisis. Generally his declaration was a holding forth rather than private conversation. Notwithstanding the popularity by which he was surrounded, his opponents and enemies were numerous, owing to the stand taken by him to defeat the establishment of "The Western Gasconader" under the management of Danderton Hitch, and his denunciation of slavery in any form.

Bad feeling grew up between him and Danderton, not only on these grounds, but also on account of the secret adoration each entertained for Grace Finnestare, as heretofore mentioned, the Eastern man knowing full well that his rival could not live in the neighborhood of the lovely girl and not regard her with affection. The instinct of the two

men became powerful factors in shaping their thoughts in
this direction; and the imagination, adding its quota to the
facts, produced so huge a cause that they became noted
enemies, whose hatred one for the other admitted of no
compromise.   Nor did this source of contention remain
long waiting for a stimulant from current events.

In November, Mr. Lincoln was elected by a popular vote
approaching two millions, having a good plurality over the
favored Democratic Party of the North, and showing the
pro-slavery party of the South, the Southern Democracy, as
well as the Know-nothing Party, to be mere factions.
Herondine heard the news with delight.   He boasted on
the street, in the presence of a mixed congregation of poli-
ticians, that the American people would no longer be
classed as slave owners, and that such of them as heretofore sought to establish a reign of justice and law would
now stand forth together to receive the commendation they
deserved from the civilized world.   They had spoken
through the polls and proclaimed their strength.   Herondine's enthusiasm, as a matter of course, only increased the
animosity of his antagonists.   The defeated parties grew
more restive, and it was freely predicted that the Republican victory would now more than ever advance the chances
of war.

On the night that his friends assembled to congratulate
him on the success of his party, there was a large assemblage at Finnestare's.   The Judge, as host, appeared to
advantage in his faultless suit of blue; but there was an
expression of care on his countenance, indicating how
deeply he felt the troubles gathering around him, which
threatened even the stability of his home, and probably
the absorption of his fortune.   He sat in a high armchair

in the northeast corner of the living room, where every one could see him, and questioned Herondine closely on leading subjects as they were introduced.

Grace Finnestare presided at the piano in the early part of the evening, but, singularly enough, as debate increased, the music died out, and she remained before the instrument a silent listener rather than disturb the glow of thought peculiar to the occasion.

Madam Gloriana, accustomed to activity and garrulous explanations, folded her hands together and gave a sigh of resignation as she found herself securely flanked by two elderly women, who poked their elbows into her ribs alternately as some expression in the discourse aroused the latent humor of their souls to the striking point. Felice, too, might be seen in the passage leading to the kitchen, anxious to understand the drift of the conversation.

On every face there appeared anxiety; from every tongue came assertions of wonder or dismay as one part or the other of the situation was contemplated. Nay, more; as the night grew dark, persons uninvited collected on the outside near the front door, which stood open, eager to catch the news as circulated within. One of these figures standing in the gloom looked very much like Danderton Hitch, for the night watchman, who was there also, made him out clearly to his own satisfaction, and wondered what he was up to. Some of Judge Finnestare's questions tested Herondine's reasoning powers to their utmost capacity.

"Are not the rights of an individual foremost of all things connected with human affairs?" he said.

"It is true," responded Herondine, "but in considering the case of master and slave you should remember there are two individuals, one for whom the supreme rights referred to are claimed without reservation, while the other has no rights at all. Your proposition, therefore, is merely sectional or circumscribed."

"I desire to remind you, my dear Alton," returned the Judge, "that the case of the master, or slave owner, was to be examined on its merits, separately. If individuality amounts to anything, it must apply to him as much as to any favorite of yours. Inequality in condition must exist among people always, because it is natural. The responsibilities of some are greater than others. The surroundings, or environment, the laws of business, and circumstances demand and impose such distinction."

"You are again correct, Judge," answered Herondine. "The standpoint or platform on which you reason is good enough as far as it goes. In other words, you have not stated the whole truth, but only a portion of it. The slave owner has undoubtedly individual rights; but, mark you, no privilege of that kind should be maintained when found trespassing on the rights of others. This is the great utility of law, to adjudicate justice between man and man. Should it fail to accomplish this purpose on account of circumscribed design, it is no longer law, but mere party legislation, disreputable and treacherous, whose operation should be stopped with as much force and interest as if it were a torrent of destruction. Bear in mind that the execution of law is not necessarily freedom from distress. Calamity is liable to strike any person, no matter how well fortified he may be against it. This is inevitable. Therefore the slave owner is as liable to suffer loss or hardship by the laws introduced for the government of individuals as the slave. If people complain of law because it does not make them rich or happy, they should remember it does not operate out of its sphere any more than a wagon or a balloon. Under the greatest law, life, there is the hardship, death, demonstrating to us clearly that our world and our conditions are subject to a give and take policy where complete immunity from distress is impossible.

" We propose to give a class of persons heretofore unjustly dealt with, the privileges of freedom that the higher moral law would concede were it in general practice here. Should this action produce stringency or loss to the slave owner, justice, no doubt, would demand compensation for it ; but in case such terms were not acceptable, then the liberty of the slaves should be proclaimed anyhow, because the apparent injustice to the masters would be trifling and insignificant side by side with the long array of social happiness and improvement to be enjoyed by the colored people set free. Besides, such legislation is in consort with nature to restore equilibrium where disturbances are presented.

" Let it be understood, a man with a moiety of truth is not so far advanced as one with the whole truth, whatever may be the case ; and a part, compared with the entire, is of little use. It is singular how many persons are found in this world grasping at a little and rejecting much, who select the less good for the greater and the ideal for the real. Some stake all hope on a single idea, others in the efficacy of an imperfect contrivance, while hundreds go before the country ventilating visionary projects of reform which are branded false and delusive as plainly as those spoken of in the Apocalypse who shall carry on the forehead the mark of the beast. In liberty we possess the greater good ; in charity, the greater virtue. The freedom of all classes of mankind agrees with natural law, provided the second condition be fulfilled of reconciling each class and individual to its proper position in order that the whole be made harmonious. This is individuality and universality one with the other. Nature's law requires this strange condition, and mankind must follow or fail. If men persist in attempting to rule the business world and society by mere opinions, regardless of imperishable law, the fabric of the human race will fall into chaos and finally produce total extinction.

"The harmony of parts produces beauty; the harmony of sounds, music. Men who speak for the individual alone and demand legislation in his interests are only half-way right. If the relationship of other individuals be denied and the prosperity of the country at large ignored or abused, the plan of nature is broken, the conditions have not been fulfilled, and disappointment and discontent must be the inevitable result.

"Men of themselves can make no law; they only define it, like a sculptor who hews a statue from the block. We are afflicted at present with ignorant opinions run riot over questions of right and wrong which threaten disruption to the nation and a blockade of republican institutions. You must urge what I have outlined in this speech — the sub-mission of individuals to the will of the majority — until the truth becomes apparent. Our opponents may precipi-tate war on the pretense that the rights of the individual have been disregarded, but in meeting them we hope to be animated with the consciousness of being on the side of sound principle held sacred in the trust of the supreme powers that control the destinies of nations."

Judge Finnestare made no reply to this statement of his prospective son-in-law. The features of the company present told of the awe by which they were inspired, and the old man sought not to induce further discussion on a subject that called forth such fearful possibilities as fratricidal war and its consequences. The conversation, however, became general, as is usually the case where the opinions of a miscellaneous gathering of people are temporarily suspended in favor of a person of superior attainments.

Madam Gloriana heard with the deepest concern what the two elderly women near her had to say on oratory in general and of some shining lights of their respective families in particular — how "Jim," the husband of one, and "Ned," the husband of the other, exceeded all men as linguists, especially when under excitement or with a little drink aboard, and would have astonished the world at large if it had not been for accident which kept them back and turned themselves and their talents into unfortunate channels, where they were now found.

Following the example of others, Herondine led Grace Finnestare to a seat near her father, and the three exchanged ideas in low tones on future arrangements and anticipated events. Figuratively speaking, they scanned the gathering clouds of war as they approached realization, and shuddered at the ordeal through which they must necessarily pass before the coming of peace again.

The young man could not help debating with himself if it were really just to marry his affianced at this time, for personally he must live up to the expectations of his political friends and quit his home for the field when necessary. On this account he revealed to Grace Finnestare and her father all his plans and obligations, all his feelings of love for her and his country, and awaited her decision. When this decision came, it was characteristic of the faithfulness of womankind as a rule and of the patriotism of the American girl. She would leave her home, she said, and follow him to the field, or wait and work until his return.

Then the auspicious day of their marriage was named — December twentieth — with preliminary arrangements for the occasion settled, amid thoughts of earthly happiness and forebodings of evil. It was also determined that Judge Finnestare would dispose of his property and banking interests in Omaha so as to move into Herondine's New York home, where, with his daughter and the two aunts, besides Madam Gloriana and Felice, who would accompany them, he would be as carefully tended as ever before, and the last years of his life comforted by their presence.

When the serious part of the business was concluded, Herondine announced to Grace and her father that he had received a letter from Aunt Frill which he would read for their entertainment, or such portions of it as deserved notice.

"Alton dear," she wrote, "we elected Lincoln. He wasn't my choice from the start, because I went my pile on Douglas, as you are aware; nor was he the man Aunt Funton was hankering after, bein' so much taken up with Constitutional Union; but, as I said before, we elected Lincoln for all that was out. We knew it would please you, for you were dead stuck after him and would bet your bottom dollar to win.

"Since the time we met that Riddleton young man in Union Square, it was plain to my mind you would drop common sense and catch on to science, whether it was south, west, or crooked.

"I gave Aunt Funton a piece of my mind about it privately, telling her it might be the ruin of you, just as much as if you went into spiritualism or the scow business, but she wisely answered that in such cases there was no remedy worth a picayune. Aunt Funton is clear-sighted; there's no backing out of that.

"It is rumored the pro-slavery people are going to hold a barbecue in Washington about next Christmas. We don't know how true it is. Do you? If you attend (but of course not), send us notice, and we'll be happy to reciprocate and thank you all the same. It is only right that such should be recognized.

"Now, about the suggestion to attend your wedding when we get word of the time: we have considered it. You are good to think of your old aunts in the emergency, but in consultation it was decided unwise to travel all that distance while Aunt Funton is feeling ill. The complaint of her stomach comes on at periods about the dinner hour, and if it were not that I had the proper remedy always ready at hand — generally beefsteak or prime roast — I do not know what actually would happen. So we'll postpone it. I may say, however, she is quite well otherwise, and tips the beam at one sixty-nine three-quarters, which is quite encouraging for a delicate woman."

After the reading of Aunt Frill's letter the discussion of minor details was continued until the company began to move away. Among the first to depart from the outside was Danderton Hitch. He had heard Herondine's speech, and it evolved new ideas in his mind. His hatred of the young man increased on being convinced that he was a person of ability, commanding the respect of his audiences, and, as a matter of course, endearing himself still further to the heart of Grace Finnestare.

Danderton's measure of revenge was not full. The doubtful conditions defined by his father regarding Whifton's method of procuring dynamite seemed unsatisfactory. The plan might fail and the bird escape. If war was inevitable, the general disturbance accompanying it would aid him in his purpose to slay Herondine.

This Eastern emissary, proud of his knowledge and confident of success, must fall ingloriously. He, Danderton, would see to that much single-handed. There need be no such explosion as that suggested by his father, which, if promoted, would cause widespread consternation and comment. The work must be done without noise and in the dark — conditions favorable to escape. Under this feature of the case, it was not necessary to consider mitigating circumstances. The act should be thorough and fiendish, with a record only of a dead man and an undiscovered assassin. On the night of Herondine's marriage, while sauntering on the porch, Danderton would stab him in the back without fear of detection. Then, afterwards, he would watch the fate of Grace Finnestare, and, if chance offered, marry her when her protectors had disappeared and all her hopes of happiness were dead !

These ideas originated with him as he sought repose on that night, and during the days intervening between it and the twentieth of December he revolved the plot in his mind. His morbid nature fed upon the outlook as something necessary for its condition, and it grew in strength and importance until it seemed a substantial reality that could not fail of accomplishment.

In the meantime, Crow Whifton, in his lone dwelling at the crossroads, had little suspicion of the actual approach of war. Relying on the information or opinions of the night watchman, he believed that, at most, the contending parties would settle the difficulty by arbitration. The conduct of Hamilton Hitch, however, entered largely into his thoughts, and filled the entire field of his imagination with a combination of pain and pleasure, like a landscape over which drift light clouds and sunshine on a lovely day.

Owing to the persistence of this train of thinking, the man became his ideal companion whose presence could not be shut out from the memory. This strange individual was not only the skeleton behind the door in Whifton's antique room, but the guest at his table, the visitor at the fireside, and the spirit of his mental vision in the darkness before he slept. He could not reconcile with his doubts and misgivings of the man the insinuating manner, the friendly smile, the liberality and benevolent acts associated with him. There was something unfathomable in his nature which tended to darken the brightness that a clear conscience heretofore sustained around the little trader in trifles, and caused a painful sensation at his heart, occasionally, as great almost as the recollection of his unrequited love.

The starting point of this trouble came from the incident before recorded, where Hamilton Hitch requests Whifton to conceal a crime to save a criminal, and makes the obligation deep and lasting by giving a bribe to seal the compact. Whenever Whifton thought of Hamilton Hitch as a gentleman, a good fellow, or a genial acquaintance, the little man invariably went back to this circumstance as if forced to do so by an unseen agent. This tampering with the mysterious continued almost without intermission from the time of the event until now, when we see him calculating on the chances of success or failure as others do, and viewing the clouds of distress or discontent as they appeared to accumulate above his head with the near approach of winter.

Doing his best to avoid consideration of it, he ended by permitting its full force to play with his intellect and bind his will to the subtle influence which it displayed. Free to all appearances, he was, nevertheless, bound even to more than this irrevocably as if chained to a rock. The very thought of filing charges against Hitch shocked him. He felt that the dark power in league with the man could be brought into action with impunity and destroy his existence with the unerring certainty of a bullet in his heart. Besides, he felt an inward loss of courage or purpose which could not be overcome.

The advent of this condition was slow, but, when fully developed, there was no doubt regarding its significance. At first the pursuit of the theme brought to his mind the idea that he himself had committed an error, and then that it was a crime. Originally a minute thing, it now assumed immense proportions, like the inflation of a balloon. From doubts of the integrity of Hamilton Hitch, Whifton turned upon himself. He had not forgotten he aspired to be a judge, and here was a case that could test his ability.

"Whifton," he said, "answer the court, are you guilty or not?"

"Not guilty, your honor; it is really so," he replied. "There was no criminal intention at the time the act was committed, which exonerates me to some extent. Other motives prevailed, such as personal safety, profit, and loss; but I agree that after due deliberation there was guilt in retaining the bribe."

"What have you to say, sir," continued Whifton, questioning himself, "about the growth, or multiplication, of small offenses: their liability to lead into serious or great crimes?"

"I plead extenuating circumstances, your honor, and ask for a stay of proceedings."

"On what grounds?"

"Repentance, your honor, which is equivalent to the punishment or restitution required by the civil law. I repent, and assure the court I shall never again be found perpetrating such wrong."

"Ah! but," said the court severely, "mark what follows your weak-kneed policy. Hamilton Hitch negotiated the purchase of dynamite through you, ostensibly for scientific purposes, but who could tell if this statement, or declaration, was true. The pursuits and public character of Danderton, his son, would not point to any such belief — quite the contrary. Now, if, when received, the dynamite should be used not for scientific purposes, but to destroy life and property, your resolution would be of little avail; and the first step in crime, of which you repent, would be advanced to a stage where criminality on a large scale could not be denied. You should eradicate the first cause if you meant to be really and truly just."

"The court has wise discernment; it is really so," said Whifton gravely; "but I have not sufficient power to institute proceedings against a man where there is so much doubt. Anyway, I shall keep the secret and take the risks."

"You are tempting fate to call forth disaster which could have been easily averted by disclosure."

"I judge for myself to the best of my ability."

"It may be false. Suppose the dynamite procured by
you should be employed against Grace Finnestare?"

Whifton groaned. He stood up, and, glancing through
the window, pointed to an old tree which appeared in the
plain some distance from the house.

"If it please the court, the penalty would be paid *there*,"
he said; but it did not transpire whether he meant that
Hitch or himself would be hanged on the tree.

"We perceive," resumed the court, "you have been
overshadowed by a mysterious power, an evil one, at the
command of the individual. You have been bound to
play a neutral part, while he has gone forth free to prosecute
his nefarious principles. In your heart you are guiltless,
yet you hold the gist of a secret which may one day lead to
disaster and death. Your case resembles that of a spirit
suspended between heaven and the abode of darkness.
You are neither up nor down, this way nor that way.
Now listen; I shall define your position, clearly, for the
information of thousands of other persons similarly situated. You are In the Depths of the First Degree of crime,
but so imperfectly implicated as to escape detection.
Should you advance with other acts of a like nature, your
career would never change its criminal course until warned
by some well-timed accident or punishment in the hands
of the law. You have decided wisely to stop and take
chances whether your original trespass on morality will die
or yield a much greater crime. Let us hope you may
escape. While this impending trouble is suspended above
your head, you must remain in the depths of the first degree, where innocence loses the charm of its glory in exchange for degradation, and virtue hides her head in
shame; where victory is checked, freedom compromised,

and the gifts of God to man sullied so as to appear incon-
sistent with the power and greatness of Him who gave
them.''

Whifton bowed his head as if saluting the decision of
the court. Other men feared the rumors of war, but he
dreaded more than anything else the coming of the dynamite ; and, behold, the time was at hand !

CHAPTER IX.

THE RECORD BROKEN.

H ERONDINE'S wedding day was typical of the
period, having brightness and gloom alternating.
The air was keen with frost, the ground hard, and far
above in the sky small clouds congregated as if preparing
to descend in snow. Public traffic on the streets had
become visibly less, as was usually the case at that time
of the year; and many people were content to remain
inactive during the absence of business until the opening
of spring. There seemed to be an ominous silence abroad
portending the coming of some momentous disaster.

It had been arranged that Herondine and Grace Finnestare would be married in her father's home when the
lights were set in the evening, and the guests assembled to
witness the ceremony and participate in the festivities.
The good old-fashioned way of having a sumptuous supper
was to be observed, with the bride and groom seated in
their proper places at the table, followed by toasts, singing,
and dancing. In connection with this program, it may be
said Madam Gloriana never appeared to greater advan-

tage than on this occasion when the persons invited appeared upon the scene and saw her handiwork displayed in the decorations and general management of the festival. It was superb.

At the time appointed, Herondine entered the large living room from the east side, while Grace Finnestare came from the west. Both were accompanied by a train of attendants. The two groups stood beneath a canopy of blue silk, whose supports and fringes were decorated with delicate winter flowers and strings of creepers. Besides the brilliant display of lights and colors, the place was full of perfume.

Judge Finnestare, entering, advanced and gave away his daughter without any perceptible emotion, so much did he confide in and reverence the character of his future son-in-law. Then the ceremony proceeded and the words necessary to make the couple husband and wife were pronounced, followed by the most sincere and hearty congratulations ever offered anyone in that district.

Some of the leading people of the company, turning from the happy bride and groom, bent their heads in the direction of the dining room, where the next most desirable performance would be enacted; but at this point their progress was temporarily arrested by a noise coming from the city which resembled a public commotion in the streets instigated by incidents or news of an unusual character. Every one stood still and listened. The loud shouting of a multitude of people could be distinctly heard, supplemented by hoarse calls, the clattering of horses' hoofs on the hard road, the quick footsteps on the pavement, the buzz of general conversation, and occasionally the report of a pistol or shotgun discharged in the air.

Herondine stood motionless with his bride, hand in hand. A painter would have seized the situation to delineate a picture where awe overspread the features of two beautiful persons in the climax of their happiness. They had reached the heights of bliss, and lo, tribulation suddenly appeared in the valley following their footsteps. One of the guests stepping into the street returned soon afterwards with the important news.

"South Carolina has seceded from the Union! A convention authorized by the state legislature adopted and promulgated an ordinance of secession this very day. The news came in by telegraph."

No one in the party understood the significance of this announcement better than Herondine. He knew it indicated not merely obstruction to republican advancement but a partial cancellation of the work performed by his forefathers, who fought and died for the political liberty, such as it was, which America enjoyed.

Lest his abstraction should incommode the company in any way, Herondine, taking the bride on his arm, led the way to the dining room, where discussion of the news became secondary to the admiration for, and enjoyment of, the viands so lavishly spread on the tables. Indeed, many persons seemed to regard it as of little importance, and settled the question of secession in South Carolina for themselves by saying, "Let her go. What's the odds, anyhow?" Herondine did not coincide with these opinions. While at supper he dilated on the subject at some length to his wife.

"This act of South Carolina," he said, "cannot be maintained on legal grounds. Separation, or secession, of one state from the others, to be lawful must be agreeable to all. The law of the case could have been enunciated by a child learning its first lessons in reasoning, so simple is it. The original design on which the Constitution and existence of the United States have been founded is the universal law before mentioned, where the individual liberty of a state, in harmony with the general interests of the others, unite in consolidating and perpetuating a great nation endowed with facilities for the maintenance of peace and prosperity among the children of mankind. The idea was probably borrowed from old Rome, although in the operations of nature there is nothing so clearly defined as this contrivance. Hence we must hold the law sacred, for upon it depends the stability of our national existence. Rome fell because she swerved from its observance, led by ambitious men ; but if we come to such a fate, it shall be when our citizens are too ignorant to reason and too perverse to be obedient to the law. There are not yet many indications that such a period is approaching.''

While the company was at the height of enjoyment, Herondine walked into the night alone to ascertain if there were any serious troubles abroad. In his opinion, anything might happen, from the shooting of an individual to open rebellion. The noises in the town, however, were no longer heard. The atmosphere was cold and the darkness impenetrable. Silence happily reigned conjointly with it above the scene. Now, if his archenemy, Danderton Hitch, happened to be near, his opportunity had come. No one would witness the deathblow. How Herondine waited as if actually tempting fate and placing his life at the mercy of the foe, but, as the reader is aware, all unconscious of danger ! He listened ; there was no sound : he moved ;

there responded no pursuing footstep. Finally he returned to the dining room.

Where was Danderton?

There were cogent reasons why he did not appear on this occasion. The necessary preparations had been made by him, as before sketched. His dress was tight fitting, confined at the waist by a belt so that no loose clothing should obstruct his movements. Even the point of the dagger he intended using was carefully examined, and he sat in the front apartment of his home looking out at the gathering twilight, ready for action. His father was closeted in his private room upstairs, where he spent most of his time studying devices which harmonized with his thoughts and applied to some ulterior design against the well-being of society. It was at this time the news of secession was given out in front of the telegraph office and caused such widespread consternation afterwards among the citizens.

Like worms frightened out of their beds by a thunderstorm, father and son rushed simultaneously to the front door. Danderton, promising to return in a short time, bounded over the nearest way to the center of the city, intent on ascertaining the cause of the trouble. He was not long absent. When he came in and went into secret conference with his father, the joy that filled his soul deprived him of intelligent speech. Seizing the man's hand, he babbled something like gibberish.

They had come to the identical place and situation where, on a former occasion, it was decided that Herondine must die on the night of his marriage. The father waited with a grim smile over his features. Presently Danderton was able to say:

"They got it in the neck this time, good. Secesh is here. South Carolina is free !"

"The d——!" said Hamilton Hitch, tersely.

Then, as the significance of the news came upon him like the reappearance of a dissolving view, his enthusiasm rose to fever heat. He grew wild and dramatic, walking hurriedly around the apartment with clenched hands and occasionally breaking into laughter. His conduct was plainly diabolical; if not idiotic.

"See here !" he said to Danderton, spasmodically pointing his finger at his son's face. "That cancels everything. Our small plans must come to a standstill. Now is the beginning ; because there is a country we can call home, and my old record can be broken to pieces, with the prospect that it never will be renewed."

"It is away up," remarked the son, "but, dad, what are you going to do?"

"Vamoose the territory. Clear out while our enemies are dumfounded by the news."

"You ain't going tonight, are you?"

"Ain't I, though? Why not? Every man likes to escape from prison when he can. You do not know what it is to have shackles on your ankles and wrists, or to be a suspect that dreads the coming of daylight. Once in a while a bad man gets in his big licks ; luck strikes him like a shot. It is our turn now. I have been patient under the burden of vile surveillance, because there was no help for it ; but now I can pitch the record to the winds and free myself by a little caution and the run of a few days."

"Do you forget that this was Herondine's night?" said Danderton, lowering his voice.

"Naw," answered the father, derisively. "Herondine

and all his truck ain't a drop in the bucket compared with the golden opportunity now offered me for escape. Such a chance occurs only once in a lifetime; therefore leave him alone. He'll turn up again. On the peril of your life, don't touch him! Do not approach the house where he is or be seen in the vicinity, lest my course should be blockaded. I want obedience to this injunction observed with greater care than anything I have ever spoken.''

In what a singular way just men are sometimes preserved from violence! Here was Herondine, who had been condemned to death by Danderton and his father, now as safe and sound as if guarded by a hundred deputy sheriffs, and the two would-be assassins, as bloodthirsty as ever and with as many facilities to carry their vile scheme into execution as before, yet powerless to act. Some would say it was due to a special providence. Let it appear so. It was due to law—to the one giving the larger share precedence over the less, and endowing the greater incident with power to control the minor ones so as to claim most attention and precipitate itself through the sphere of its existence in its true character. Advancing to the window, the father threw up the sash and continued:

''Look! the night is actually as thick as mud, as if to favor me. It will not be fooled. I'll take the chance. Besides, I would have you to know, we can make our own terms with the new government in the South and get anything we have a mind to. There is a great prospect for us; we'll be in it this time. Now, while I go forward at once in the darkness, you follow at early dawn. Our destination is Charleston.''

''And the property here?'' inquired the son.

" Biles, the real estate man, will take care of it. He has my instructions and knows what I want. Biles is a careful thinker, and works closely. We can depend on him. He may rent the house for a while, and then sell the entire property. I shall invest the money in the bonds which, no doubt, will be issued by the Southern government for the purpose of meeting expenses; and we, in this way, may become creditors of it and persons of consequence."

This glowing account of the father inoculated the mind of the son with visions of future greatness, and reconciled him to the failure of his plot against Herondine. Both men began preparations for departure. As it was early in the night, the father could easily clear the city and suburbs without exciting suspicion or even curiosity. He could procure a good mount for a trifle from one of the stable men, who was a friend of his, and, like Whifton, in the depths of the first degree. He held a secret in trust, and was faithful. Hamilton Hitch had many such friends. In an ordinary emergency they were useful, but on the present occasion invaluable.

It did not take the old man much time to get ready. A money belt round the waist and a brace of pistols in his hip pockets were the only additions made to his everyday apparel. With the caution peculiar to his former trade, he slunk to the back door and peered into the prospect beyond, lest there should be any person there watching for his exit. As he became satisfied that the place was unincumbered by the presence of a detective, he motioned to Danderton a farewell and disappeared.

A few hours afterwards some farmers returning from Omaha to their homes on the Iowa side of the Missouri River were overtaken and passed rapidly by a solitary horseman unknown to them. To their salutation he answered not a word or gesture; but appeared to bend with greater eagerness than before over the animal's mane, urging him, no doubt, to quicker speed. The direction of his course was southeast, and the clatter of his horse's hoofs was heard long after he had disappeared from view.

Danderton took greater pains with the event of his departure. The trunks intended to be sent after him as freight, with personal effects, were examined and brought together so as to facilitate their transit when Biles's messengers came to handle them. Like his father, he seemed to ignore the necessity of baggage, for a gripsack, a money belt, and a revolver were the only articles he designed to carry or own on his intended journey. After a few hours' uneasy rest he donned his best clothes, left the house by the front door, and dropped into a restaurant adjoining the stage office, where, when breakfast was concluded, he left messages for his agent with the proprietor of the place. Then, about the time the dancers at Herondine's wedding were going home from Finnestare's with the impression that there was at least one happy couple in the territory, Danderton entered the first outgoing stage, sank heavily into a corner seat, and with melancholy aspect saw familiar objects pass him in review as if for the last time; while the cumbersome vehicle, oscillating in the air, proceeded forward, carrying him away from a home he might never see again.

Whifton rode into Omaha about noon, not so much on account of the nature of the general disturbance, of which he had heard something, as to make inquiry at the post office for mail matter. It will be remembered this was the date on which he expected to receive the dynamite for

Hamilton Hitch, and the circumstance troubled him more than he was willing to admit to a third party. Time, however, with its variety of remedies for poor souls and distressed bodies, lessened the burden of his cares on this occasion. There was a letter for him all the way from Europe telling him the explosive for which requisition had been made was not available. The experiments tried had not yet produced the article in a satisfactory shape; but when perfected, it said, a Boston firm, which was named, would place it on the market, and then he might supply his wants to any extent required.

This statement relieved his anxiety. So full of satisfaction did he become on account of it, that he determined on having an interview with his good friend Hamilton Hitch, to whom he would communicate the contents of the letter. In this connection, he believed the time had come when it would be appropriate to call at the new residence and be entertained there instead of meeting around the corners of the streets or in a restaurant. In his estimation this was progress, whether his doubts and suspicions or the warnings of his instinct regarding the man were true or false.

Imbued with this opinion, he directed his steps to the Hitch residence; but what was his surprise, on arriving there, to behold a sign in the front window on which was inscribed in large characters the words "To Let," and other appearances indicating that the house was unoccupied. But this was not all. Transferring his glance to Finnestare's, he observed active preparations around that domicile as if the inmates were about to leave. A portion of the fence had been thrown down the better to facilitate the removal of furniture. Crates and boxes ready for shipment were standing in the open spaces, and others receiving their quota of personal effects from skilled packers specially employed for the occasion. A little apart from these appeared a flaring notice, brief and to the point, supported by a pole stuck into the ground, announcing the place "For Sale"; and it was evident on all sides that the venerated landmark was doomed to experience great changes in the near future.

"Ah!" exclaimed Whifton, turning away from the sad scene, "they're going to clear out, bag and baggage; it is really so. What will become of the place, anyhow?"

Passing the bank on his way downtown, he saw that the establishment was in new hands, held, of course, on the old secure lines, and the management would soon, one of the directors told him, commence the erection of a substantial structure where the business would be carried forward on a larger basis and be a credit — meaning an advantage — to the city.

The subject of Grace Finnestare's marriage recurred to his mind, but it aroused, instead of resentment or bad feeling of any kind, sadness bitter and deep, such as a child would feel on being deserted by its near friends. He wept a little, silently, when no one saw him, and remarked, as he pressed the tears from his eyes with his handkerchief:

"*I* would be no match for her, anyway. Why should I? How foolish I was ever to dream of such a thing! So beautiful a girl to be the wife of Crow Whifton would be quite an impossibility. It is really so."

When the decision was rendered in the bracing atmosphere of the afternoon, he felt better. Then his attention was directed into other channels. Remarks made by citizens collected on the sidewalks regarding secession reached him as he proceeded downtown, and he soon began to realize that this was the all-absorbing topic of the hour. Every one of his acquaintances introduced the subject to his notice, and he was still listening to opinions on the probable results of it on society and the government when Honeybone, the night watchman, appeared before him.

"Whif, by gosh!" said he. "How's secesh?"

"Just getting the news all in," replied Whifton.

Then, acting on a secret sign from Honeybone, which consisted of a wink of the left eye so well pronounced that the lower part of the cheek was drawn up as in spasm, he grasped the arm of his friend, and they stepped off together intent on reaching their old haunt at Cuffins's, where cocktails and lemonade became the order of the day. Whifton was quite liberal on this occasion. He felt it his duty to act in this manner to meet excitement halfway and also because some of the weight or mental strain on his mind and heart had suddenly become less than heretofore.

He lent a willing ear to Honeybone while that doughty night guardian described in unequivocal terms the shortcomings and inconsistencies of society along his beat as interpreted by him, and made no sign indicating surprise or emotion when the questionable conduct of Danderton Hitch on the night of Herondine's speech-making was spoken of. With a studied calmness which would be noticeable to any one but the imbiber of cocktails, he asked:

"Have you any idea what was he doing there at Finnestare's?"

"Lookin' in," promptly answered his companion.

Whifton did not pursue the theme. He believed in letting well enough alone. The failure of the dynamite to arrive and the departure of the Hitches for parts unknown removed all traces of incipient crime from him, or what might have originated in disaster if not fortunately interrupted. Now he need only keep silent, and he could yet pass as a man free from suspicion as well as be accorded a first place among the best citizens of the country. Thus did he remain faithful to the deep designer who had bound him to secrecy, and imagined his conscience free for evermore, forgetting that his resolution confirmed the previous arrangement whereby he existed, body and soul, in the depths of the first degree of crime, without, apparently, a hope of complete freedom from them in the future.

When everything pertaining to the times had been freely discussed and viewed from the standpoint of opinions held by the speakers, the friends separated.

CHAPTER X.

WHAT HISTORY MUST RECORD.

FOLLOWING the overt act of secession, South Carolina continued the initiative of provoking war. Before the end of December, the authorities of the state had seized Castle Pinckney and Fort Moultrie, military works in Charleston harbor, and the United States arsenal in the city of Charleston, with the public property contained therein. Thus to secession were added aggression and spoliation.

It became evident to the people of all classes in the United States, as well as to the world at large, that these aggressive acts were performed principally as examples for other seceding states; that they indicated the policy to be

pursued by the combination, or confederacy, in future;
and, finally, left no hope for a peaceful solution of the
question at issue to be entertained. The wisdom guiding
the seceders was at fault here. It would be no infringement on the sovereign rights of a free state, assuming
South Carolina to be such after secession, to permit the
United States to hold title to territory or military supplies
within its jurisdiction until an agreement had been reached
regarding its disposition. The appropriation to itself of
property to which it was not in any sense entitled would
be a sufficient cause for war, if nothing else had transpired
to induce it; and the haste displayed in preparation for
hostilities seemed conclusive evidence that the men urging
such policy were fully alive to its responsibilities and what
it must inevitably entail.

It must be plain, also, that the overtures made by the
state commissioners about this time for formal independence could have no weight under the circumstances;
because war was actually in progress on their side, and
must be atoned for or resisted on its own principles and
with similar weapons by the authorities in Washington.

An opinion gained currency in the North which was
held by many worthy people — that the South desired the
establishment of an oligarchy whose power would be more
extended even than the jurisdiction of a limited monarchy,
and whose pronounced class legislation should be as firmly
held by the sway of the sword as if it consisted of, and had
been modeled after, the eternal laws of the universe. The
arrogance displayed by the South in the first days of secession, the exhibition of substantial force contrasted with
the absence of any military organization in the North, the
confiscation of the enemy's supplies wherever encountered,

and the resolution to adhere to slavery as heretofore, went largely to confirm the truth of this opinion.

In imitation of South Carolina, other states seceded during the month of January — Mississippi, Florida, Alabama, Georgia, and Louisiana — and the Lone Star State, Texas, February first. These acquisitions to the new power enabled the leaders of it to organize a convention, or representative body, which was afterwards known as a provisional congress, with powers to elect a president and vice-president and adopt a constitution suitable for its requirements.

When these preliminary acts were completed, resulting in the consolidation of the Confederate States of America and the proclamation of its constitution and principles, the enthusiasm of the people who espoused such cause rose to immense proportions and permeated the public mind of the civilized world. Statesmen, soldiers, scholars, and other patriots flocked to the standard of the Confederacy vowing they would sacrifice every consideration of emolument or convenience for the sole idea of offering assistance to their respective states in the hour of trial. Many a man had no other reason to give for his precipitate flight south than that it was his native home, the place where he was born, or that he could not deny his services to his native state in the day of her distress.

These popular sentiments, well known to have been associated with the history of mankind since the beginning of tradition, are held in higher esteem than the niceties of correct law, and constitute a potent cause for the division in public opinion on the important question here noticed. Perhaps a battle for love of home is as justifiable or meritorious as for absolute right, if the consequences be of more importance in the one case than the other and more likely to secure substantial benefits to the parties concerned; or, perhaps, the invisible powers surrounding man never contemplated having absolute right made a perception in human understanding — the better to enable that department to operate in the limited sphere of its destiny — but to be merely an admirable atom capable of being discovered among the many brilliants at their disposal.

Like an incoming tide that sets afloat the multifarious craft lying idly on the shore, the growing strength of the Confederacy induced thousands of wavering spirits to espouse its cause. Congress, in Washington, made an effort to conciliate the dissatisfied and disaffected by a guarantee of non-interference with slavery as it then existed in the states; but this endeavor proved too weak before the uncompromising measures of the South in its haste to establish independence. The seizures and confiscations continued in all the states pinning their fortunes to South Carolina.

Mr. Buchanan, the President of the United States, while deprecating secession, was not satisfied that Congress had inherent power to make war on an individual state that chose to secede. This seemed to afford a pretext to the new Confederacy for believing its existence would be sustained by the authority of civil law. Moreover, assurances of support came from sources outside the United States. Heretofore the South had been a market for the importation and sale of English goods, and it was freely asserted that substantial aid and recognition from England would be forthcoming at the proper time.

Nothing seemed to be wanting to this young nation in its arrogant assertion of independence, coupled with disrespect of others' privileges such as was claimed by the North and disregard of the truth of principle. Yet the hope, the enthusiasm, the concentration of power, and this fair field of human expectation were blighted by the calculations of false guides. The men who instigated secession and fulminated war were responsible for the conduct of the men who afterwards fought and bled for a cause they believed sacred and just, and lost. At the cry of "country" and "birthright," the soldier naturally would not stop to inquire what nice intricacy of universal law, superior to these watchwords and God-given to the world when time began, was available by which he might escape a fight; nor would the statesman be deterred from action, even if he knew of a higher motive for his conduct, on seeing his country rent by barbarous usage and the folly of ignorance. Hence, how terrible it is to lead a division of mankind into an untenable position doomed to failure and then witness the consequences — the graves of the brave men who fell, the wreck of friendships and family ties, the vacant places that would never again be filled by loved ones, the desolate homes, the suspension of industry, and the cruel heart-burnings that spare neither age, sex, nor condition !

It was not through patriotism that the idea of secession was conceived, nor in the calm reasonings of philosophy, but by furious personal pride and ill-tempered assumption of despotic right. It was the "mammon of iniquity," the red hand of selfishness unrestrained by God's law, that sought eternal rule for traffic in human beings and the liberty to be unjust. Perhaps the men responsible for it, in the first instance, belonged to a past age. Perhaps an enemy scattered its baleful seeds on sensitive minds incap-

able of resistance, or designed as a scheme to advance his
ulterior purposes to the detriment of America. Whatever
had been the cause of its origin in this particular case it
acquired notoriety, strength, and political recognition to a
greater extent than any other delusive project foisted on
the people since the acquisition of national independence,
only to betray the spurious nature of its birth, claims, and
pretensions.

If the delusion nursed by the followers of the Confederacy at that time appeared on a large scale, the lesson
taught by its results has been far-reaching and instructive
to the world at large. It will be understood hereafter
that in any enterprise contemplated by men something
more than mere opinion or self-interest will be necessary
to guarantee complete success; otherwise, the invisible
powers shall strike the operators with the rapidity of lightning, through the laws of circumstances or others equally
irresistible, and lay their plans in the dust.

One of the first officers of note assigned to military duty
under the Confederacy was General P. G. T. Beauregard,
a native of Louisiana, having been born near New Orleans
in 1818. He was not only a soldier of the first class, but
a man qualified to lead the army of any race or nation in
the world as general-in-chief. Graduating second in his
class at West Point Military Academy in 1838, he was
assigned to the artillery of the United States army, and
shortly afterwards transferred to the engineer corps, where
he distinguished himself for many years by careful attention
to his duties in the vast field of operations demanding
his presence and that of his associates.

In recognition of his worth and to show the estimate of
his ability held by the Washington authorities, he was

detailed Superintendent of West Point towards the latter part of the Buchanan administration. This position he resigned the following month in order that he might enter the service of the Confederate government; and, as a result of this movement, he was assigned to the command of the Confederate works in Charleston Harbor, South Carolina, the day before the inauguration of President Lincoln in Washington. This seemed to presage great things for the South; for General Beauregard was well known in every state in the Union, and people believed his military skill would go far in strengthening the party of his choice.

The immediate effect of secession on the people loyal to the North was the infliction of a kind of stupor, like an individual who receives a sudden blow from an unexpected source and becomes unable to determine how to proceed either towards protection or retaliation. As the term of the administration approached the end, public opinion relieved it of the obligation to meet the new difficulty with the earnestness of an incoming one; but it must be said that measures within the scope of its judgment were executed promptly in the interests of the public spirit of the North. Among these may be specially mentioned the hasty summoning of General Winfield Scott, the veteran general-in-chief of the United States army, to Washington by the President, and the careful preparations made under his supervision to ensure the safe inauguration of Mr. Buchanan's successor on the fourth of March.

There was a remarkable division in public opinion in the North as to the righteousness of the Confederate claim to independence, which pervaded all classes of people, making it exceedingly difficult for the leaders of the Union cause to distinguish friends from foes. The regular army, a little over sixteen thousand strong, had been distributed through the vast territory of the United States and could not readily be withdrawn without neglecting the frontier duty to which it had been assigned. Disaffection appeared in the ranks of some of the militia and volunteer organizations surrounding the national capital, and wild rumors were circulated that the aggressive policy of the South would be pushed so far as to attempt an interruption if not a suppression of the government of the North altogether or make it subservient to its dictation.

The patriotic spirit of the North did not long remain in abeyance. Men could endure desertion and the raising of a new standard in the South until reason should decide the merits of such acts; but when to every other offense heretofore enumerated was added the threat of invasion, with supplementary measures such as would prevent the new president of the northern states from taking his seat, then patience had reached its limits. Many a gallant man arose in his might and vowed he would dispute the passage of the invaders single-handed if no one else rendered him assistance. Hence, out of the lethargy of awe patriotism began to strengthen itself. Like the long roll of distant thunder on the approach of a storm, the murmurs of defiance went back to the South as if they were the echoes of its boldness.

It was at this time that Abraham Lincoln assumed the duties of President of the United States. It may be said no one of his predecessors in office was ever encumbered with such enormous responsibilities as he, or around whose individuality so much public care was congregated — not on account of the absence of willing hands to support his

administration, but because of the delicacy of the principles he had been called upon to sustain, which, if suffered
to vary in the least particular, would change the current of
future events in the United States adversely forever without hope of recall.

Abraham Lincoln was born in Hardin County, Kentucky, February twelfth, 1809, and was therefore fifty-two
years of age at the time of his inauguration as President of
the United States. His ancestors came from England
and settled in Massachusetts but gradually moved southward through New Jersey, Pennsylvania, Virginia, and
Kentucky, following the general habit, or law, peculiar to
all men of each generation, seeking new homes. In those
days Kentucky was covered with vast forests, and afforded
a speculative field for explorers and men of enterprise.
Under the inspiring example of Daniel Boone, a celebrated
hunter and pioneer, Mr. Lincoln's grandfather emigrated
to that state and joined the common lot of those who undertook to transform the wildness of territorial inaction to
the prosperous condition of husbandry.

When only seven years of age, Mr. Lincoln experienced
one of those changes that had characterized the previous
history of the family. His father moved to Indiana for
the purpose of establishing a new home in a still wilder
territory than the one just vacated. After two years' residence here, his good mother died ; and, his father marrying a second wife, the boy, so far from making any complaint or becoming testy or stubborn under the new regime
in the household, began rather to exhibit that wonderful
individual magnanimity which afterwards distinguished
him through life. Like the great character mentioned in
Christian history, he became subservient to the condition

of his surroundings and faithfully discharged the duties of
his position.   These were of an arduous character, including the sturdy feats of a pioneer, which were sufficiently
aggressive and tedious to neutralize the ardor of the most
willing mind; yet the youth did not bend beneath the
burden imposed upon him, but, on the contrary, grew to
great strength and stature, attaining a height, when twenty-
one, of six feet four inches.

The characteristic attached to him of being a good son
was only one feature of his individualism.   Wherever his
opinions were heard, they indicated a depth of penetration
into philosophic truths uncommon to men of his time, and
a scope or broadness of views on current topics far beyond
most of his political contemporaries.   It may be readily
conceded, therefore, that he was a lover of knowledge and
sought its attainments under the most difficult circumstances, and, it may be said, without cessation.

Not being fully satisfied with the Indiana homestead,
the elder Mr. Lincoln instituted a further change in 1830,
and began the preparation and construction of another
home of a similar character in Macon County, Illinois.
The son, then grown to manhood, not only favored the
simple earnestness of his father to afford him all the gratification possible, but, yielding to the necessities of the
case, began the work of reclamation on the new land with
the physical powers and energy of a giant.   Nothing,
perhaps, in the whole course of his career is so suggestive
of a noble nature as this act, or series of acts, performed in
the paternal interest.   He raised no doubt as to the wisdom of the undertaking, intervened no counter opinions
likely to detract from the merits of the original design, or
stipulated regarding compensation for his own extraordi-

nary efforts. No: on the contrary, he praised the excellence of the place and left nothing undone on his own part to bring all the details connected with the arrangement of the farm to a successful termination. When his work was finished, when his father's heart was happy in contemplating the realization of his wishes through the instrumentality of his son, young Lincoln left the paternal home to seek his fortune in a world distracted by rival issues and party strife.

The history of his career during this period reaching to the nomination for the presidency reveals the struggles of a man inspired by the love of rectitude fighting on the front line for all that men hold to be just, noble, and humane. The two characteristics tending most to distinguish persons in this world — namely, honesty and truth — were held by him in an eminent degree. It was not difficult, therefore, to understand or mistake his character with these far-famed qualifications as the leading points of it, for his purposes were so molded in rectitude and his speech so emphatically true that he stood above reproach before friends and foes alike. Crafty men sneered at him; but their ridicule became insignificant in his presence, like the imbecile howling of dogs in the moonlight.

There was deep design in selecting such a man as standard-bearer for the party from which so much justice was expected. The world at large would estimate his weaknesses and his worth by old or new standards according to the degree of intelligence with which it was endowed, and the factions controlled by these decisions might gloat over the one or the other as best suited their ideas; but such pronounced virtues as those above mentioned could not escape recognition, even by the most illiterate, any more than the sea could be denied immensity or the earth fruitfulness.

It was singular how his conduct stood, unchanged, the crucial tests of place and power. What he had been in his native state he was in the glory of the highest position the world could bestow on any individual — a modest man, sensible and upright. The pride which follows and encompasses title, the enthusiasm that obstructs the votary of party in the pursuit of knowledge, and the malice generated in the heart of an enemy were not with him. In his conscience and in his soul he possessed the freedom of a man who stood near God; because he aimed to disseminate justice to the world as that justice came from the Supreme Power, undeterred by flattery or threat. What need had he of the tinsel which bedecks the apartments and the official gown of the great, the strut of consequence, the exclusiveness of vanity, the disrespect of arrogance, or the red eye of bloated pride, while the purity of principle encompassed him and the dignity of law was the guide of his actions?

In his official life, the same definite purpose and freedom from confusion of ideas could be discerned. No one misunderstood his policy. All the requirements of his party, supplemented by what he himself demanded, appeared under two headings: " The Integrity of the Union " and " The Abolition of Slavery." These were as plain as the decalogue, and more concise. Substitute, compromise, and trickery were out of the question, as well as the doubts of friends and enemies as to the justness of his course, while his determination to adhere to his policy was not influenced in the least degree. He must have seen the subtle design of God and nature for the union of mankind, regulated by just law in each nation, state, community, family, and individual, but more especially the moral right of every one to be free from cruel bondage.

Beyond the barriers thrown up against him he saw the great light that must come to the world by means of law, making men and women lose their dissensions and uncharitableness — so as to mingle with the spirit of the universe, in peace, justice, and love. This was the vision that upheld his soul in the hours of trial such as he was obliged to endure; this the force which propelled his will, self-balanced in right, under circumstances appalling to the bravest heart and capable of subverting to inferior claims and purposes the most brilliant intelligence of the age.

Nothing can surpass faithfulness. It is an attribute of the Supreme Power, the energy that never sleeps but operates on the design of motion in material without the loss of an instant in a thousand years. The individuality of Mr. Lincoln merged with it into the great powers above the common methods of solving questions of the day; therefore he could not be moved by or made to descend into shades through which the light of his future world had not yet penetrated. It was not a faith that inspired him; what he fought for he knew. It was the real instead of the ideal; that which was practicable as against mere theory; the further resolution of chaotic disturbance into order; the bringing of man's rules to a parallel or to harmonize with the eternal law of the universe.

Stimulated by Mr. Lincoln's confidence and courage, the North went vigorously to work in the preparation for war. Men of great patriotism appeared, ready to give their lives as well as their fortunes to sustain the Union. It soon became evident that the celerity and boldness of the South were not enough to dissipate belief in the Union cause in the minds of Northern men. There would be some delay in organizing forces, but the North would meet the South to test the issue the latter had induced by the strength of arms.   Noncombatants saw the signs indicating the near approach of battle until suspense became painful; then, in fear and trembling, listened for the sounds.

———

CHAPTER XI.

AN IMPRESSIVE TRANSFORMATION.

THE precipitate flight of Hamilton Hitch and his son Danderton from Omaha was not executed with greater energy than Herondine's movement to the East at the call of duty.   Being one of the leading spirits of the Republican Party, and having accomplished much of what he had journeyed westward to perform, he recognized the utility of immediate consultation with his associates so as to strengthen the government at Washington with as much voluntary assistance as possible.   The time had come when theory and speculation must give way to stern reality, and patriotism be made to bear the test of danger and hardship without complaint.

It was then the members of Herondine's household awoke to the full realization of what war required.   They had been congregated into the New York residence under the most friendly auspices.   Aunt Frill and Aunt Funton had given a royal reception to Herondine and his lovely bride; had assigned the most comfortable quarters in the establishment to Judge Finnestare; made Madam Gloriana happy by installing her housekeeper and Felice cook;

as well as that they reached out and pressed an arm of choice society into service so as to furnish entertainment or amusement suitable to the persons interested. Now, however, when the genial influence of the management of his good aunts began to be felt like the sunshine of happy hours, Herondine arose and announced his intention of offering his service to the Federal government. It seemed a great hardship to deprive this family of such a man under the conditions named, yet there was no remedy by which his departure could be averted consistent with his former professions of patriotism. His country claimed him, and he must go.

It was about two months after their arrival in New York when this important change took place. The morning Herondine left his home there was sobbing in almost every apartment of the house. Grace Herondine, his wife, was pale and anxious-looking while her husband had been making preparations to depart; but when she saw his manly form disappear in the street, leaving her lonely and desolate, she burst into loud wailing. The aunts also appeared broken-hearted, knowing full well the significance and the results of an encounter with the pending dangers of war.

"I would be reconciled if it was anybody else — myself, for instance," said Aunt Frill. "The idea of allowing such a fine man, who, after all, is only a boy, to go to the war to be killed is pitiful — just outrageous."

"It is the quintessence of effervescence of reminiscence, or the diabolical made plain to the mind's eye," said Aunt Funton, who, when laboring under unusual excitement, generally made use of learned language so as to emphasize her sentiments in the hearing of her associates. "This comes of his not staying with Constitutional Union."

"My dear Funton," replied Aunt Frill, "while I acknowledge you in the right, say rather it was an ill wind that blew him into the party that now claims him; and, laying all matters aside, he should have run on Douglas if not on the square."

As these remarks were made in the presence of Grace, she answered:

"Let us be reconciled to what suited him best according to his own convictions of right, and it will please him hereafter to know it when he shall be menaced by danger and difficulty."

Then the household, under the old management and the new, began its allotted duties, so as to relieve the members of it of the pain which Herondine's sudden departure had created.

In the meantime Herondine journeyed to Washington without delay. His heart beat in unison with the popular sentiment of the loyal men of the North, and his ideas burned with fervor for its institutions. He was prepared to undertake any duty, no matter how arduous, to prove the sincerity of his attachment to his country's cause, if further proof was necessary after seeing he had given up home for it and all else dear to him in this world.

When he arrived in Washington, the city appeared to be overrun with transients — men destined for all branches of military service, as well as strangers from outlying cities and states, besides hucksters, bummers, loafers, pimps, thieves, and camp followers. The noncombatants of the latter type here enumerated had been forced from their usual haunts at other points by the prospect in store for them during the inauguration of President Lincoln, which would take place next day, and the disturbed condition of society at the national capital thereafter owing to the war spirit of the times.

Looking leisurely at the city itself, he concluded the plan of it had been designed for future generations instead of for the people of the present; its streets were unusually wide, some of the public buildings remained unfinished, and the population appeared limited far more than his previous conceptions of the place indicated. However, he was fairly pleased with the situation, which was level and extensive, flanked by a noble river, the Potomac, on one side, whose placidity and solemn grandeur appeared conspicuous. He was favorably impressed, also, with the size and make-up of the capitol, whose white walls glistening in the sunshine made a resplendent vision, especially as it stood on elevated ground at the head of Pennsylvania Avenue, which people called *the* avenue, although there were others in the city.

Having met some of his political friends in the capitol as previously arranged, and accepted a position relative to the ceremonies projected for the following day, he stopped for a few minutes in the rotunda, which is under the dome, for the purpose of examining minutely the large painting there of the surrender of General Burgoyne. It was while turning away from the picture that he encountered the smiling face of a man who stood in his path and, raising his right hand, gave the military salute to indicate he was at Herondine's service.

"A bummer," thought Herondine, as he scrutinized the fellow's campaign hat jauntily set on one side of his head and the dark blue clothing worn by him, which stood much in need of repairs. As he remained passive an instant, Herondine continued to examine him from the standpoint of his ideas as held at that time.

He was of medium size, by no means soldierly looking nor athletic, but one who seemed formed to create merriment on some stages of life if not in a theater. He exhibited capacity to produce facial expressions of a comic character, was demure to the extent of being noticeable, and of a cheerful disposition although evidently in embarrassed circumstances. Seeing him once, his identity could easily be established afterwards on account of the bridge of his nose being curved instead of straight, the convex part of the curvature projecting toward the left side.

"What do you seek?" inquired Herondine.

"A friend," answered the man promptly; "and," he continued, "service."

Herondine reflected as if stunned by an objective thought: he would, no doubt, need the services of a man, no matter what his situation in the future, for, pay or no pay, he could afford it on his own account; but would this strange specimen of mankind meet all requirements? Would he be reliable and fearless? Because in the present emergency and on future occasions he could not tolerate a coward. Roused by these thoughts, he continued the dialogue.

"What are your qualifications?"

"I practiced shuffling a good deal in the past," said the man. "In taking change from a woman, for instance, or from a person not well posted in counting, I generally moved the coins around on the counter or table until the other party became confused, when I would insist that the amount coming to me was short. In this way I gained a trifle."

"Was your name connected with this kind of business?" asked Herondine in surprise.

"Why, yes; and largely, too, let me tell you. In New York, which is my birthplace, although I spent a good deal of time in Missouri, it was a common remark of people in sending some of the family to market, 'Take care you do not meet Furflew the shuffler!' My full name is Bannister Furflew. I could not be convicted of theft, because I pretended I was doing right. A large part of the world is at the same game. I know them. Shufflers every one of 'em."

Herondine appeared utterly astounded at the cool deliberation of this speech. The audacious assurance of the man was most provoking.

"Do you imagine," he said, "I could possibly take a man of your character and antecedents into my service?"

"Oh, yes," replied Furflew in a light manner. "I'm honest with you. I tell you the whole truth from the start, which is more than your men of good character would do. Besides, this accomplishment may be of some use in future. The times demand every class of persons and all they are capable of doing. This was not my regular profession, however."

"What business did you follow?" asked Herondine anxiously.

"Trick of the loop," said the man with a bland smile.

Herondine groaned. The airing of such degradation deprived him of the partial control of his powers and induced the production of the involuntary sound above mentioned.

Furflew resumed:

"I turned my wits into the wrong channel, you'll say.

It amused me, like men who fish and hunt in a fair field. I did not force people to play the game. If they lost, they got some value for it — pleasure and experience. On this account it may not be so bad as people make out. They want something to remind them they commit foolish mistakes sometimes. When a greenhorn supposes he can win from a professional and tries his hand at it, he is guilty of such a blunder."

"You are amusing, to say the least," remarked Herondine, who began to relax the rigid aspect he had shown in his first judgment of Furflew. "What other praiseworthy accomplishments are you master of ?"

"I do a little at juggling, sleight of hand, and ventriloquism."

Herondine laughed until his shoulders shook with the bubbling of the merriment within him; then, suddenly becoming grave, inquired :

"Are you courageous?"

"Not much. I would run away in a fight or dodge it if I had a chance."

"I want a thoroughly fearless man," said Herondine, with a lofty air.

"There ain't no sich critter," returned Furflew sarcastically. "You may suppose you have him, like attempting to catch a notorious insect; but when you examine the place where he should be, he ain't in it."

As the expression on Herondine's face indicated hesitancy, Furflew urged other reasons in his own favor, as a last resort.

"When I get a place and regular pay, I'll drop my lawful profession," he said. "If I was careful before while carrying on a little game on the side agreeable to the players, whose business was it? Not the 'cop's,' if I know myself. I knew men who spoke against me play a dog- gone worse trick and yet thought they were some pump- kins. Don't find fault with me on that account. I'll attend to things, you bet, and tell you the bottom facts of every case,—which will come in handy for you."

"But," said Herondine, who was going to add that Fur- flew's conduct in the past would disgrace him in the future and on this account could not possibly employ him, when he was restrained from such course by counter thoughts ap- pealing to his charitable nature in favor of the unfortunate man. Besides, he could, of course, discharge him at any time, and withhold the description or record of his former career from his wife or friends.

Whether Furflew understood the nature of Herondine's reflections or believed his own tactics to be insufficient to accomplish his present purpose, he changed the tenor of his appeal.

"I was taken by your appearance," he said, "because you resembled a friend of mine. Not a relation, but a young man I used to meet in Union Square, New York, who listened to all my foolish ideas and advised me what to do. You should have seen him! He was such a gentleman! Wouldn't say you were a doggone fool on no account. Full of smart talk and learning of every kind was that youngster. He could read your thoughts like a brick. You are surprised! I tried him at it. I guess he held his own and wasn't put out. He could look through you; that was the extent of it. When we got acquainted I made him laugh every time. I walked with him round the square, mind you, often, but he never showed the least sign that he didn't want me."

During the delivery of the above narrative, Herondine's cheeks grew purple, and at its conclusion he asked:

" What was the name of your friend ? "

" Rob Riddleton," answered the man.

" Dear me ! " resumed Herondine, " how odd that is ! Riddleton is a special friend of mine — indeed, one for whom I have the greatest regard. I received valuable instructions from him, for he is a ripe scholar. We exchanged visits, dined occasionally at noted places of public resort; but latterly I have not met him. Where it he ? "

" Went south a year ago. Said he would serve the North in the coming troubles, and hinted he was in the employment of the rising political party."

" I am glad to hear it," said Herondine. " I suppose you will now expect Rob Riddleton's friend to give you the means of making a living. Well, call on me the day after tomorrow, and I may find something to suit your case. Remember you must be faithful to your duties, whatever they be."

" You bet your bottom dollar," said Furflew earnestly.

After handing the man a card on which his address had been written, Herondine turned away, and soon after left the capitol, while Furflew rubbed his hands with such manifest delight that those who witnessed the exhibition believed him temporarily insane or a born lunatic.

When the inauguration of Abraham Lincoln as President of the United States was completed without the interruption of malicious disturbances as expected, Herondine visited the War Department. As he did not desire a commission in the line or staff of the army or service on board a man-of-war, he was offered the control of the Secret Service Bureau, an institution little known to ordinary people, but one that rendered most important services in the time of need. Not only did the operation of this bureau extend from the Saint Lawrence to the Rio Grande, from the Atlantic to the Pacific, but the friends of the administration even were subjected to espionage, so decidedly obtrusive in its character as to be dreaded as much as a plague.

The highest position given under the auspices of secret service was commissioner ; the lowest, spy : although both might be convertible in an emergency. The genius displayed in the business of the bureau was excellent, and would have done honor to the strategic inner work of a secret society. All agents were to act in an independent manner and be known only to the director at headquarters ; but they carried certain signs whereby men in a lower rank or class might procure assistance, when necessary, from those of a higher one, if present, who understood them. The headquarters of the Western Division was at Saint Louis. Declining the chieftanship as tending to confine him inordinately to office work in Washington, Herondine chose to accept a roving commission as best adapted to his wishes, and through his solicitation was empowered also to employ Furflew as attendant, or helper, with the rank of spy.

When the man reported at the appointed time, Herondine made him acquainted with some of his duties ; in fact, he delivered a speech with a far more serious air than if he had an audience of five thousand people before him.

"Bannister Furflew," he said, "consider yourself under pay from this date. The amount will be one hundred dollars per month, with perquisites. These additional allowances shall be subject to my examination and approval. While in my service, you must hold no allegiance for any one else. You must be mine, soul and body. Our business will be to collect information of the movements or intentions of the Confederacy, so as to aid our own government in similar undertakings. Ask me no questions, write no letters, give no opinion to strangers about the North one way or another, and conceal your real character by every means in your power. Undoubtedly we shall be in the midst of war very soon. In that case, if your profession was known to the authorities of the South, you would be shot on sight. This, however, gives only half of the perils to which your condition may be subject: for instance, betray the trust reposed in you by me, and death will be the forfeit of your treachery."

"I had an idea once," said Furflew, "that shuffling was a dangerous game; but gracious! it was the pink of perfection compared with this. I won money at trick of the loop by giving the hand a simple turn of the wrist; but golly! there ain't no loophole to crawl through in the new job any more than if I was screwed up in my coffin."

"Be careful," resumed Herondine, "and you will be exposed to less danger than if you were in the field. Play a dual part; that is, be two men in one, but never what you really are."

"I might shove my old trade on the side," said Furflew.

"I approve it," replied Herondine, promptly. "I believe it will be legitimate for the first time, under the circumstances. Now, furthermore, you must always deliver your reports verbally: write nothing on paper. When we are in secret session, the sign that I am ready to receive reports will be my two hands held up with the fingers apart. At these sessions you will be at liberty to ask questions."

"It would be handy to learn the dumb language," remarked Furflew, with a long face.

Herondine smiled, but resumed in a business way:

"Are you ready to take the ironclad oath?"

"Oh! ah!" stammered the man, "it's risky, but the pay's good. One must do something for a living, and if killed today you cannot be killed tomorrow; so here goes."

Furflew then held up his hand while Herondine read for him the celebrated ironclad oath which persons in the employment of the government at that time had been accustomed to take. Then the instructions continued.

"Our first expedition will be to Charleston, South Carolina; you will go there in advance of me and employ rooms. I am to be known as Brother Fishington, preparing for the ministry of the Methodist Church, and therefore desirous of seclusion, the better to prosecute this design. Say I'm a Southern man, born in Louisiana, where you knew my father and grandfather, as well as my cousins on the mother's side, the Rungates. These details should be given to the person in the private house where I am to room and board, preferably a lady of the Methodist persuasion, so as to harmonize with the character assumed. Avoid the hotels. You can take up your quarters in a boarding house or move round from house to house to suit your convenience. Let no place accessible escape you. Hear everything and forget nothing. Meet me in the suburbs of the city, the last station on the railroad, so as to get me into quarters without having to submit to the scrutiny prevailing at the depot."

"There is one thing I'd like to know, just out of curiosity," said Furflew. "Why is it necessary to give the secret sign if we are alone, anyhow?"

Pausing to reflect an instant, Herondine answered:

"I might have some one in the closet, you foolish man."

"Ah!" exclaimed Furflew, seriously, "ain't I doggone, though? It never struck me before."

"Now," resumed Herondine, "such questions only waste time and do not properly pertain to your duties. Every regulation of this kind has been instituted for more reasons than one: therefore in future if you should hear strange sounds, instead of asking for explanations ascribe them to the family jar next door; or see curious sights, rub your eyes and believe a mirage is coming up. Don't be a fool if you can help it."

After this wholesome lesson, and armed with the necessary expenses, Furflew·departed for the South. The disposition he possessed previously of enlivening dull life with mirthful sallies and good jokes seemed to have been brought up to a round turn or changed within a few hours to the deep gravity of a man who had heard a series of sermons on death and damnation. Unquestionably Furflew exhibited a long face and a sickly pallor while journeying to his destination, and kept closer to his corner in the smoking car, where he had gone to escape observation, than at any other time during his life.

He debated with himself. Would he ever return? Was escape possible? His final answer to these questions was, "yes"; but mark you what a glorious thing it was that he knew the arts of shuffling, juggling, trick of the loop, and ventriloquism, for upon these he depended to secure the desired immunity from detection. Ah! what vile men there are in the world, he thought, who tried to persuade him he was iniquitous, whereas he was only painstaking. See what he would do in the South. Turn the minds of the people on to his entertaining exhibitions, thus affording them profit and amusement and security for himself! Reflections like these soon inspired confidence, and with confidence soon came buoyancy of spirits. When he entered Charleston he could smile. Remembering the character that Herondine was to assume, Furflew went to work with a will to secure quarters for him, after he had engaged accommodations for himself at a commonplace hotel. His method was quite efficient. Based on information received from his host, he visited the Methodist church in the evening during the progress of an entertainment to liquidate the pastor's indebtedness. There he inquired of some of the congregation for the most responsible lady in the community who would be likely to room and board a man preparing for the ministry. He was told there was a Mrs. Whirlston, wife of an elder — a widow, however, as the poor man was dead. She lived in a neat house on a retired street, and was actually the life of society. Nothing could go on — or off, for the matter of that — without her.

Next day Furflew saw the lady and her house and her rooms. He told her how Brother Fishington had run against him in Louisiana at one time and he wanted now to reciprocate in hunting up for him respectable lodgings. The lady seemed well pleased with the proposition; so the room was engaged.

Then Furflew turned his attention to Herondine's arrival. As originally arranged, he stepped off the cars in the suburbs of Charleston. Furflew saw him approach as he sat in the waiting room of the station, and actually opened his mouth in wonder at the transformation he had undergone since seeing him last. The long black coat, the white

necktie, the felt hat, the broad, flat boots, and the sanctimonious air were present; and, taking off his hat, it
might be seen that his hair came in bangs over his forehead
—a fashion much courted by professional men, not excepting some generals, authors, and circus clowns, probably on
account of a wise provision of nature which fascinates the
minds of its victims so as to be able to bring them all, in
this manner, on a level.

"Brother Fishington," said Furflew, taking Herondine
by the hand, "How do you do since I saw you in Louisiana?" Then he winked his off eye, the one farthest from
observers, and said in a low voice: "You beat me; you're
perfect."

"Very well, I thank you," answered Herondine in a
general way. "Ah! by the bye, what is your name?" he
continued.

"How soon the brethren forget!" said Furflew. "My
name is Curler."

Then the conversation drifted into topics such as citizens
of Charleston would be most likely to pursue at that time,
until they reached the house where Herondine was to stay.
When the landlady appeared, Furflew, advancing, said with
a great show of ceremony:

"Madam, this is Brother Fishington. Brother, Mrs.
Whirlston."

Then he turned and went away; but as soon as he found
himself alone in the street, he threw up his hands before
him with the fingers open, to signify to himself he was in
secret session, and said:

"If that ain't the softest billet in this here town, I'll be
doggone!"

CHAPTER XII.

WHAT CAME FROM THE DARKNESS.

H ERONDINE found Mrs. Whirlston an estimable woman, with large motherly sympathies, good household ability, and an active watchfulness directed towards the coffers of her acquaintances for the benefit of the church. In person she was of medium size, weighing about one hundred and fifty pounds, comfortably fat, vigorous in health, jolly tempered, and showing little, if any, signs of physical decay, although her only daughter, Cynthia, was marriageable.

One might suppose that Herondine, or Brother Fishington, would be given the best room in the house, not only on account of his relationship to the church but because he appeared the superior man in the well-fitting disguise assumed by him ; but his landlady thought otherwise, for the reason that this sacred precinct of the establishment had been reserved for the accommodation of company or transient visitors, without whose society she did not think it possible to exist. Besides exchanging visits with a set scattering from good to medium, she entertained. Hence the apartment referred to, known as the front parlor, where these meetings or entertainments took place must be as free from ordinary intrusion as the region of the gods. It was also tastefully, if not sumptuously, furnished. In the earnest desire to keep out flies, fresh air, sunshine, and light were more or less excluded, giving the place a vault-like odor as well as a sepulchral aspect. However, all these appearances were fashionable then and there, and may be elsewhere.

Herondine's accommodation was by no means neglected. His bedroom was on the second floor; and Mrs. Whirlston's own sitting room, a cosy apartment on a line with the parlor, but inward, backward, and sideward, would be at his service on all occasions, which went far to show that he actually fared better in the end than a person would imagine at first sight.

Miss Cynthia, to whom he was introduced, appeared delicate and somewhat passive in her manner or methods; devoted, however, to church meetings, Sunday schools, and kindergarten work; and exhibited no interest whatever in the manly form of Herondine, which was heartily appreciated by him. He was informed in confidence by her mother that Miss Cynthia had an admirer named Tuppins, a small man with sloping shoulders and a tallow-looking face, living with a small farmer beyond the suburbs of the city. He had come once a week, generally on Sunday evenings, for years without indicating in any way what his intentions were or what he proposed to do. It was believed he had been spellbound, both by the splendor of the parlor when illuminated and the charm of the young lady's society, and could not move one way or another, backwards or forwards. As he was the sole support of an aged mother, the usual excuse offered for such imbecility, his visits were tolerated; besides, there were no rivals in the case: better have him, perhaps, than none at all.

The form of entertainment given to Tuppins resolved itself into one program the year round. First, on entering, Miss Cynthia played and sang for him the celebrated melody, "Carry Me Over the River"; then there was an interval for conversation on hopes and fears. The second part was filled up by "Weigh Your Anchor with the Tide," followed by reports or opinions on the conduct of others, unjustly termed "scandal" by the outside world; and the night's amusement closed with "When We Meet in Zion." After this, Tuppins went slowly into the night like one half asleep — a condition presumably correct, seeing that the time of his departure was midnight.

A few days' experience in his new character convinced Herondine that he never had made such a miscalculation as when he imagined he could live a secluded life as the roomer of Mrs. Whirlston. When it became known that a brother preparing for the ministry was boarding at her house, the place was besieged by visitors, and, what was most embarrassing, all wanted to see him. His name became like a familiar word that had been echoed abroad. It was Brother Fishington here and Brother Fishington there, the student this and the scholar that. Mrs. Whirlston told the people interested that he would be pastor the next term. Therefore hope ran high in expectation of hearing him preach, as he was a fluent speaker and a handsome man.

All this brought a cloud over the inner life of Herondine. He actually considered how he might escape notoriety by falling downstairs and dislocating some of his joints so as to be confined to his room without interruption or scrutiny. He abandoned the idea, however, on calling to mind the case of a popular man of his acquaintance confined to his residence by sickness; how the doorbell had to be muffled with the piano cover, the blinds drawn down as if the individual were dead, the stairs strewn with additional carpeting, and a guard placed at each door of the house to prevent forcible entrance, while the invalid trembled beneath the bedclothes with fear as if he had the ague. No, it would be better, he thought, to remain in condition, so as to be qualified to run should the pressure brought to bear on him be too hard or unendurable.

Day after day his situation became more unfortunate. When introductions were growing less, and the nine days accorded gossip to ponder over the wonders of such an arrival as his had given place to more sober reflection, Mrs. Whirlston proposed, to the utter astonishment of Herondine, that he conduct the services at the church Sunday in the absence of the regular pastor, who had taken a vacation for the benefit of his health. At first, Herondine expostulated, begged, craved to be excused, but all to no purpose. Then he pleaded incapacity, twisted in his seat, coughed, fumed, stormed, stamped on the floor, in the vain endeavor to escape from the trying ordeal. Mrs. Whirlston smiled, then laughed outright at so good a joke.

"Brother Fishington, I have you in hand," she said. "I'll make a man of you. We must not disappoint the congregation, because I have already assured them you will be there. A pastor never has any will of his own, remember, but is led by the brethren."

"Led by the nose," remarked Herondine, in desperation.

Mrs. Whirlston's merry laughter at this sally rang out like the clear sound of a bell.

"I'll make it easy for you," she said.

Fortunately for Herondine he had witnessed the method of conducting services in church on former occasions; so he finally consented to officiate as requested. Lest, peradventure, he should become too conspicuous, he prepared for the occasion. He ruffled a portion of his hair, wore colored glasses, and marked his face in such a way that the natural expression of it was completely changed, especially when seen at some distance. Mrs. Whirlston was a little shocked at the transformation, declaring it was mean of him to hide his good looks, but was reconciled when informed he did it out of pure modesty.

What seemed a climax during the services on the occasion occurred when a Southern enthusiast stood up in the congregation and asked Brother Fishington if he would not say a prayer for the success of the new government, the constitution of the Confederacy having been adopted in convention at Montgomery, Alabama, a few days before. Herondine, without hesitation, raising up his hands, said:

"O Lord, scatter the enemies of our government. May they perish like grasshoppers in a Kansas storm. May the withering blight of incompetency afflict their designs so as to make them incapable of injury to us. Through contentions and dissensions may they suffer defeat in battle, until they are wholly subdued and become the sport of the civilized world. Amen."

Herondine's earnestness arose from the fact that the prayer was said for his own government, whereas his Southern hearers believed it had been dictated for theirs. When the murmurs of applause which greeted this effort had subsided, Mrs. Whirlston, with a kindling eye, remarked to a lady near her:

"I knew it was in him. I can tell every time."

To which the other answered:

"A small blame to you. Who wouldn't with such a man?"

At the evening services there was a large assemblage, after which it might be seen that Tuppins stood at the outer gate waiting to accompany Miss Cynthia home and listen entranced to the regular program beginning with "Carry Me Over the River." This laudable design left Mrs. Whirlston to be escorted by Herondine.

The night was dark. The feeble light of the gas lamps extended little more than ten or twelve feet, leaving the gloom to prevail in the intervals. The sounds of footsteps were dying out. Occasionally a front door would be heard to slam as the last straggler entered the house and hurriedly shut it as if a robber were at his heals. The deep silence of temporary death was beginning to assert itself when they heard a quick footstep, evidently of a man coming towards them on the same sidewalk. It was yet some distance to the place where they were walking.

"Seems to me I ought to know that step," said Mrs. Whirlston. " I study the tread of people, do you know?" she continued.

"For what purpose?" inquired Herondine.

"As an index of character," she answered. "As the mind directs the footsteps, it is possible to determine its character through closely contemplating their movements."

"That is an original idea," returned Herondine. "It is mind-reading through a medium. No doubt something might be gained by the process. What have you read from the sound of my feet?"

"I have not heard them when off your guard," she answered. "Some day I may; but the man approaching is dangerous. I do not know how the information comes. It is, no doubt, intuition. He is a stranger."

They had reached the outer edge of a circle of light surrounding a lamp-post just as the man came through it from the darkness on the other side. They saw him clearly, and Herondine started so violently that Mrs. Whirlston, who had hold of his arm at the time, felt the shock.

"Brother Fishington," she said solemnly, "you know that man."

"Yes — no. I only thought it might be one that I had seen before."

"Where have you seen him?" inquired Mrs. Whirlston keenly.

"Where?" answered Herondine, seeking some way of evading a direct reply. "In the cars at the wharf."

Mrs. Whirlston laughed at the absurdity of such an answer; but before the conversation was resumed they entered the house, and Herondine went direct to his room upstairs, through whose open door the strains of "Weigh Your Anchor with the Tide" was pouring from the front parlor below, where Tuppins sat dumfounded as usual.

Herondine, after adjusting the window blinds and lighting the gas, examined his face in the mirror. He was pale and a trifle nervous. Even on the part of a brave man, these signs were excusable, for the person who had emerged from the darkness and whose footfalls had been interpreted by Mrs. Whirlston, was his archenemy, Danderton Hitch!

During the following few days Herondine kept indoors, pleading indisposition, and Mrs. Whirlston began to suspect that the appearance of the stranger on Sunday night had something to do with it. However, she did not press her inquiries further. On Thursday of the same week, Furflew called and made his first report. It was decidedly sensational.

He had wandered freely through the city practicing ventriloquism as a starter, reserving his other accomplish-

ments for future use, lest the civil authorities might take
exception to them and cause his arrest. It was gathered
from him that the feeling against the North was very bitter.
Indeed, he had heard some speeches whose virulence,
denunciation, and threatenings struck him dumb with
fear, for never before did he understand what force could
be infused into language. Traitors and spies were specially mentioned as obnoxious, and several times he was
questioned as to his political opinions and sympathies.
On this account he suggested the propriety of joining a
military organization, which would have the effect of
removing doubts of his character from the minds of Southern men, to which Herondine consented.

The special information he had to communicate was
most important. It was that preparations were being made
to bombard Fort Sumter, in Charleston harbor, which
was held for the United States government by a mere
handful of troops. He had seen General Beauregard
actually superintending the construction of some of the
offensive works; and, from all he heard said about the
matter, the fatal day could not be far distant.

When Furflew left to return to his duties in the city,
Herondine sent a night dispatch in cipher to Washington
as follows: "Sumter is threatened. Beauregard pressing
matters to a crisis. Relief is needed at once."

Now that he had given sufficient reasons to be permitted
to enjoy seclusion during his preparatory course of studies,
he smiled to think he would not be disturbed in future;
but alas! he little knew how cleverness is frequently defeated by stratagem moving in the opposite direction.
While his original design had been concocted so as to
enable him to live in the enemy's country without being

seen except at rare intervals, Mrs. Whirlston's purpose
appeared to be to have him known, understood, and admired by every man, woman, and child in Charleston;
whether for the good of society, the church, or herself
could not be easily determined. On the present occasion,
when he returned to the house after sending his dispatch
to Washington, she had news of great import to communicate to him.

"General Beauregard," she said, "will be given a public
entertainment tomorrow night, and you and I are going.
I bought a new hat for the occasion. See! here it is.
Isn't it lovely?"

Being in the sitting room, Herondine staggered into a
seat like one intoxicated. This announcement struck him
like a cannon ball. Some one in the crowd would doubtless know him, even if Danderton were not there, and such
recognition might lead to serious consequences. The lady
continued:

" I have friends that are related to the General, and I
can introduce you to him. We must make you acquainted
with the principal men in town so as to be social and
agreeable."

Herondine could offer no objection, seeing how thoroughly he had been trapped in his own net; but he
thought of his wife in her loneliness and wondered if she
dreamed of the difficulties that now were beginning to
meet him, threatening exposure, capture, or, perhaps,
death. Yet his duty called for all these and more; hence
he told his landlady he would be happy to accompany her
on the occasion named.

The reception given to General Beauregard by the
people of Charleston was handsome and enjoyable. On

the brink of a precipice they were merry, which, perhaps, is one of the great secrets of living well. The manhood, the intelligence, and the fashion were there to greet the soldier. Mrs. Whirlston, besides being on the arm of Brother Fishington, had remarkable twinkling light in her eyes, and laughed at the least display of wit. Her high bosom on these occasions rose and fell like the tide reaching to catch the maximum point of its course on the shore. Cynthia accompanied Tuppins, but was not of her mother's party.

The hero of the hour made a circuit of the hall accompanied by a few chosen friends. When in the neighborhood of Mrs. Whirlston, one of her lady acquaintances met the General and secured the desired introduction. When Herondine was presented, Beauregard, remarking the soldierly appearance of the man, said:

"Brother, I would have been well pleased if you had selected the military instead of the religious profession. Your shoulders seem better fitted for the field than the pulpit."

To which Herondine replied:

"Thank you, General. Had I known you were to command, I might have done so."

"It is not yet too late," said Beauregard seriously. "I shall —"

"Oh no, General," said Mrs. Whirlston, suddenly coming to the front in a beseeching manner. "*We* must have him."

The General smiled good-humoredly, and before moving on said in so low a voice that none but the lady heard him:

"Yes, madam, *you* must have him."

"Ah!" ejaculated Mrs. Whirlston, turning to Brother Fishington and clasping her hands with delight, "how penetrating he is! He actually can read one's thoughts; but isn't he a love of a man?"

"He is very affable," replied her companion, "which is, perhaps, the most noticeable sign of a gentleman to be met in public."

Herondine, scanning the features of the people eagerly, saw no one but strangers. Danderton was not there. From parties conversing with his landlady, he gathered that Fort Sumter would be attacked without further delay, as the preparations for its reduction were completed. This news made him sad; seeing which, Mrs. Whirlston entertained him with lively descriptions of many society people in the hall until they returned home.

The rumors whispered from house to house regarding the contemplated siege of Fort Sumter were true. Furflew confirmed them in making his second report to Herondine, soon after the night of the entertainment. Furflew had enlisted in the Confederate service, the better to obtain information, and was attached to a battery on James Island. He intimated that there were two other places in the harbor besides this where batteries had been placed — on Sullivan's Island and Morris Island, the former containing the historic Fort Moultrie, which mounted thirty guns. There was also an ironclad floating battery, carrying four guns of large size. All these would play on Sumter. The Southern authorities hoped the officers and enlisted men composing the garrison of the fort would join their cause and thus prevent a battle, but they were disappointed.

Major Robert Anderson and his command, consisting of two skeleton companies of the First United States Artillery, about sixty-five men, remained true to their duty and to the United States.   Anderson, although a Southern man and a slave owner, was the first conspicuous example showing the nice points of honor and genuine manhood under the circumstances surrounding him, and the severest test to which human life may be subject. His method of conducting the defense of his charge, his patriotic sentiments for the government which had honored and promoted him, his courage under fire, and the broad views of right and justice which were his in the darkest hours of his great trial— proved beyond a doubt that he was then and would be forever a noble man.   His individualism disappeared for the general good of the United States.

Furflew, before leaving the presence of Herondine, had something special to propose.   It was this: if he desired to witness the bombardment, Furflew could give him the exact time at or near the wharf.   General Beauregard had his headquarters in Charleston, from which place he dispatched messages to the detachments under his command. Furflew had gained the confidence of the officer empowered to make details, and requested to be one of the men sent to the city on special duty; hence he would meet Herondine at an intermediate place.   As Beauregard's officers had already begun to demand the surrender of Sumter, it was probable that action would commence next morning at daybreak, in case of refusal.   Then the men separated.

Herondine in the intermediate time discoursed with Mrs. Whirlston on the dreadful nature of war, and added he wished to see for himself the opening of the campaign, so as to moralize on it for the benefit of religion.   With her knowledge, therefore, he left the house after dark, and, promising to return soon, proceeded to the wharf for the desired information. It was near midnight before Furflew put in an appearance, but when he did he merely pushed a piece of paper into Herondine's hand and passed on without speaking. The paper when unfolded contained these words: "At daybreak."

Satisfied with the result of his watchfulness, Herondine returned to his lodgings — not to sleep, however, but to await the coming of the greatest event ever witnessed in the course of his life, one that was to awake the people of two sections of a rich and powerful nation to a consciousness that the fratricidal strife had begun which would desolate many a fertile plain and bring to premature graves the bravest and the dearest of the manhood of their families.

It was April. The genial spring had descended from heaven, bringing with it verdure, blossoms, perfume, and balmy air to mankind, irrespective of condition or party. Notwithstanding the fascination of its presence, the hearts of men were filled with malice and the bitterness which produces murderous strife. Herondine, at the open window, towards the dawn of the fatal day, looked into the darkness and contemplated the two powers here at work — the hand of God with its incomparable gifts, and man with the sword ready to slay his brother. Surely this irreverent exhibition, so palpable even to an unphilosophic mind, must end in terror, ruin, and destruction. Above there was glory in the atmosphere, as if the souls of mankind were invited to enjoy a felicitous state without tasting death; while below, in the midst of beauty and competence, there stalked premeditated carnage, hatred, and all the worst passions that brutalize the nature of the human kind.

A light mist arose from the waters of the harbor before morning, as if it were the last attempt of the Infinite to prevent a conflict: but it was not sufficient to totally obscure objects; it only chilled the air and made the actors uncomfortable.

Herondine occupied an elevated position. As he stood watching the obscurity changing its character by the admixture of gray, and marveled on the great silence pervading the city, he saw a red light like a rocket rise suddenly out of the darkness at one point, describe an arc of a circle in the air, and descend again to the earth, bursting at the point of contact. Then a deep, loud report followed, resembling a thunderclap, which rattled the glass in the windows, shook the buildings in Charleston, and awoke the inhabitants. It was the first shot of the war; and Herondine, understanding its significance, trembled. In a little time another report was heard, and then several at the same instant, indicating that additional batteries had joined in the action. The scene was one to inspire terror, knowing that the destruction of human life was the principal object.

The people dressed hastily and crowded into the streets intent on seeing all that could be seen or to inquire into the particulars of the bombardment. Many sought elevated places, to gain a view of the display — the flashing of the guns, and the clouds of thick smoke which rolled over the surface of the earth and were then carried off by the wind.

Notwithstanding their sympathies in favor of their own cause, the faces of the people were blanched by the reflection of some indescribable horror. The void roused by the presumption of man struck back by a method that even the bravest felt to be fearful. The uproar in the heavens resembled a great storm supplemented by a conflagration involving both earth and sky. When daylight appeared, the batteries of Fort Sumter returned the fire and added to the general confusion. The echoes of the volleys increased the sounds fourfold. Many sensitive people felt sick, and others occasionally thought of the brave band of men within the fort fighting for honor and nationality against fearful odds.

Mrs. Whirlston dressed hastily, and joined Herondine at the window soon after the firing began. She was so much alarmed that speech forsook her for the time being. In deference to her good heart, it may also be said she wept silently over the misfortune of the war and the inequality of the contest going on in the harbor. This inequality seemed tò imply guilt to the larger party, which even the usages or privileges of warfare could not palliate.

Next day the Federals surrendered and the South scored the first victory.

CHAPTER XIII.

AN OLD CRAFT SIGHTED. ·

TAKING advantage of the general good feeling among the officers of Beauregard's army on the fall of Sumter, Furflew obtained three days' leave of absence from his battery. The news he brought Herondine read like a novel, it was so interesting.

Furflew was present at the firing of the first shot. It was a shell discharged from a ten-inch mortar belonging to one of the batteries on James Island, which is washed by the confluence of the Ashley and Cooper rivers, these streams bounding Charleston farther to the northeast. The order to fire came in about four o'clock in the morning. The men of the battery, excepting a small guard, were asleep, but were aroused immediately by some of the non-commissioned officers going among them and pulling them out of their bunks. When everything was ready for action, the privilege of firing the first gun of the war was offered a gentleman present, who refused on conscientious grounds; but immediately thereafter some one, a civilian, stepped forward, and, saluting the officer in charge, said:

"Captain, I shall be pleased to fire the first shot."

"We have men enough in the battery to perform that service," was the reply; "but who are you?"

Furflew could not hear what the stranger said, and then another individual coming up made an explanation. This seemed satisfactory, as the captain asked no further questions, but at half past four fired the mortar himself.

The first man, who, in the manner above described, became conspicuous by making the request, was tall, dark-complexioned, with a high shoulder, and eyes that trembled in their sockets. He seemed to be well known to the men in power — a circumstance that induced Furflew to learn the particulars of his history. It appeared the man in question came into the state with his father last winter. They were Westerners, and possessed ample means, for they engaged rooms at a family hotel of good reputation and moved among the men who proposed to govern the South. The father, in order to secure confidence and some social standing, made arrangements for the purchase of Confederate bonds, investing his entire fortune in them, thus becoming, to all intents and purposes, an active member of the Confederacy. For this act, and also on account of the eagerness with which he espoused the hostile feeling against the Federal government, he and his son were given important positions. They were kept in close relationship with the authorities in Charleston, being attached to a detective agency similar to the one at Washington in the interests of the North, and were rising rapidly in the profession on account of their knowledge of Northern men whom they were instructed to shadow.

Herondine was astounded at this news. While he was aware that Danderton Hitch was in Charleston (for the person described by Furflew was no other than he), it seemed incredible he should have gained such favor in the South and appear so soon in direct opposition to the business at which Herondine was engaged. It looked as if it were the old trick of Greek against Greek or a fatality. There could be no doubt now of the danger encompassing him, for, if once recognized by either Danderton or his father, he was sure of being arrested and tried for his life.

After instructing Furflew as to how he should act in case of an emergency when ordered to retreat, Herondine turned attention to his own case. He determined in future to remain in the house except at night, and then, when abroad, to keep out of public thoroughfares and social gatherings.

When bringing the subject to the notice of Mrs. Whirlston next day, he insinuated the probability of the authorities claiming him for military service if seen much in public, which had the desired effect of making that lady as anxious to conceal his identity as he was himself; although this did not prove she was not patriotic, but only that she loved the interests of the church better than those of the state.

This master stroke of ingenious stratagem did not come a minute too soon.   While the two friends were yet deliberating on the feasibility of hiding Brother Fishington if absolutely necessary in one of the clothes closets or under the bed upstairs, an ominous ring was heard at the front door.   Mrs. Whirlston knew it to be of this character because none of her acquaintances ever rang in that way, and, besides, it was not the time for callers, neither could it be considered the ring of a peddler.

The feeling of Mrs. Whirlston in moving quickly to answer the call assumed that the person on the outside was in authority and had come to make some demand.   On opening the door, she was not wholly disappointed.   An elderly man, slightly bent, with white hair, thick features, round head, and a scowl by no means prepossessing, stood there.   He did not smile when encountering the inquiring look of the lady, but in a frigid way asked:

"Have you a roomer called Brother Fishington, madam?"

"I do not know you, sir," Mrs. Whirlston replied, "and I am not in the habit, anyway, of telling my business to others, especially to those who come to my house uninvited."

The lady paused, but her face exhibited an expression indicating she had given the newcomer a thrust that would require some ingenuity to parry.

Herondine arose on hearing his name mentioned, and, peering through the interstice of the door, saw the man but could not recognize him, as his face was then turned to one side.   The position of Mrs. Whirlston's sitting room, where Herondine was standing, was favorable for the purpose.   The view crossed the dining room, entered the doors of the front parlor transversely, and passed through the open front entrance. Herondine could see and not be seen. The man, nothing daunted, continued:

"I understand Brother Fishington is preparing for the ministry; at least, it is so said."

"And who doubts it? Do you?"

"I have not come here with any doubts. From the description given of him, I infer he is an acquaintance of mine."

"I would not imagine that fact could benefit him much," said Mrs. Whirlston, with a forced laugh. "If you are a friend, leave your card and he will be ready to meet you if he thinks it's good for him."

"If he should consider otherwise, what then?" inquired the man.

"I suppose in that case he need not meet you."

"Is it true that this Brother Fishington is a stranger?"

"If there is anything in that, you have the advantage. I know him, but I never saw you before."

"Madam, you would not wilfully harbor an enemy of the Confederacy?"

This was a phase of the subject Mrs. Whirlston had not considered. While she understood her duty to the civil power, the church absorbed her liveliest interests. So pronounced, or steadfast, was she in her opinions of Herondine, that even this assertion had no effect in awaking any doubts in her mind concerning him. She answered promptly:

"Those who have resided in my house have been honorable and true, and I have no reason to fear for them."

"We are not certain about your guest. There is only a suspicion. The power controlling the forces now getting ready to demand and hold the independence of this state should know how every individual here stands in relation to it; therefore I shall insist on examining your premises."

In this instant the stranger faced the doorway, revealing to Herondine the obnoxious physiognomy of Hamilton Hitch, an account of whose political tendencies and questionable character had been given to him in Omaha, as well as the knowledge imparted by Furflew that he was now a spy in the South.   Mrs. Whirlston remained firmly intrenched in the passage, however, as if to dispute it to the last.

"Who are you?" she asked, "and by what right have you come here to force an entrance into my house?"

"I am a detective, madam, and this is my right," the man answered, producing a paper with the seal of a court and the signature of a judge authorizing the bearer to examine premises where suspicion existed that they contained a person or persons inimical to the new government.

"Well," said the lady, while her face grew exceedingly pale and her limbs began to tremble, "this is very strange, and I do not know how to account for it; but, as the scripture says, 'An enemy hath done this,' a secret emissary of evil, who, doubtless, is no churchgoer."

She held the door open, invited the detective to accompany her, and continued:

"Let us go to Brother Fishington's room upstairs, and you can examine it.   I do not know exactly where he is at present."

Mrs. Whirlston said these words in a loud voice, hoping to be heard by Herondine, so that he might take warning and escape, for she really believed the present investigation had been instituted for the purpose of forcing him into the military service, the idea being strengthened as she recalled the remarks made by General Beauregard at the entertainment already noticed.

Herondine's room was commodious and neatly furnished. It was clean and had an odor of fresh flowers, blossoms gathered by Mrs. Whirlston's own hands for the handsome vase on the mantelpiece. There was no baggage, Herondine having brought with him only a satchel containing one change. This receptacle was there, open. There were a few gloves, collars, handkerchiefs, socks, but no papers or pictures.

"Brother Fishington is clever," said Hamilton Hitch, seeing his examination resulted in disappointment.

"We need clever men nowadays," returned Mrs. Whirlston, with some sarcasm, intending, no doubt, to reflect on the detective's methods.

"Now, madam, do you really think him handsome?" he inquired, with a show of intimacy quite tantalizing.

"My individual opinion is my own. It would not agree with yours in anything," she said.

"The remark was made also that the brother was tall; could you not give his height?"

"I never measured him," evasively answered the lady. "If he has been an acquaintance of yours, further information on the subject would be superfluous."

The man laughed in a derisive manner. Still, he proceeded downstairs, looking wistfully at the apartments as he went along. When they entered Mrs. Whirlston's back sitting room, it was empty, very much to the relief of the lady. Then the detective prepared to depart. When at the front door he stood an instant irresolute, as if about to speak, but impolitely turned away without word or motion and soon disappeared down the street.

Then Mrs. Whirlston went through the house flying, on the supposition that her good Brother Fishington would turn up or turn out ot his hiding place at every moment. Alas! nothing but deep silence met her earnestness She went from room to room, looked into the closets — aye, under the beds, sometimes — calling " Brother," but Herondine did not respond.

From the sitting room where she last saw him there was a door leading backwards into the kitchen, another from the kitchen into the yard; from this space one might proceed into an alley, and thence into a street.   Following this course, she found his footprints in the dust of the alley.   He had evidently taken that way while she was conversing with the detective at the front door.   This was substantially true.

With the discovery that Hamilton Hitch was on his track, Herondine knew his time in Charleston must come to an abrupt termination.   One moment's delay, one miscalculation, one false step might deliver him into the hands of the unscrupulous detective, from whom no mercy would be expected; therefore, when he saw his face at the door, he decided at once to escape while there was yet hope that he himself was only known by hearsay.

Herondine's plans had been well arranged.   He did not travel by the regular routes.   From north to south there had been a line established along which agents of the secret service were to move and on which they would receive aid, including shelter, food, and conveyance from station to station.   There were signs and passwords and other paraphernalia, necessary adjuncts of the system ; but the men connected with it were unknown to each other except on occasions when it could not be avoided, and then there were no questions asked or information given, as this was reserved for the chief in Washington.

Before leaving Charleston, Herondine, seeing a news-boy, desired to send a message to Furflew, who, as may be remembered, had been given a furlough, but was now room-ing at an uptown boarding house. Taking a paper, he marked on the margin of it the letters " T. I. G." Then he folded it carefully and wrote thereon, " Private Curler, Bummer's House, Charleston," asking the boy when he went that way to deliver it as addressed, also to state in explanation that it came from the Brother. Then Heron-dine paid the boy, who volunteered to deliver the message at once and did so.

Furflew, on learning that the paper came from Brother Fishington, knew that it must be a document above the average. Lighting a cigar and taking a seat near the clerk's desk in the office, with one leg over the other, he opened the paper and began to scan the news. Nothing appeared therein that he could see connecting either him or Herondine with the incidents related. Finally he came to discern the letters on the margin.

" Hem!" said he to himself. " What's this? What's those — 'T. I. G.' ?"

He reflected some time, puffing, however, the smoke of his cigar with unusual energy, as if the action might not induce a solution of the difficulty. Then he returned to the question and proposed an answer.

" 'T' stands for tea, 'I' is I, and 'G' stands for jug, — tea I jug — tea in a jug. Well, if that ain't odd, I'll be durned. He got tea in a jug somewhere and wants me to know it. Bully for you."

With this conclusion, however, Furflew did not grow satisfied, for, reason on it as he would, nothing reached his intelligence that looked one way or another like a probable message or a fact worthy of note.   He replaced the paper in his
pocket and walked into the street.   This was the first message
sent him by Herondine, and must therefore be of unusual
importance.   What could it mean?   They had not agreed
on signals or cipher communications, and this one was without doubt written on the spur of the moment.   Hence he,
Furflew, must wait in order to deliberate on all sides of the
question.   After an hour's tussle with the unknown, a spark
flew out of the void that illuminated his mental perception.

"Ah!" said he, suddenly catching at a thought and
dragging the paper from his pocket.   "Durn the luck! if
it don't read backwards—'G-i-t'!   Now, we know what
that is, anyway.   Git; clear out; skedaddle; make tracks.
Holy frost! there's something up!   I should smile!   It's
too hot here, for sure; but look at me, will you?   When
I 'git' this time, I'll be a deserter.   I reckon the life that's
left in me won't be worth suds.   I guess I couldn't get
insured, nohow.   Shot on sight for being a spy!   I'll be
shot then and there before I'm seen at all."

That night Furflew called at Mrs. Whirlston's.   He went
through the alley to reach the back door in order to avoid
detectives who might possibly be watching the front.   He
found the lady in a high state of excitement, owing to the
disappearance of Brother Fishington.   She related the incidents of the morning and expressed a belief that her guest
must have been induced, one way or another, to join in the
war, as he did not return.   .

"I was kind of anxious to see him," said Furflew, "because he was a durned good fellow when we met in Louisiana."

"Yes," answered Mrs. Whirlston, "I noticed you were friendly."

"I always said — to myself, of course," resumed the man, "for I had no one else to say it to—he'd turn the hearts of the women towards him if he ever got a pulpit; he had the knack of it."

"Oh, his ability was very marked," rejoined the lady, "more, perhaps, in directing devotional exercises to God than seeking praise for himself."

"I wouldn't give shucks for the woman that didn't dote on the ground under his feet. It was plain to be seen he was as handsome as plum duff on a Christmas table," said Furflew, endeavoring to keep the conversation from taking too much of a religious turn.

Mrs. Whirlston made no reply to this comment. Her ideas of Brother Fishington were too refined to be jostled about with those of other people, even his own acquaintances. If she knew the Brother was handsome, she would recognize it as a secret too good to give out or let out. Hence she asked Furflew somewhat suddenly:

"What will you do?"

"Do?" inquired the man.

"To find him," she answered. "Will you not go here, there, and everywhere, look into barracks, see the men on parade, examine the depots, and scour the streets?"

Furflew seemed confounded by her earnestness, but did not answer.

"And when you find him," continued Mrs. Whirlston, "send him back here."

"I'll say," resumed Furflew, "that there woman in Charleston is sweet on you—"

"We want him to be pastor."

" She has a thing in her eye that won't fall out nohow "—

" The congregation admires righteous behavior and piety."

" She's worried to death on your account."

" We miss him."

" Say," continued the man, becoming more confidential, " when the war is over, I'll try my best to run in with him on the first cheap excursion train and plank him right down before you without charge, and no questions asked. Mind your prayers while we are away. There is danger around. Keep your weather eye open, for in the mean-time that same detective what was here might take it into his head to brew trouble for you without malt, and no mis-take. So long."

Before Mrs. Whirlston could make further remarks, Fur flew had departed. He was convinced that his chief was on his return journey to Washington, and that the mes-sage he himself had received required a similar movement. As in Herondine's case, Furflew knew the secret route and pursued it, although his pass would have entitled him to safe conduct in any case for the ensuing twenty-four hours.

Among Mrs. Whirlston's friends, the disappearance of Brother Fishington was considered a mere item related to the all-absorbing subject of the war. Examples of this kind were numerous, and some a great deal more distress-ing, for men quit their homes who were the sole support of large families, thus leaving them to struggle with difficulties and absolute want. The people who crowded into the front parlor where Tuppins had seen and heard so much that was felicitous, offered their condolence regularly, more on ac-count of the loss sustained by the church than anything ascribed to the feelings of the lady; but when, in a few days, it became known that detective Hamilton Hitch had revisited the house and charged Mrs.Whirlston with treason to the state in that she had sheltered and made much of a man in the secret service of the North, their puerile sympathy was changed into consternation. Then it was that she drew company in earnest. People came by the score, and filled every room in the house downstairs at a sitting. It is wonderful how the full measure of earthly joy to many is invariably tinctured by sorrow.

Mrs. Whirlston was the wonder of the hour; and as her individual rectitude was not questioned, all members of the congregation, as well as hundreds of others, were wild to meet her and hear from her own lips the strange story then circulating.

Oh ! how she loved the multitude ! But ah ! at what a fearful cost was her ruling passion gratified ! With the repletion of her desire came notoriety, and the pleasures of the one seemed overwhelmed by the other. Besides, she must appear in a public court and give satisfactory evidence that she was not the miscreant represented by detective Hamilton Hitch. Add to this, for the whole truth must be told, every ounce of tea, every caddy of sugar, every bottle of wine, and all her preserved fruit were swept away as if a hurricane had stricken the pantry and scooped them out to satiate the appreciative palates of her general visitors. They were gone, but she was satisfied. Then she relapsed into a meditative mood, and, as the people said, "was better to be alone with her sorrow"—and the empty pantry.

In this connection it must be said, in vindication of the chivalry of the male sex, that Tuppins made a remarkable effort in the search for Brother Fishington. His plan was to post notices on dead walls and country fences, as they do in the case of lost sheep, so that people seeing them would desert their legitimate occupation and run him down or fish him up, as the case might be.   Full of this idea, Tuppins began the writing of the notice with Mrs. Whirlston's consent, for she said, " No one knows what might come out of it "; but alas ! the document never went forth. It was incomplete, dying a premature death.

"Lost or strayed away," wrote Tuppins, "a man not blind, not lame — "

Then he stopped, unable to proceed further.

" Put in," said Cynthia, " no fool."

This phrase being added, Tuppins read and reread the notice until his brain began to ache, when he abandoned the effort altogether, and, as he expressed it, " let things look out for themselves."

CHAPTER XIV.

" THE POOR MAN OF CHRISTENDOM."

HERONDINE'S headlong retreat from the South induced him to reflect and determine that the power at his command in his present profession was not absolute.   Evidently his first patriotic effort in his country's behalf had been given a serious repulse by one whom he regarded as a nonentity, but whose action, in the varying chances of war, had become like a tornado, forcing the enemy to flee to his home for refuge as if the operator were the superior instead of the inferior man.

Herondine could easily perceive that the original cause of quarrel between North and South was expanding to immense proportions, involving not only legitimate war but also feelings of bitter hatred among the individuals of both sections. The scenes presented to his view as he journeyed northward were animated by military movements in anticipation of active service in the field. The cry " To arms ! " might be heard on all sides in the streets of cities, on the public highways, among the pleasure-seekers of popular resorts, in the cars, on the steamboats, in the farmhouses, on the common of the quiet hamlet, and at the doorsteps of the family residence, as if the echoing guns bombarding Sumter had awakened also the retributive spirit of the North so as to retrieve its sullied honor and wreak a deadly retribution on its enemies.

On account of the vast amount of business accumulating in the bureau at Washington and the necessity existing for every man to be at his post, Herondine had barely time to visit his family in New York before launching into a new expedition. This was none other than to ascertain, if possible, from members of the Confederate government or their friends, the strategic movements contemplated for the government of the Southern army within the next few months. The principal places of operation in this connection would be Richmond, Virginia, and Montgomery, Alabama, which at that time was the capital of the South and possessed many advantageous conditions in its favor. As a matter of course, Furflew would actually bear the chief part in the undertaking and from the skill displayed by him recently in Charleston it was believed much valuable information would be derived through his assistance. It was a hazardous duty in any circumstances, but especially so at that time, when those who played with war after such a fashion lived incessantly in the shadow of the gallows.

Before leaving the national capital Furflew had executed an improvement in his person very much desired as tending to disguise his identity in the new field of enterprise to which he was assigned ; namely, an artificial bridge on his nose so as to straighten out that organ and enable him to assume foppish airs such as might possibly turn the heads of the ladies in Montgomery, seeing that the Grecian bend was then in full vogue among them. The artistic workman who devised the appendage above mentioned had been seeking opportunities for the display of genius through the instrumentality of invention, and, hearing from Furflew the nature of the article required, literally flung himself into the project, regardless of time or expense. Hence, in an uncommonly short period there was produced something that is rarely, if ever, seen in an ordinary show window, or, indeed, for the matter of that, on a man's face — an artificial nose, of fine imitative color and consistence, apparently sensitive, like other organs of the same class, to the praises or censures or odors of the world.

Carefully examined, it was seen to be an external case composed of gelatine having a pair of spring spectacles surmounting the middle part or astride of the bridge so as to grasp the facial organ or such portions of it as were available. The edges coming in contact with the face were concealed by narrow strips of steel which appeared to be necessary adjuncts of the spectacles, and the point of contact above, under the forehead, was covered adroitly with a piece of plaster, to give the impression to the observer that there was a slight wound there and to divert scrutiny away from the nose itself. Each orifice at the lower end was so arranged as to be carried into those of the wearer, and the line beneath was covered by a thick mustache which clothed the entire upper lip and completed the design.

Under this new piece of face gear Furflew reveled in beauty and self-importance. The harmony of proportionate lines had been established on his exterior front. The pride of vanity kindled in his eyes, and he assumed a waggish gait like men who feel physical power developed in their shoulders impelling them to strike forward. Knowing that Herondine would follow him as a supporter in a few days he departed for Alabama in good spirits, believing his arts would fully sustain his character if everything else failed.

As for Herondine, the part he was to play on this trip had been carefully selected, as danger to men of his class was increasing daily and the most trifling incident or omission connected with his arrangements might betray him into the hands of his enemies. He personated a commercial traveler soliciting for orders for the English firm of Blistor Winkle & Company, successors to Periwinkle, of Birkenhead and Liverpool, founders, manufacturers, and ironmongers—the special branch, or department, in which he was concerned being wrought and cut nails, galvanized sprigs, tacks, and spikes. He carried samples of these articles with him; and as English goods were then popular in the South, there would be no difficulty attached to his representations for the period required.

A few days after his arrival in Montgomery, Furflew appeared on the streets of that city in all the glory of an itinerant fakir giving exhibitions of his skill in ventriloquism, supplemented by feats of jugglery; and when the scenes thus presented came to a close, he collected from the audience, by the old-fashioned method of sending round the hat, what each individual was pleased to bestow in recognition of his ability or worth.

At stated periods he reported to Herondine all the in-formation he had gathered among the citizens relating to the war. The confidence of the fellow seemed the most wonderful part of his performance. His smiles were gen-uine. He looked the people square in the face and straight in the eye, in contradistinction to the theory that one in opposition to the constituted powers could not do so with-out betraying symptoms of fear. He laughed ; and those who heard him said among themselves, " This is an honest clown any way you take him."

Standing on a chair, with his back against a wall, his hat tilted on the side of his head, and his face decorated with the artificial bridge and attachments heretofore men-tioned, the rest of his body being encased in respectable clothing, he went through each one-hour performance with the utmost spirit, and satisfaction to himself and his audi-tors. Sometimes he rose to greatness, when he produced the humming of the honeybee both during its freedom and captivity, the siss of the beefsteak on a hot frying pan, and the changes the sounds undergo when the steak is being turned, and finally the snap which terminates the process when the gravy is turned out from the pan to the dish.

It soon became evident to Furflew that his favorite pro-fession would prove remunerative as well as provide him personal security, for, on counting his collections for an average day, the good round sum of fifteen dollars was reached, thus giving more proof of the soundness of his own opinions and the errors into which the world had fallen in regard to the pushing of a fancy trade. Nor was

this all: when luck takes a favorable turn it becomes mu-
nificent. It was so in this case, as may be seen presently.

During one of Furflew's performances there stood on
the outer edge of the crowd in front of him two men
whose facial contortions, induced by laughter, proved
beyond a doubt that they were heartily amused. The
physical signs associated with these jolly fellows portrayed
a condition of easy circumstances. Without being osten-
tatious or showy in dress, they were comfortably clad.
They wore neat-fitting boots, clothes, and hats, and carried
themselves so decidedly within the lines of prudential
decorum as not to be mistaken for members of the swell
mob whose fraternity is supposed to have as many claims
on society as the phylloxera or the army worm on the
vegetable kingdom. Notwithstanding the similarity of
their dresses, consisting of business suits of the same
material, the difference between the two men was very
marked — not that either appeared crafty with the other
simple, but that one seemed a greater fool than his companion.

The elder, the more conspicuous man, must have been
at that time over fifty years, of medium height and build,
mild in aspect, but ready to be shaken by mirth at any
moment. He wore bushy whiskers shaped after the manner of Englishmen; had a pert, upturned face, florid complexion, and a disposition to wink his left eye occasionally
in order to incite others to laughter. This individual was
none other than Saracen Gay, called also "the poor man
of Christendom," a character well known in the South for
his philanthropy or eccentricity, and accorded all the
privileges of the best society on account of his social
standing. He was a millionaire, but, owing to mental

weakness, had been placed under the directorship of friends, so as not to be imposed upon by sharps or other evil-disposed persons. He feared to be accounted rich, having some hallucination that he would be murdered for his money; and hence his immediate companion, pandering to his delusion, called him at first the poorest man in Christendom, which the public made special by the title, "the poor man of Christendom."

The man who accompanied Saracen Gay on the occasion here mentioned was his valet, Risbon Flappins. Much care had been bestowed on his selection, and due regard paid to the peculiarities of the gentleman he would attend in future. "Ris," as he was often called, seemed to possess all the qualifications necessary for the position, or any other, for the matter of that. He was strong and fearless, yet gentle as a woman, sober, industrious in the affairs of his employer, and fully alive to the obligation of humoring his opinions and fancies. Flappins proved an excellent attendant; he encouraged his master to travel to the great cities and points of interest in the United States, kept him safe and comfortable throughout each ordeal, and had a jolly good time from year in to year out.

Saracen Gay rented a villa in the suburbs of Montgomery, but owned several in other places, so that, as a rule, he was constantly moving. This arrangement diverted his mind and made life endurable. At the time of his appearance before Furflew in the streets of Montgomery, he was expecting the arrival of a carriage which he had ordered at some other point. His opinions about its transportation will show a phase of his oddity.

"O Flappins," he said, "don't you think the carriage could be drawn behind the train?"

"Of course it could," answered the man.

"The wheels are strong."

"Quite right; the wheels are strong."

"If the road be level, the carriage will make as good headway as the train itself."

"Certainly; besides, Saracen, there ain't no hills on a railroad."

"But in case of trestles, don't you see what would occur?"

"The carriage would bob up and down, that's all."

Saracen Gay laughed.

"It would be funny to see it," he remarked, "but, Flappins, do you think it strong enough to endure such usage?"

"Of course it is."

"Well, what did you do? Did you tell the railroad people?"

"I knew exactly what you wished done with it," replied Flappins, assuming a serious air; "I told them to hitch the carriage on to the hind part of the train and let her come up that way."

"Ah! Flappins, you are very wise. You always know just what is best to be done. I tell you a good thing, though: when that carriage arrives, we might get this clever fellow into it"—alluding to Furflew. "He could practice his art for a while and pass as a millionaire, but in the meantime I could come up on the street as a poor man and apply for a ride, when you could take me in. Do you catch on?"

"Do I? I should say so. It's just the thing. In all my experience I never heard any proposal half so good. Besides, Saracen, if a shot is fired at the carriage, he'll be hit, sure."

Although not wanting in sympathy for his fellow-man, Saracen Gay laughed at this prediction until tears came into his eyes, because it favored his own plan and presented a ludicrous situation to the mind.

"You're wonderful," he resumed, addressing Flappins, "to point out the danger before it happened."

"I tell you what I could do, though," replied the man, boastfully. "If I saw that bullet coming towards you, I could catch it in my hand."

Saracen Gay never questioned the accuracy of this statement. He merely remarked in a quiet way peculiar to him:

"Good gracious! how smart you are!"

After the performance Flappins moved up to Furflew and addressed him in an undertone. By the aid of a few sentences he explained the standing and character of Saracen Gay and the plan they had agreed to for adding to their party so as to have a good time. As a matter of course, this suited Furflew admirably. Touching Flappins in the ribs with the point of his elbow, he said: "I'm in it. Bet your bottom dollar. We'll paint the town red, and lay it on thick. Now," continued Furflew, "let us meet him, and hear me go through the first act." Coming to the place where Saracen Gay was standing, Furflew resumed:

"What poor man is this, my dear Flappins?"

"Him?" answered Flappins, in well-feigned surprise. "Why, he is a poor fellow that's off and on here, now and again and between times, until you imagine there is nothing left of him. There ain't his like nowhere. In fact, he is the poorest man in Christendom."

"Bless me! how distressing that is!" said Furflew. "By the bye, Flappins, I tell you what we might do.

When my carriage comes round tomorrow, we might take
him up and give him a lift.''

"Just the thing," said Flappins.

Saracen Gay, extending his hand to Furflew, answered
for himself like a gentleman.

"Thank you. Your goodness may meet its reward
when least expected. The poor man will be glad to
accept your kind offer." Then, as Furflew turned away
departing for his lodgings, the speaker resumed, addressing
Flappins, "You're a great manager, Ris. Who would
have thought it? that fellow goes home with the conviction that I am as poor as a church mouse.''

"And he never dreams that he might get plugged,"
rejoined Flappins, laughing.

"That's the best joke of all," returned Saracen Gay;
"but," he resumed, "you are truly a wonderful man."

Whatever were the private opinions of the actors in this
drama as to the congruity or incongruity of the persona-
tion each had assumed, the following day carried with it
a full measure of amusement for them all. Furflew, seated
in the center of the carriage, with the most important air
he could assume, viewed the crowd with a critical eye;
Flappins, with a broad grin on his countenance, occupied
the box seat and held the reins well, while Saracen Gay,
appearing behind, seemed delighted with himself, with the
situation, and the people at large.

Knowing the peculiarities of "the poor man of Christendom," a vast congregation assembled on hearing that
he had taken up the ventriloquist and permitted public
exhibitions from his carriage. The applause was immense;
he was lauded to the skies. It was a great day for Furflew,
and a vindication of his belief in the business of a street

fakir. Once he saw Herondine in the crowd, which reminded him of his real character; but he said within himself patriotically, "I could capture this place without firing a shot." Into the work before him he threw his whole energy and spirit. He squealed like a hog caught under a gate, held dialogues with persons in the air above him, imitated the calls of birds and beasts, and sang humorous songs in half a dozen different tones.

While the amusement was at its height some one spoke to Saracen Gay. As the people saluted this man with much deference, it was evident he was a character of some importance. Indeed, we may say without betraying confidence that he was a member of the Confederate government. The occupant of the carriage by a motion of his hand invited him to a seat, which was immediately accepted, for Saracen Gay was personally acquainted with the most conspicuous men in the South, and assisted them in prosecuting the war. As it appeared just at this time that Furflew should be afforded a rest, Flappins drove through the city leisurely; while Saracen Gay and his new friend began a conversation of more than ordinary interest, especially to Furflew.

"Well, poor man," said the late arrival, "we're moving."

"Saracen Gay, believing that this assertion referred to the motion of the carriage, looked down at the vehicle and having been reminded of yesterday's unfinished conversation with Flappins regarding its transit, suddenly asked that worthy:

"How did it come, Ris? You never told me."

"Didn't I, though?" answered Flappins. "For that oversight I'll kick myself when I get down; you may rely on it. What do you think the fools did? Instead of hitching the thing as I directed, they went to work and carried it, wheels, body, seats, and all."

"Did you ever!" exclaimed Saracen Gay, laughing heartily at the supposed absurdity of the railroad people.

The newcomer resumed more impressively than he had begun:

"I mean, Saracen, that we are moving in the war."

"O! ah! sure enough! How far have we gone?" exclaimed the party addressed.

"Beauregard thinks we can reach Washington in three months, and hold it as long as we please," replied the other.

"I believe we can," responded Saracen Gay gravely.

"Although he is our leading general at present, there are persons in high places who have some one else in their eye for general-in-chief. For my part, I'm a Beauregard man."

"Quite right," said Saracen Gay; "he's good enough for anybody; but tell me — what is there on the boards?"

"We are going to establish the capital of the Confederacy at Richmond, Virginia; Beauregard has been ordered to push north with a large force; and Johnston goes to the Shenandoah valley, so as to check any advance of the enemy in that direction. We are yet in the lead."

After further discourse on the subject, the gentleman desired to return home, as he had a large mass of correspondence to answer, and was driven to his residence: but Saracen Gay was not tired of amusement; so the carriage continued in motion, carrying the three curious characters heretofore described, so humorous and yet so dissimilar.

" Can you tell me, Flappins," asked "the poor man of of Christendom," "why I don't get letters through the post office like that man ? "

" Ah, Saracen, that is a puzzler.   Why, indeed?   Perhaps our friend Furflew knows ? "

It appears that Furflew answeied to his real name when starting for Alabama, believing it as much unknown as any new one he could assume.

" Why, I know," replied Furflew; "because you are poor."

Saracen Gay chuckled with delight on hearing this statement, it fitted his thoughts so accurately.

" If you can foretell things to come, perhaps I could find out when I will get a letter," he said.

" You will get one tomorrow," replied Furflew, resolving secretly to send the desired communication himself.

" Ris, isn't he wonderful ? " said Saracen Gay, addressing Flappins.

" Never struck his equal," answered the man.   "I tell you, Saracen," he continued, "now is your time to find out things.   You often ask me questions as far out of my line as the man in the moon is from his Sunday clothes, but you have your chance at last."

Flappins's proposition came upon his listeners with the terrors of a thunderclap, the weak mind of Saracen Gay being confused by it, which prevented him from concentrating his thoughts on a single idea, while Furflew knew in his heart he could not answer correctly any ordinary question beyond the knowledge he possessed of a few common things.   In his dilemma Saracen Gay appealed to Flappins.

" Ask him, Ris; you know what's good for me," he said.

Flappins, reflecting a moment on the nature of the difficulty imposed on him, asked with an air of great wisdom:

"How can you know a man with swelled head?"

"He has always his pants turned up in rainy weather, and wears a large charm on his watch chain," answered Furflew, doubtful whether he had stated a truth or a falsehood, but trusting to chance to carry him through the ordeal to which he was then subjected.

"Hit the nail on the head!" exclaimed Flappins, with approval.

"Oh, how true he is!" said Saracen Gay; and he added, "Thank heaven, I never do it."

After a further exchange of pleasantries, it was agreed to meet next day in order to mature a plan which Furflew had partially formed of extending the sphere of his usefulness as a universal merrymaker. He determined on renting a large hall in which he could display his genius and accommodate the business public in the evening after the manner of a theater.

That night his interview with Herondine was long and animated. A dispatch was sent at once to Washington containing most important items of news concerning the movements of the Confederacy. Moreover, Herondine mentioned Furflew's efficient services and recommended him to receive higher pay, as well as promotion, when the requirements of the grades above him admitted of such.

Then Furflew, seating himself at a desk, wrote the following letter to Saracen Gay: ·

I'm out of my way, Saracen Gay, to write to you. It's a long time since you heard a word from me, because this is my first letter; but I feel for you, my poor man, as much as I can, and therefore wish you the right to vote in your own defense on pretense of being worthy.

What the people say, Saracen Gay, must be true about you. You're the poorest man in Christendom — or anywhere else, for the matter of tliat. The postman will not bring anything to the door of the poor when 'tain't there, nor the police chief give relief should your leg of mutton spoil in the boil.

All this goes to show, when you know, there's one thing you should do. Get Furflew and follow him through thick and thin to the bitter end. There is nothing like it. He'll amuse you. He'll make you think in a wink of more fun than you would gather in a year without him on a run. You may smile in a while at others of his ilk at a bilk —but with him you can soar to a roar or quaff till you laugh the mirth of fifty clowns.   FROM YOUR OWN CORRESPONDENT.

This epistle having been dressed and pointed by Herondine so as to make it a combination of prose and doggerel poetry, to harmonize with Furflew's humor, it was forwarded to its destination, and the two secret operators separated for the night.

CHAPTER XV.

A TAKING DESIGN.

FURFLEW'S estimate of himself increased in proportion to the success of his exhibitions of the art of ventriloquism. He began to imagine he could readily overshadow legitimate enterprise by the glamour of buffoonery, and compel society, as it were, to reverse the decision made against his trade, which had become so widespread and deep-rooted as almost to defy the ultimatum of human effort no matter how wisely or efficiently exercised. In former times trick of the loop and jugglery were his favorite operations or methods of making a living, the spirit of vagabondism which they entailed having a peculiar influence over his mind that was not by any means distasteful or distressing, but, on the contrary, quite desirable; and hence the eagerness with which he pursued them : but after engaging in the service of Herondine he found it necessary to accept the practice of ventriloquism to the exclusion of other tricks so as to stand within the boundaries of the law.

His success in this department became so marked that it fired his genius to advance after new glory and fresh fields of wonder or delight. The ease displayed in the capture of Saracen Gay and his man Flappins gave him a potent factor on which to base valuable data for future work. He concluded there were many persons who when confronted by minds stronger than their own would willingly obey their behests and feel a kind of pleasure under their influence or restriction. Even the strongest people are sometimes childlike. This was a great fact to seize and utilize by one so illiterate as Furflew; but the crafty nature of the man made him as bold in research as a scholar in philosophy or a thief after gain.

The plan submitted to Saracen Gay and Flappins when they next met Furflew was both amusing and sensational. The first named two men were to obey Furflew's dictation and the direction of his ideas wholly during the time devoted to the exhibition as if their minds had no self-capacity or power of control. If he asked them to see strange birds on the stage, they should show proper signs of admiration for these creatures, as if they really existed; or, should he declare that a section of the Tower of Babel was in their presence, they must forthwith extend their hands for the purpose of feeling the consistence of the ancient relic.

Saracen Gay became delighted with the prospect of fun based on such flimsy pretenses as those advanced by Furflew; but, shallow as his mind appeared to be, he believed the public generally were given to delusions and would not hesitate now, nor would it add much to the discomfiture of

mankind to introduce and promulgate a new one.   Hence
he entered vigorously into the design and consented to
follow Furflew's instructions to the letter, guaranteeing the
same for his man Flappins.   In giving his views on the
occasion, Saracen Gay remarked :

"It's like catching a man on the hip, or worse."

"Just the thing," answered Flappins.   "We might
call it the science of hipism."

"Or hypnotism," added Saracen Gay.   "How considerate you are, Flappins, to give me the suitable word and
then approve it ! — but you were always great."

Furflew, not to be outdone in courtesy, said :

"The name is O. K.   Now, to make the public stick to it
we'll do this : whenever you stand up in answer to my
calls, walk as if you were bound in the hips, or hip-screwed.
They will see at once that the secret power raises Cain with
the hips to begin with, and spreads over the rest of the
body afterwards."

That night there was a large audience to greet Furflew
in the public hall which had been rented for the occasion.
Having become popular on the street, the opening night,
the first of his evening performances, was well patron-
ized.   Harassed by civil war on the one hand, the people
favored anything likely to amuse them on the other.   If
they wept today, it was their intention to laugh tomorrow.
Such is human nature, true to natural law ; which gives us
sunshine and showers, growth and decay, consolidating and
loosening life and death.

Furflew rose to eminence when the curtain went up and
he stood face to face with those who were willing to pay for
mirth.   Not only had he devoted more attention to his dress
to meet the importance of this the greatest triumph of his

life, but he exceeded his previous efforts at mimicry and
fairly bristled with genius. It was towards the close of the
series of performances already announced that he undertook
to introduce his new scheme. Extending his right hand
towards the audience as if he meant to exercise conjuration
over it, he said :

"If any one here feels my secret power, let him or her
stand up."

The surprise which this proposition evoked was barely at
its height when one equally great followed. Two men
responded to the invitation and stood rigid in their places,
one on each side of the hall, awaiting further instructions.
At a glance it could be seen they were Saracen Gay and his
man Risbon Flappins. The incident gave rise to great
merriment. The house roared. It was a new thing, a
taking design, and succeeded even beyond all expectation.

"Come forward," said Furflew.

The men moved in obedience to the command, but it
was noticed they slid their feet over the surface of the floor
as if unable to walk freely or that they were suffering from
rigidity of the joints. When they reached the stage and
began to perform in obedience to the suggestions of Furflew, the house went into new bursts of applause and merriment. Saracen Gay and Flappins danced to the strains
of imaginary music, pulled bell ropes that had no existence, and threshed corn where there was none, besides
executing several other remarkable feats under the spell of
enchantment by which they seemed bound. Nor did the
amusement of the occasion falter at this point. Something
else appeared that transcended all other incidents witnessed
that evening, and wound up in a climax long to be remembered.

During a lull in the performance, a tall, dark-visaged man was seen to enter the lower end of the side passage leading the entire length of the hall from one of the street entrances to the stage. He seemed to have just arrived and to want to transact a little business of importance with the performer; for he held his head high in the air, hummed to himself a favorite tune, glanced furtively, if not carelessly, at the audience, and smiled when he saw the men on the stage in the full glare of the gaslight. It was evident from his nonchalant manner he felt quite at home and sure of his purpose. He even stopped and leaned against the wall so as to permit the people to enjoy the full measure of pleasure which appeared to be their portion on that night.

Furflew saw the stranger the first instant of his appearance. In the glory of his triumph, it was some time before he realized anything odd or unusual in the circumstance. When, however, he began to see clearly what the dark man's presence meant, he stood up first in awe, then trembled like one in front of an executioner. He turned red; then grew white. His companions heard him mutter a sound resembling the combination of a curse and a groan, but believed it was due as much to exultation as anything else, so little do some people know of the reality. His look was so intently fixed on the man in the alleyway that the people believed the latter a fresh neophyte of hypnotism, whereas, unfortunately, Furflew in this case was the victim. He was not only caught on the hip, but through the heart and on the head, metaphorically speaking, by him who had been the terror of his life and who had appeared once more to seal his doom forever — Danderton Hitch, the detective!

In the big pocket of his overcoat Danderton rattled something like a chain. To some ears the sound was interesting, if not musical; but Furflew knew it to emanate from the links of a set of handcuffs with which his enemy loved to play before seizing his prisoner. It was like the ominous stroke of a hammer in the construction of a gallows to him who was about to be executed. Before his first paroxysm of fear ended, he felt his wrists alternately with each hand, contemplating their power of endurance, and looked around the stage as if seeking a precipice into which he meant to fall, like one pursued by a vicious dog.

It was singular and terrible how he had become the sport of circumstances. Raised to a great height by success in one instant, only to fall into ignominious defeat the next. Yesterday the idol of the people, today a prisoner—for he would be one presently, with the prospect of a dark cell in the enemy's prison awaiting him and certain death immediately thereafter. He shuddered; and Saracen Gay thought the current of air through the hall was making him cold. This was the first time he had encountered real danger, and, naturally, the situation astounded him; but by a great effort he preserved a calm demeanor and ventured to look up a plan of escape. There could be no doubt Danderton had the advantages in his favor, compared with Furflew, in the present emergency. He possessed the secret of the performer's identity, knew he had been a soldier in the Confederate army in Charleston harbor, and strongly suspected him of being what he really was—a companion of Herondine and a spy in the service of the North.

When the interval of rest terminated, Danderton advanced towards the stage. At the same time, Furflew, stepping to the footlights, addressed the audience. He said:

"You see, fellow-citizens, my followers are increasing. Now, this third man will act rather strangely and therefore must be held by the others until he grows tame under force. He has caught on lively. Got a full dose, you bet, and is in it. Flappins and Saracen, you see to him."

As Danderton stepped on the stage, Flappins seized him by the collar, and a wild tussle ensued amid the uproar of the house. The struggle was fierce for a short time, during which Danderton endeavored to draw his revolver; but Flappins had anticipated the movement and held his arm with his right hand, while with his left he gave him a straight punch in the stomach that came near doubling him up.

"Give it to him good, Ris," said Saracen Gay, delighted with such fun, as he hopped round the contestants, but was afraid to touch either lest he should be sent sprawling to the floor.

"Saracen, you leave him to me," said Flappins. "It ain't becoming for a poor man as you are to handle such game as this. I could settle three like him."

Saracen Gay laughed immoderately at this assurance, being unable to speak through excess of feeling. It could be easily seen that Flappins was gifted with great power, and delighted in giving it a test. Danderton was strong, full of endurance, and athletic; but in the hands of Flappins he was a mere boy.

"Keep that little gun in your pocket," said Flappins, after he had convinced his opponent how useless it was for him to attempt to gain superiority by the exercise of brute force, "because it might hurt yourself. Little toys of that kind are liable to do some damage in the hands of children."

"Do you know who I am?" asked Danderton, with some pride, while he trembled from chagrin and pain.

"Hear him, Saracen," rejoined Flappins.

"I know him, Ris," answered Saracen Gay. "He's an old pumpkin."

"I tell you I am a —"

The conclusion of this sentence was drowned in the burst of laughter which the two friends sent forth and that was taken up by the audience as an assurance that they were fully amused by the vagaries of hypnotism as shown in the new convert.

But where was Furflew? Looking around the stage, Saracen Gay found he had disappeared, but, strange to say, ascribed his absence to natural causes rather than to the fear of impending danger. Hence, when the janitor came forward and announced the performance at an end, no one suspected there had occurred anything outside the sphere of ordinary stage business.

The people rose and crowded into the passages, jostling against each other good-humoredly in their efforts to get out, and laughing at remarks pertaining to the evening's amusement. Flappins discharged Danderton with an admonition not to attempt interference with "the poor man of Christendom" or his affairs in future, otherwise he would come to grief soon and sudden; and then with his master mingled through the crowd, believing they would meet Furflew on the following morning.

It must be said of the Northern man that the chief incidents of that night were the boldest and most skillful acts of his whole career. Even during his retreat, with his glory extinguished like the snuffing of a candle, he chuckled at the cleverness of his venture — how he managed to

escape capture. When Flappins laid hold of Danderton,
Furflew withdrew through a door at the back of the stage,
and, meeting the janitor in the corridor, told him his
assistants were at the last act and when they had finished
he could step on to the stage and announce the performance at an end. As payment in advance had been made
for the use of the hall, the request would be complied with,
the man said; and Furflew left the building. Then his
make-up came down piece by piece. The artificial nose
was crushed into his pocket; the mustache disappeared;
his hat was given an ugly bruise to knock it out of shape;
and he pulled the collar of his coat around his neck as if
suffering from malaria. In this condition he appeared
before Herondine, who recognized instantly that danger
must be near at hand.

"I am ready," said the chief.   "What is it?"

"The old thing; Danderton is on the track," replied
Furflew; and he added, "just fifteen minutes to get out."

"Pooh!" rejoined Herondine, "more time than we
need. The bills are paid, the line is clear, and nothing
further to detain us. Come."

They left the hotel hurriedly together and five minutes
afterward were in the secret route on their way to Washington.

"I wonder where is Furflew," said Saracen Gay, looking
round and addressing Flappins after they had waited in
vain on the street for his reappearance next day.

"I bet a dime the friends of that dandy fellow we had a
tussle with last night ran into him. They'd do it to get
even for giving him the hypnotize."

"That's it, sure, Ris. How many do you think went
at him?"

"Oh! about seventeen, all told, from the grandfather down to the third cousin far removed."

"It was lucky we were not in his company when it happened."

"Lucky for them, you mean! I should say it was. I'd have whipped the entire crowd in two minutes and a half. After that you could see nothing of them but the dust they raised while flying from my vengeance."

"I say, Flappins," said Saracen Gay after a hearty laugh, "didn't the new fellow take to it in great style, though?"

"Never saw the beat of it, Saracen. Why, I could feel the darn thing on the inside riling me while I held him. It was nothing else."

"Flappins, I'm serious. Could we not open business on our own account?"

"Of course we can. In these later days I never heard anything so novel as this suggestion of yours."

"We might follow in our comrade's footsteps, be his disciples, and take on to the profession."

"That is a remarkably bright idea, Saracen."

"We could make money, you know."

"Barrels of it; but, as you will never be more than a poor man, I could take the coin as my share."

"And what would you call mine, Ris?"

"Let me see," answered Flappins reflectively. "I'd name it 'the honor of the thing.' You are the soul of honor. That is all you need, and that's all you'd get."

"Oh, how wise you are, Flappins, and considerate! but tell me — would we attempt ventriloquism?"

"Naw," returned the man contemptuously. "There is too much uphill work and squeaking in that job. Plain

hypnotism as received from the professor is all we'll do;
for, let me tell you, Saracen, of all the easy trades to learn
in the world that stands first."

"Suppose some of the converts become unmanageable?"

"Put on an extra hand — one of the unemployed."

"Do you think, Flappins, it will be easy to find persons
to act as we did — under the influence of hypnotism, you
know?"

"I'll manage that part, you bet. Get 'em by the dozen.
If in no other way, run 'em in at a dollar a head."

"Then we need not bring them along like circus people
or those of a box-show?"

"Not much. We can find a new set in every place.
You and I will be professors, dress in long coats with fur
collars, wear flesh-colored gloves, carry riding whips, have
our handkerchiefs scented every morning, up to snuff, and
let our hair grow down to our shoulders. O Saracen,
won't we have the gay old times!"

Saracen Gay laughed until tears came into his eyes at
the golden prospect outlined by Flappins. When he recovered sufficiently to speak, he said:

"Ris, you're wonderful. I believe you are the greatest
there is."

"I have something more to spring on to you, Saracen.
We'll get out bills. I'll engineer it in this way. I'll pile
up the biggest sell out — all for fun, of course. This is
what will meet the public eye: 'The Greatest Attraction
of the Age. Wonders of Nature Revealed. Saturday
evening at South Side Hall there will appear for the first
time Professor Risbon Flappins assisted by Professor Saracen Gay in their soul-stirring exhibitions of hypnotism
which have lately captured public attention by their won-

derful and mysterious power. Come early and secure seats.' "

" Now, really, Ris, will the people gather in response to this invitation and pay money besides? "

" Will they? If the hall ain't crowded to the door never call me Flappins again, but ' fool.' Why, Saracen, you have no idea the way people spend hard-earned money; but, as it's none of our business except to take it in, mum's the word."

In order to complete his preliminary arrangements for the contemplated performance, Flappins left Saracen Gay at home and proceeded to the city alone on a tour of investigation. He was desirous of ascertaining how far he could be successful in the enlistment or engagement of persons willing to act as if under hypnotic or exterior influence, paying them, of course, a stated sum for their services. It occurred to him if those skilled in singing or dancing were selected and paid a higher rate of wages than ordinary workers, the introduction of hypnotism as their additional accomplishment on the stage would add largely to the general amusement. In this design they would, he thought, exceed the details of Furflew's masterly entertainment, and he was quite correct. The evidence of his success appeared next day when he and his employer sat in the anteroom of the hall where their theatrical venture was to appear. About noon, Flappins, beckoning to Saracen Gay as a sign that he was to accompany him, said:

" Come, Saracen, let me show you something." Throwing open the door, the man continued: " Look."

The passage was full of people: nay, on reaching the front entrance they saw a multitude on the outside, of all ages and conditions, awaiting with apparent eagerness some expected event.

" Flappins," said Saracen Gay, in amazement, "do tell me what are these people looking for ; what, in fact, is their objective point ? "

" Those," replied the man, speaking guardedly in a low tone so as not to be heard by any one but his companion, " want the hypnotize bad, for all that's out. I gave a few pointers last night in several places just to see how the thing would work, and here we are as full of business as a green grocer on a Saturday night. Oh! the way they catch on is a caution."

" How did you do it, Ris ? "

" I told them we'd pay a dollar a head for rough ones, and upwards for better — or worse, as the case might be."

" Are they willing to act ? "

" Like a charm."

" Won't tell the secret ? "

" Naw, any more nor you or I."

" It's wonderful," said Saracen Gay reflectively, and he continued : " How can we get out of this scrape ? "

" There ain't none. We will employ ten new hands every night while the play lasts, and tell the others to call again."

The performance presented by Flappins and Saracen Gay that night was a brilliant exposition of the new science. " The poor man of Christendom " was delighted beyond description, for he had found a profession suited to his condition and tastes. Henceforth Flappins need not worry about discovering new sources of pleasure to amuse his charge, because Furflew's ingenious contrivance covered the whole field. In speaking of their success, Saracen Gay remarked:

" Ris, our friend the professor was great in more ways than one. Don't you recollect how he foretold I would get a letter next day? Well, sure enough, it came. That was the most wonderful insight into the future I ever knew or heard of. Did you ever hear anything to beat it, Ris?"

"Never, Saracen; nor anybody else, to my way of thinking."

"It came from our own correspondent. I never knew we had one, Ris. How did you get him on?"

Flappins seemed puzzled by this question, but, after some reflection, replied:

"I gave him a trial to see how he'd make it, engaging at the same time that we would call quits after the first letter. I said I didn't want to see him work himself up, like one man I knew in a newspaper office, who resembled a chimney sweep—he was blacker at the top than he was at the bottom. He couldn't write anything better than his first, or worse at any stage of his elevation. Therefore I advised him to keep as dark in the future as he was in the past."

"You're a wonderful judge, Ris," remarked Saracen Gay, as the two professors moved off to their quarters so as to prepare for the enjoyment of a good dinner.

CHAPTER XVI.

SOME SECRETS NEVER TOLD.

HERONDINE and Furflew returned to Washington after their second hazardous expedition in the midst of popular excitement and active preparation for war on a large scale. There was little delay in reaching a new duty. Herondine was designated an emergency aid-de-

camp to the commanding general in the field.   This assignment was not known to the public or spread on the records;
indeed, the commander had no conception of the number
or identity of such aids in his service ; but it was a fact,
notwithstanding, and deemed advisable by the Secret Service Bureau as a precautionary measure rarely if ever omitted
on important occasions; and, besides, accorded entirely
with the man's own wishes.   Thus Herondine would in
time come face to face with death on the battlefield.   Furflew
attended to his chief's horse as well as his own, which carried a pack saddle filled with necessaries.

One peculiarity of the secret service is, the agents of it
are free to wander where they please, guided by their own
judgment.   Although Herondine and Furflew had specific
duties, yet they were bound to no man nor restrained in
their movements by any general or special order.   Hence
their preparations were made to partake of as much comfort and satisfaction as possible without trespassing too far
on official privilege.

While in Washington, they listened to the news somewhat after the manner of children awed into silence by
the deep reverberations of thunder.   Every day — nay,
every hour — came charged with sensational events.   Virginia, the grand old state, with its comely physical features
and famous historical record, plunged headlong into secession, carrying with it the future general-in-chief of the
Confederate army and a host of soldiers.   The Sixth Massachusetts Regiment of militia, on its way to Washington,
was attacked by a mob in the streets of Baltimore, showing
the sympathy prevailing at that point for the cause of the
South ; and that portion of public opinion heretofore
muzzled by the law, now broke loose without restraint into

one long tirade of abuse against order, decency, and justice.

People began to imagine the pretensions of the North regarding the Union could not be sustained in the face of all these significant signs; and even men of superior ability, whose opinions had been consulted on these questions, held it wise to let the South go.

The information obtained by the Federal government, through its agents, of the plans of the Confederacy pointed to an early movement on Washington with the intention of capturing that stronghold and thus forcing a settlement of the war in harmony with Southern aspirations; and it soon became apparent that this belief was well founded, for not only did the Southern executive change its situation from Montgomery, Alabama, to Richmond, Virginia, but the veteran general Beauregard, with most of the available troops of the South — about twenty-five thousand men — appeared in that state and began the construction of a fortified line of defense along the river Bull Run, extending in a direction southeast to northwest, within two days' march of the Federal capital. While this movement was not necessarily the inauguration of a siege line or a storming party, yet no one could predict to what uses it might be applied in future if disaster overtook the Union soldiers.

The situation was decidedly menacing. General Beauregard's headquarters were at Manassas Junction, a point of meeting for the Orange, Alexandria, and Manassas Gap railroads; and Bull Run was situated about three miles in front, in the direction of Washington. To the right, thirty miles distant on the lower Potomac River, was a Confederate force of three thousand men under General Holmes; while on the left, sixty miles away, appeared the

Army of the Shenandoah, under the command of General Joseph E. Johnston, eight or nine thousand strong. This force rested on the upper Potomac, and completed an irregular crescent whose principal points not only threatened Washington, but also commanded the approaches to Richmond.

The part of Virginia where Beauregard's army then operated was one great plain, relieved to some extent by the ridge of the Blue Mountains, forming the eastern boundary of the Shenandoah valley. The passage of the James River, on which Richmond is situated, was guarded by two Confederate forces; and altogether this first strategic display on the part of the South seemed to indicate immense success in the near future.

On the other hand, the executive in Washington, advised by the veteran general Winfield Scott, pushed forward troops to check the further advance of the Confederates and protect the people of a few doubtful states from the baleful influence of secession. General Patterson, an experienced and reliable officer, commanded the Federal right wing — about fifteen thousand men — in front of Johnston. General B. F. Butler occupied the left with a force of Union patriots, while Irvin McDowell, promoted to the rank of brigadier general for the occasion, assumed control of the center, designed to test the prowess of Beauregard's army.

It was a fair adjustment of principals, where the men in whom the North confided were as staunch and brave and reputable as their opponents; and no decision could be deduced from appearances or conjecture as to how the palm of victory should tend in the first great battle of the war.

General McDowell claimed Columbus, Ohio, as his birthplace. He was a classmate of Beauregard's at the military academy of West Point, and after graduating with honors at that institution was assigned to the artillery branch of the United States army. Besides his educational courses in America, he had spent some of his earlier years in the college of Troyes, France; so that his varied accomplishments and the broad scope of his knowledge fitted him for important military services in his native country. He was instructor of infantry tactics at West Point, adjutant general of General Wool's column in the Mexican War, aid-de-camp to the general-in-chief at Washington, and inspector of troops. On General Scott's recommendation he was promoted to the rank of brigadier general in May, 1861, and assigned to the command of the Department of Northwestern Virginia, where the troops constituting the center of the Federal army were congregating.

General McDowell was a whole-souled patriot and soldier, faithful to his country in the hour of her peril, with the instincts of a gentleman, the ability of a scholar, and the honesty of one in whom the nation at large could implicitly trust. His command began to form on the south side of the Potomac River opposite Washington some time before his assignment to duty with it, and in numbers finally reached about thirty-five thousand men, with forty-nine pieces of artillery. Besides being burdened with the weight of a critical public opinion, ever ready to censure or question his movements if not in harmony with the current of its spontaneous views, McDowell had other difficulties to meet in the formation of his army, the most important being that the three-months men enlisted in April would be entitled to leave the field in

July; and if any considerable number of these soldiers made a homeward movement on the eve of a battle, it might probably result in disaster to those remaining if not supported by fresh troops. However, a large class of the people of the North was eager for active field service; and, stimulated by the cry of "On to Richmond," McDowell gave the order to march.

Herondine and Furflew were among the crowd of civilians present with the army on the morning of that memorable day, July sixteenth, 1861, when the bugle sounded the call to arms and the long roll of the drums beat the summons to "fall in." It was noon before the line of march was taken up, the men being cheered by the inspiring sounds of martial music and the sight presented to view of moving columns of comrades in gay uniforms. Nevertheless, it must be admitted the soldiers sweltered under their equipments. The weather was hot, the roads dry and dusty, as well as blocked up by trees, causing much delay and the expenditure of extra labor in clearing the passage. Besides, although the general conformation of the land seemed flat, there were inequalities in the surface of it, tending to impede the steady advance of troops; yet nature supplied some relief to him who turned to her in that hour.

The view on each side of the route was pleasing, diversified by the appearance of trees in groups, picturesque ravines, and pleasant-looking homesteads. One could see the solemn aspect of spruce, cedar, and·pine among the woods, and the far-famed evergreen holly decking the upland near the houses. Clusters of ferns flanked the trail, interspersed with honeysuckle, lupine, and fairy flax; and in the orchards, which were numerous, the appearance of fruit gave evidence that the coming yield would be abundant. In the still atmosphere the songs of birds were heard, as if intended to be an accompaniment to the sunshine; and many limpid streams of crystal water came gushing to the feet of the invaders, echoing the music above.

The Confederates fell back without offering much resistance, in obedience to the orders of their commander, whose strategic plans had been matured some time before the Federal advance. Tyler's division of the Federal army, with orders to push beyond Centerville, where McDowell's headquarters were stationed, and appear as if intending to move on Manassas Junction, the place where the Confederate army was supposed to be, was made abruptly aware of the true position, for, while reconnoitering on the eighteenth with Richardson's brigade, Tyler came upon the enemy at Blackburn's Ford, on Bull Run, fully three miles northward of Manassas. Attempting to force a closer inspection of the ford, Tyler was driven back, suffering some loss in killed and wounded. Other reconnoissances and reports came in giving evidence of the fact that along the banks of this beautiful stream the battle must be fought, for Beauregard's forces were here prepared to dispute any further invasion of their territory.

The Confederate line of battle followed the serpentine course of the stream for a distance of eight miles, the right resting at Union Mills, southeast, while the left held the passage of the stone bridge, northwest, over which the public road ran from Centerville to Gainesville and thence towards Manassas. This road was also called the Warrenton turnpike. Between the right and left, the Confederate forces had been distributed in groups — brigades — within supporting distance of each other. This plan became feasible on account of the character of Bull Run, its banks being rocky and precipitous, flanked by thick brushwood, as well as that the stream itself was impassable, owing to summer rains ; but at the intermediate points referred to sand bars and gravel had formed tolerably fair passages for teams, on which, generally, there appeared but a few feet of water.   These passages were called "fords." Thus, while General Ewell held the right at Union Mills, Jones guarded the passage of McLean's Ford ; Longstreet, that of Blackburn's Ford ; Bonham, Mitchell's Ford ; Cocke, Ball's and Lewis's fords ; and Evans, the stone bridge.   Besides, General Holmes came up on the eve of battle to support Beauregard's right, and Johnston's army, from the Shenandoah, to strengthen his left and center ; while McDowell received no addition to his army from one point or the other, although numbers of his men had fallen out of ranks since the beginning of the march.

It was Sunday morning, July twenty-first, 1861.   The dawn broke over the eastern sky with a sympathetic expression for the condition of the earth, regardless of the petty turmoil agitating the minds of men.   It smiled sweetly at the appearance of night retreating over the horizon like some contemptible wretch anxious to seek the cover of an underground resort.   Vibrations of light danced in mid-air, creating a feeling of joy in the beholder.   The long, low bluff known as Bull Run Mountains, with Thoroughfare Gap in the center, became visible from elevated points; and the dark patches of ground occupied by small woods or ravines were enlivened by new and more cheerful coloring.   There was a balmy feeling in the atmosphere, and a delicious odor, as if intending to induce rest and refreshment on this Sabbath morning; and far in the distance were views such as might originate dreams of happiness in the breasts of the unfortunate and the hopeful if mankind had been a little more civilized or had studied more extensively the benign lessons of Mother Nature.

Before the door of a cottage by the wayside between Centerville and Bull Run, a man might be seen through the gray light of the morning, actively employed in grooming two horses, and varying his labor by the application of accouterments such as were deemed suitable for stern service in war. The man wore a campaign hat jauntily fitted to the side of his head; was fairly well attired, having a white linen stable frock over his blue clothes; and wore serviceable boots with the spurs of a cavalryman, although, on looking at him more closely, one could see that he was no other than Herondine's attendant, Furflew, the lifelong shuffler and ventriloquist—so much does war change the aspect of things in human life.

Suddenly the deep boom of a cannon filled the quiet atmosphere with terrific commotion; for there was generated a feeling of terror in all who heard it, the air trembled, the earth felt insecure, and the combatants within reach of the sound understood that the battle had begun. It was the thirty-pounder rifled gun attached to Carlisle's battery, and was fired under the immediate supervision of Lieutenant Haines, United States Artillery, at half past five o'clock in the morning, as a signal that General Tyler, with his division of the Union army, occupied the position assigned him in front of the stone bridge on Beauregard's left.

In an instant Herondine appeared on the scene, with a serious expression on his countenance, but ready for the saddle. He had just completed the breakfast prepared for him by Furflew a short time before. It may be said in explanation of his presence here, that he had rented the cottage temporarily from the owner, who had been advised to move away to a less exposed district until the issues in the present trouble were settled. They were modest but comfortable quarters, and protected from danger by hills although quite near the stone bridge and the Gainesville road, along which bodies of troops were marching.

"We're in it for sure," said Furflew, addressing Herondine, as he threw up his head between the horses, whose nostrils were sniffing the troubled void as if to ascertain the extent of the commotion.

Herondine, pointing to the door, signified to the man that he was to make a hasty repast, while he would mount and wait his return.

"I'll go in to please you," answered Furflew, while suiting the action to the word, "but I could no more eat on this here day than fly across Bull Run. That there sound is enough for me, and no doubt we'll get more of the same kind purty soon. I'll take a couple of cold sandwiches with me. They'll come in handy before the day's out, you bet, if we don't git cold lead in place of 'em."

When the preparations for departure were completed and both men on their horses faced the route over which they were to travel, something of a marvelous nature arrested their attention. It was a horseman at full speed whose appearance and activity indicated that his errand must be of great moment. He was coming on the parallel line to Bull Run from a southern direction toward the northwest, and would presently pass Herondine's headquarters. Herondine suspected he was a courier from some of the gener-

als on the other side, but wondered what his business would
be at this early hour and in such a place.

"Look to your pistols," he cried hastily, addressing Furflew; and, reaching to his holsters for his own, awaited the
stranger's arrival.

When only a short distance from the place where they
had halted, rider and steed presented a splendid appearance.
The man was over the medium height, displaying great
strength and confidence in his physical powers. His face
was a little pale but enlivened by a manly expression in
which the well-formed features participated individually
and collectively. His brown hair clustered in thick curls
around his ears; he sat erect in the saddle like one master
of the position; and the will power impetuously urging
him forward seemed to communicate with the spirit of his
horse and induce it to push with a mad energy through all
sections of the journey, whether easy of access or dangerous.

Notwithstanding his dress — a gray suit, long boots, and
campaign hat, such as Confederate officers wore — Herondine concluded he was a Northern man. Nay, he smiled
as he saw the stranger give the sign, proving that he belonged to the secret service in which Herondine himself
was engaged; and glancing at Furflew he became aware
that the individual mentioned was stricken with awe, as if
he had seen the whirlpool of Charybdis swallowing a ship
without hope of rescue.

"Cap," said Furflew — a term applied to Herondine on
the new expedition on account of its near approach to the
military — "I'll be doggoned if this ain't that there young
smarty we met in New York — the clever one — that Riddleton feller, the book eater and aunt fancier. Oh! look

at him, will you, without winking! Ain't he a daisy, though ?''

It was indeed Rob Riddleton grown strong and bold through hard exercise and the impulses of an active mind. Pulling up, he recognized Herondine at a glance, and the two friends exchanged very cordial greetings. Then, turning to Furflew, he shook him by the hand until he laughed in admiration of the man, although the boom of the thirty-pounder was again heard, and the rattle of musketry, showing that the skirmishing lines of both armies were at work. At a sign from Herondine, Furflew fell back some distance to permit the unrestrained conversation of the two chiefs brought together under such peculiar circumstances.

"At our headquarters in Washington I did not hear of you," said Herondine, "and therefore am somewhat surprised at your knowledge of our service (alluding to the sign made by Rob Riddleton at his approach) as well as that you appear in a Confederate dress."

"My rendezvous is Saint Louis," answered Riddleton ; "besides, this," and he pointed inwardly to his tunic, "is not a whit more questionable than the garb of Brother Fishington, recently discarded by you."

"Why, Riddleton, you astonish me," said Herondine. "I always gave you credit for immense powers of research, but the knowledge of my method of operations looks like necromancy. You ought to be chief."

Riddleton smiled at the compliment tendered him by his friend. He rode up to Herondine until their horses' flanks touched, and, placing one of his arms akimbo as if intending to assume a nonchalant air, said impressively:

"I play the highest game on the boards. The chieftanship of one side only is a tame affair. The restrictions imposed on you, for instance, result merely in half measures of gain. I cannot tolerate any such bondage; therefore I have chosen to be two characters in one, as coming nearest the complement of my ambitious desires."

The gravity of Herondine's face became deep and dark as he struggled with the thought uppermost in his mind regarding the true character of his new-found friend.

"You do not mean to insinuate that you are —"

As Herondine hesitated, Riddleton answered quickly:

"Aye, I am. I scout for both armies. See here."

Dismounting from his horse, with a few rapid movements he turned his tunic inside out, reversed the covering of his pantaloons, and lo, he returned to the saddle in the dress of an aid-de-camp to a general in the Federal army.

"This is beyond my comprehension," remarked Herondine, when his surprise had subsided sufficiently to enable him to speak.

"In every profession there are high and low stages," replied Riddleton. "The part that I play would be impossible to others. I have capacity for it, and therefore it is as easy of accomplishment to me as a boatman who dips his oars in the water unconscious that he is executing intricate movements. Assuming a disguise and gathering information of the enemy outside his lines are meritorious enough, but going into his camp and sounding the intentions of his commanders is much better. This I have done even with less risks than one would imagine. I pass through the Federal lines with as much ease as the Confederate, because I have authority from both commanders. I supply information to both, and it is evident each is satisfied; otherwise I would be imprisoned or ordered to discontinue my visits."

"How can you give information of our army to the Confederates without being considered a traitor?" asked Herondine.

"That depends upon its character," replied his companion. "Some information is of no value; therefore it could be given without detriment to the Union: besides, I might give a little that was important if by this means I could obtain a greater share for the other side. Do you understand?"

Herondine smiled at the ingenuity of his friend's methods, while Riddleton continued:

"Beauregard commands here," pointing towards the south; "McDowell there," turning towards the north. "They are mere puppets in my hands. I hold the key of the situation. I can give victory to whom I choose."

Herondine looked up incredulously; and, being understood, Riddleton after a short pause resumed:

"Now, friend, there are some secrets never told to the public; the one I am going to communicate to you is of such a character. You will see that its importance and my high estimate of your friendship will guarantee its safety with you." Riddleton drew from his pocket a paper, and, handing it to Herondine, said, "Read."

It was a dispatch from General Beauregard to General Ewell, who commanded his right wing at Union Mills, as before stated, directing him to march on Centerville and attack McDowell's reserves.

"What have you done?" inquired Herondine.

"The delivery or the withdrawal of this dispatch will change the whole character of the battle," returned Riddleton. "I have kept it back so as to subserve my purposes. I consider it a legitimate way of making a fortune for myself, seeing the danger that surrounds me and the necessity there exists of providing for the future. I am not playing this game for Beauregard or McDowell, South or North; I am playing it for myself. I have bet my pile — about ten thousand dollars — against the united sum of a club of ten Southern gentlemen that I would win this battle for the South. Of course, it is another way of offering me reward for important services; and each one of these persons will be enriched from other sources by the transaction, anyway."

"Surely," remarked Herondine solemnly, "this is treason inexcusable."

"Oh, no!" answered his friend pleasantly. "You see, I am guided entirely by my own judgment. I have an insight into things. I disobey Beauregard's commands by not delivering his dispatch to General Ewell. This fact will be sufficient to prove to McDowell that I have operated in the interests of the North and satisfy him fully of my genuine character as his secret agent. But, mark you, my own opinion is, if Ewell marched on Centerville the South would lose the fight, because it would bring McDowell's entire army into action, in which case the issue must be very uncertain if not disastrous to the Confederacy; therefore I will be excused in the eyes of Beauregard. I deserve something for this foresight, and I am going to get it. By keeping Beauregard and his united army on the south side of Bull Run, and half of McDowell's forces at Centerville and beyond it out of supporting distance on the day of action, it is easy to foresee the result. The beauty and strangeness of such maneuvering of mine is this: by operating against both sides to their detriment I win their favor and a fortune for myself outside their jurisdiction or knowledge. This is what I call being smart."

"Well," said Herondine, "you are a remarkable man; but, for my part, I could never resort to such plans, because I would be loath to execute them."

Without intimating what his future course or speculations would be, Rob Riddleton resumed his wild ride over the country, leaving Herondine and Furflew to pursue their way at pleasure.

CHAPTER XVII.

THE CARRIER PIGEON FALLS.   THE BATTLEFIELD.

HERONDINE, meditating profoundly on the strange career of Rob Riddleton, urged his horse forward towards the extremity of the elevated ground surrounding his quarters, from which he could observe the further progress of the battle and determine on the character of his individual duties for the day. Nothing appeared to occupy the early hours of the morning but the booming of the great gun before mentioned and the action of the skirmishers. On reaching the highest point available in the vicinity of his route, he could account for these peculiarities. The great contest of the day had not yet begun. The range for the Confederate batteries in the neighborhood of the stone bridge, and, indeed, for those of the Federals also, was too long, excepting the thirty-pounder Parrott, which was on a hill, and fired over the heads of the skirmishers on duty nearer the enemy's line.

He could easily observe, also, the long lines of troops on the flank movement contemplated by McDowell directing their course westerly so as to overlap Beauregard's left. These columns consisted of the divisions of Hunter and

Heintzelman, and in all numbered about thirteen thousand men. Hunter's division consisted of Porter's brigade of three New York regiments, to which also were attached a battalion of United States infantry commanded by Major Sykes, a battalion of United States cavalry commanded by Major Palmer, a battalion of United States marines led by Major Reynolds, and Battery D of the Fifth United States Artillery under Captain Charles Griffin, and Burnside's brigade of four regiments, one being from New Hampshire, two Rhode Island, and the Seventy-first New York, with two howitzers and a battery of artillery, the latter being the Rhode Island.

Heintzelman's division contained three brigades — Franklin's, Wilcox's, and Howard's. Franklin's brigade contained two Massachusetts regiments and one from Minnesota, besides having attached to it Battery I, First United States Artillery, commanded by Captain J. B. Ricketts. Wilcox's brigade was made up of two New York regiments and two Michigan regiments, and had attached to it Battery D, Second United States Artillery, commanded by Captain Richard Arnold. Howard's brigade contained three Maine regiments and one from Vermont. Two divisions were held in reserve — Runyon's, aggregating about six thousand men, eight miles distant, and Miles's, with a like number, at Centerville, three miles distant.

Pointing in the direction taken by the troops of the flanking column, Herondine remarked to Furflew:

"We follow where these lead. The commanding general will be found there, for to a certainty the row will be settled near that point."

Furflew, shading his eyes with his hand so as to get a clearer view of the situation, replied meditatively:

"Trick of the loop had its terrors, like everything risky, but you bet it was a sight more comfortable than this here job any way you take it."

The skirmishing near the stone bridge was participated in by five companies from the First and Second Ohio regiments, of Schenck's brigade, Northern troops, against two companies of the Fourth South Carolina Volunteers and one company of Wheat's special battalion, Southern troops. After an hour's engagement it became apparent to Evans, who directed the action on the Confederate side, that the Federals did not intend to cross Bull Run at that place, but merely instituted a feint so as to gain time to execute a greater undertaking elsewhere. As he could detect the columns on the opposite side of the stream advancing to position, he consulted his superior officer, Colonel P. St. George Cocke, commanding in his immediate neighborhood, when it was determined to form a new line of battle to oppose the incoming section of McDowell's army. On this understanding Colonel Evans withdrew his troops from the stone bridge, leaving four companies to defend it, and pushed his command westward across the valley of Young's Branch, a stream running into Bull Run, and seized the high ground beyond as the most suitable position to await the coming of the enemy, who wheeled to the left at Sudley Ford, three miles above the stone bridge, and marched directly to meet the foe.

Evans's new line consisted of six companies of Sloan's Fourth South Carolina, Wheat's special battalion of Louisiana volunteers, Terry's squadron of cavalry, and David-son's second section of Latham's battery of artillery, four six-pounder guns, and a company of cavalry attached — the Campbell Rangers, commanded by Captain J. D.

Alexander. The left of the line rested on the Sudley road; and the line itself extended through a small wood, affording cover for the troops, and commanded a good view of the open ground as well as the road along which the Federals were approaching. The artillery supported the right, and the cavalry the left.

Small as this front appeared, there was a large number of troops available to reinforce it. During the previous day and night Johnston's Army of the Shenandoah came in, and its commander, General Joseph E. Johnston, assumed command of the entire field, while General Beauregard superintended the battle. Johnston's troops consisted of four brigades — Jackson's, Bartow's, Bee's, and Smith's — five batteries of artillery, and Colonel J. E. B. Stuart's command of cavalry. The whole of these troops covered and supported Beauregard's left, Bee and Bartow on high ground in view of Evans's line of battle, Jackson near Longstreet at Blackburn's Ford, but ordered to the left at an early hour. Smith's brigade came up in the afternoon. Stuart's cavalry stood between Bonham's left and Cocke's right; Imboden's battery of artillery unlimbered about one hundred yards northeast of the Henry house on a plateau overlooking the battlefield; and the Hampton Legion, six companies of infantry six hundred strong commanded by Colonel Wade Hampton, stood in the vicinity of the Lewis house to support any troops engaged there. There were also some independent troops in the same neighborhood.

All these troops could easily be reinforced by others stationed along Beauregard's line on Bull Run. Cocke, besides the five Virginia regiments of his brigade, was still further supported by a battery of artillery and one company of Virginia cavalry. Bonham, at Mitchell's Ford, had a full brigade of five regiments, one being North Carolina and four South Carolina, supported by two batteries of artillery and six companies of Virginia cavalry commanded by Colonel Radford. Longstreet's brigade at Blackburn's Ford contained three Virginia regiments and one North Carolina, supported by two six-pounder brass guns from Walton's battery. Jones's brigade, at McLean's Ford, contained two Mississippi regiments and one South Carolina, supported by two six-pounder guns and a company of cavalry, and still further supported by Colonel J. A. Early's brigade of four regiments — two Virginia regiments, one Louisiana, and one Mississippi — besides three rifled pieces of cannon commanded by Lieutenant Squires. At Union Mills, Ewell's brigade contained two Alabama regiments and one Louisiana, supported by four twelve-pounder howitzers of Walton's battery and three companies of Virginia cavalry. These troops were still further supported by the command of General T. H. Holmes, including one Tennessee regiment, one Arkansas, and Walker's battery of artillery.

The elevated position occupied by Evans while awaiting the Federal advance was called the Matthew's hill. It was here the battle began.

Burnside's brigade, being in the van of the Federal column, came into action single-handed about fifteen minutes before ten o'clock, with the division commander, Hunter, at its head, under whose orders the Second Rhode Island Regiment, Slocum's, threw out skirmishers on the flanks and in front. These gallant men, bristling with energy, broke into view of the Confederate line of battle like a party of pleasure seekers on a holiday, changing the quiet aspect of the landscape to one of intense interest. They fired to clear the copse in front and received a fire in return from Wheat's "Louisiana Tigers," also skirmishers. The balance of the Rhode Island regiment, advancing in line of battle, supported by its battery of six guns, was met by the companies of the South Carolina regiment under cover of a thicket, who poured volleys of musketry into their lines, to which were added grape shot from the how-itzers near their position. In this action General Hunter was wounded and carried from the field, as was also Major Wheat, who commanded the Louisiana volunteers on the Confederate side.

The Federals were driven back on the main body of the brigade, which soon renewed the contest. Their advance was checked, however, but they fought under cover of the woods in front of Evans's line fully an hour, during which time Porter's brigade came up to their assistance.

Gradually the limits of the battle widened, like the increase in the velocity of a great storm. There were heard the quick succession of infantry rifle discharges, or to-gether, making one loud report; the ominous hum of leaden bullets in the air, making even brave men tremble; the sonorous sounds of the heavy guns; and occasion-ally the cheers of some of the contestants, as if they were engaged at a game of football. Detached clouds of smoke arose from the field through the dust, dragging themselves heavily across the irregular plain and filling the gulches with their noisome presence. Men fell never to rise; comrade deserted comrade in the excitement of the moment; and friend was severed from friend to share the honors of the battlefield with the living or the dead.

The Rhode Island battery of the Federals, first in action, did very efficient service. The howitzers of the Seventy-first New York rendered valuable assistance; and Griffin's celebrated battery, coming up at a gallop, soon became a conspicuous object in the fight.

Notwithstanding the fine display of courage and endurance exhibited by the Confederate front, Evans, its commander, found it necessary to ask for reinforcements. His request was made to General Bee, whose brigade, as heretofore stated, together with the brigade of Bartow, stood on high ground some distance back of him. General Bee recommended that Evans's command retreat to the line occupied by him; but Evans, feeling he had gained a decided success in his own position, was unwilling to order a retreat. General Bee therefore led the two brigades across the intervening ground and threw them into action — two Georgia regiments in Bartow's brigade and four regiments (one Alabama, two Mississippi, and one North Carolina), in General Bee's brigade. There were only two companies in one of the Mississippi regiments.

These new troops lengthened the line of battle and gave renewed hope to the Confederates; but on the Federal side two of the brigades of Heintzelman's division, hurried forward by special orders, met the new condition with equal courage and equal hope. The third brigade, Howard's, had been assigned to duty by McDowell in the morning on the other side of Bull Run.

When Franklin's brigade came up, Ricketts's battery went into action with a vigor that carried terror to the enemy and made for itself a record that will live long in history. The united forces of the flanking brigades broke the Confederate line, which began slowly to retire across the valley of Young's Branch, when, as if to complete their discomfiture, the brigade of W. T. Sherman, afterwards the distinguished general, joined the Federal left and with its new associate forces drove Evans's famous line with its reinforcements and supports precipitately off the ground as if a a thunderbolt had stricken it.

Sherman's brigade was composed of the Thirteenth, Sixty-ninth, and Seventy-ninth New York, and the Second Wisconsin, regiments, supported by Battery E of the Third United States Artillery, under the command of Captain R. B. Ayres. It was one of General Dan Tyler's division, which was supposed to force the passage of the stone bridge at a favorable period of the battle and join the other forces of McDowell on the field. The three remaining brigades of the division did not actively participate in the fight. Richardson's watched the enemy in front of Blackburn's Ford; Schenck's also guarded the position held by it in the early morning; Keyes's brigade followed Sherman across Bull Run, but remained partly inactive under cover of a bluff.

The retreat of the Confederates caused a lull in the battle. The Hampton Legion was thrown into action on the Southern side, and partly saved the retreating troops from panic although suffering severe losses on its own account. The ground over which the retreat was conducted consisted of the valley of Young's Branch, then crossed the Gainesville road, or Warrenton turnpike, in a southern direction and came in upon a plateau similar to the one just evacuated. This new position was picturesque. It was dotted with clumps of trees, interesting glades, and long stretches of open ground flanked by dense woods of pine and oak.

On the northeastern corner of this elevated ground stood the Robinson house, the residence of a free colored man, and about seven hundred yards to the southwest was the home of Mrs. Judith Henry. The Warrenton turnpike ran in front of the Robinson house; and the Sudley road, coming from a northerly direction, crossed the Warrenton at right angles and pursued its direction south in front of the Henry house. Southeast by east of these houses was situated a dense wood of pines, and it was here in this friendly shelter that the new line of battle of the Confederates took shape.

The man who began the foundation of this line at a time when the utmost confusion prevailed was cool and stern in aspect. His words were heard above the uproar. Quick in his movements, resolute in command, fearless in demeanor, every sign he executed was viewed with admiration and confidence as if it possessed the power of a whirlwind. In imitation of him his men fell into line and stood like pillars of rock across a public highway. He said to those who were retreating, "Form behind me. The enemy won't pass here!" In explanation of the intrepidity of this awe-inspiring soldier, his name went from mouth to mouth. It was Stonewall Jackson! Even in that very hour he received the sobriquet of "Stonewall." General Bee, while rallying his troops behind the Robinson house, cried out: "Look at Jackson's brigade. It stands there like a stone wall!" From the brigade the name reverted to its commander.

Jackson's brigade contained five regiments of Virginians. Like their commander they were soldiers of the first class. On the present occasion their example was far-reaching in its effects on the disorganized troops just then breaking away from the front.

Generals Johnston and Beauregard arrived on the scene to witness these varying phases of war. Beauregard, with characteristic foresight, directed the standards of the confused regiments to be placed in position and then by a united effort had the men rally upon them. This method proved successful. Order was restored. The strengthening of the front was then resumed. Jackson's brigade was the rallying point. The Seventh Georgia stood to the left of it; the Hampton Legion to the right. Two Virginia regiments from Cocke's brigade took similar position, one on the right, the other on the left. In a very short time the available forces in this formation amounted to six thousand five hundred men and thirteen pieces of artillery, with large numbers under orders to join it or in motion for the battlefield from distant points of Beauregard's lines.

On the other hand, the Federals advanced to the attack with the brigades of Franklin, Wilcox, Sherman, and Porter, Palmer's battalion of cavalry, and Ricketts's and Griffin's batteries of artillery, in all estimated to contain about eleven thousand men. Burnside's brigade retired to recuperate, with McDowell's permission. Although wearied from long marching, having been under arms since midnight, the troops came up to the front in gallant style, breaking in over the plateau around its edge from the Robinson to the Henry house, Griffin's and Ricketts's batteries taking position near the latter and opening fire on the enemy without delay. These batteries were supported by the Eleventh New York Fire Zouaves and the Fourteenth Brooklyn, besides a squadron of the First United States Cavalry under Captain Colburn.

The Confederate front was supported by five batteries of artillery — Imboden's, Stanard's, Walton's, Pendleton's, and Alburtes's — whose fire raked the entire surface of the battlefield, while the bullets from the rifles on both sides filled the atmosphere with messengers of death.   McDowell, the Northern commander, viewed the action from the Henry house, while Beauregard, his opponent, rode along the Southern lines encouraging his troops to renewed acts of bravery.   The firing from right to left was continuous for at least two hours, the Confederate left and the Federal right suffering very heavily.

Beauregard further strengthened this position by additional troops, including the Second Mississippi and Stuart's cavalry, two companies of which dashed through the New York zouaves with a loss of five men.   Then an incident occurred which went far in deciding the fortunes of the day.

Beauregard, fearing that any fresh troops coming to the aid of the enemy would force his position, determined to become the aggressor.   He ordered his whole line to advance and drive the enemy off the plateau.   Fisher's Sixth North Carolina Regiment, advancing through the woods on Griffin's right, had just come up, and with the other troops on the Confederate left attacked the regiments supporting the Griffin and Ricketts batteries, driving them from their position into the valley beyond.   Still Griffin and Ricketts stood their ground, pouring on their enemies shot, shell, and canister with the persistence of a hailstorm.   Even when their supports refused to return, these gallant men were seen working their batteries without a moment's intermission, grim with the smoke of battle and feeling instinctively that the honor of the Federal cause — for that day, at least — rested on their shoulders.   Glory to their memory!   They held it until overpowered by numbers.

The action of the Confederate left was very decisive. It could easily be seen that the vigor characteristic of fresh troops was there ; besides, these troops were afforded shelter until coming quite near the Federal position. This enabled them to wholly disable the batteries. The cannoneers were killed, the horses disabled, and the firing silenced. Captain Ricketts lay on the field severely wounded, and was soon made prisoner ; Lieutenant Ramsey, of his battery, was killed ; and a few escaped. The Confederates rushed forward and captured the guns. It then became apparent that the Federals would lose the battle.

It was about this time, when great confusion prevailed on the Federal side in the vicinity of the action just related, when aids-de-camp had been completely exhausted on account of field service and could no longer be found in their regular places, that two troopers crossed the valley on the north side of the bluff occupied by the Union army, directing their course toward a group of general officers, among whom was McDowell. The troopers in question appeared fresh, and thus invited attention as being capable of affording relief in the present emergency, small as it might be reckoned. The foremost of these men, alighting in front of the commanding officer, revealed the nature of his mission in a few rapid words. He had come to offer his services at a critical moment. He was an emergency aid of the secret service—Herondine. McDowell, recognizing the importance of the provision here tendered him, wrote a dispatch on the leaf of a notebook, and, handing it to Herondine, instructed him how to proceed so as to secure its delivery. It was an order for some of the troops on the other side of Bull Run to move up without delay. Mounting his horse and making a motion to his attendant,

who was no other than Furflew, to follow him, he dashed
off at mad speed, exciting the admiration of those present
by the ease with which he held his seat and the swiftness of
his career. There was no doubt now as to the certainty of
his future fame or the character of his patriotism. He was
now as much in line of danger as a regiment in front of
the enemy.

The route he pursued inclined northeast by east — a
dangerous one, because the Confederates were close upon
it, some of them having pushed beyond their original lines
so as to prevent counter movements of their enemy. He
had traveled fully half an hour outside the Federal lines
and was beginning to imagine he would reach his destination without accident, when he rode into a strip of open
ground surrounded by a wood. When about halfway
across this glade he turned in his saddle in order to ascertain how Furflew was progressing; but instead of detecting
the presence of his attendant he saw five or six men suddenly emerge from the wood and level their pieces at him,
and the next instant he found himself rolling in the dust
and his horse struggling beside him as if in the throes of
death. Before he could regain his feet, the men were upon
him; and one of them, presenting a pistol to his breast,
cried out hoarsely :

" Surrender, or you're a dead man ! "

Then they proceeded to search him without much ceremony; and, finding the dispatch, which had been concealed in his watch, appeared to regard the capture and
discovery as something of great importance, for the missive
was carried immediately to some person on the edge of the
wood, awaiting developments, who appeared to be in
command of the party.

This character proved to be a repulsive-looking man, with heavy features, large body, one shoulder being higher than its fellow; and was mounted on a splendid-looking horse. As the message taken from Herondine was handed to him, he exclaimed:

"Another carrier pigeon caught! Good luck! Three today."

It appeared evident this party of Confederates, for such the men proved to be, had been detailed for the special duty of apprehending couriers bearing dispatches, so as to prevent the orders of the commanding general from reaching their destination, and therefore proving ineffective. Such contemptible methods always accompany war and are accounted legitimate.

One of the men, approaching the leader, said in an undertone:

"Come and see our prisoner; he's a fancy duck."

At this the horseman galloped forward saying, "I knew him a mile off," and in a few moments confronted Herondine, who, unhurt, was standing near his dead horse with his arms shackled behind his back.

From the look of commisseration which the features of Herondine bore for the noble animal that had carried him so faithfully during his recent career, there appeared, on viewing the stranger, one of dark scorn and defiance such as might be judged incompatible with his character as already known to the reader. On the other hand, it was observed that the natural scowl on the horseman's face brightened up with a species of savage joy on beholding Herondine, and he would have laughed in derision at his predicament had not some powerful emotion stopped him. Nay, he went still further: twice he drew his pistol from its belt as if about to shoot Herondine, but as often did he return it to its case, deterred from the execution of the first impulse by some plan designed to bring about a future result more in harmony with his desires.

As for Herondine, all the strength of his manhood was required to sustain him in this dark hour; for it was not alone that he felt the danger and hardship of being a prisoner in the hands of the Confederates, but he saw he was at last at the mercy of his worst enemy here in command —Danderton Hitch !

After recognition, Danderton did not remain in the presence of Herondine. He turned and rode to his original position in the wood, from which point he issued his orders. In regard to Herondine these were of the most exacting kind. He said to the men of the party:

"Bind his shackles. Run a chain from the hands to the feet. Mind, he must not escape. By h——! the man who lets him off will die by my hand as soon as I come up with him. I'll take no excuses. If he attempts to run, shoot him. If he becomes violent, use your sword-knives. Should he be abusive, knock him over with a club."

Danderton further instructed them to prepare for a movement to the rear of the Confederate army and afterward home to Richmond, where the necessities of the service required their presence. He would communicate with his chief in the field and join them on the journey. In a few minutes after these orders had been given, the entire party was in motion, Herondine having been accommodated with a seat in a baggage wagon closely guarded by two men. In this situation his thoughts reverted to home first and afterward to the uncertainties of his profession ; for he had no doubt his usefulness, from a Northern standpoint, was

now at an end, and, judging from the character of his enemy, his life was also in danger.

As the cumbersome conveyance rolled over the uneven
trail, he could yet hear the ominous sounds peculiar to the
battlefield and the united roar of wagons in motion arising
from the plain like the moaning of the sea or the passage
of a great storm through the atmosphere. Later, while a
troop of cavalry was dashing past them, Herondine heard
the following inquiry and reply:

"How is it?"

"We've whipped 'em."

Then he knew his party had been defeated and anything
like the capture of Washington or the permanent establishment of the Confederacy might transpire in short order.
From these considerations, it may be inferred, his thoughts
grew troubled as the shades of evening approached; and if
he did not afterwards sleep, it was because they became as
deep and profound as the surrounding night.

But to return to other incidents of that fatal day. Furflew had labored hard to follow Herondine, as he was not
a first-class rider and possessed little of the bold spirit
which animated the breast of his chief. At the time when
the latter disappeared in the wood Furflew was fully half a
mile behind. Then he heard the rattle of the shooting
which unhorsed Herondine, and saw the blue smoke arise
above the trees. Suspecting the presence of an ambuscade,
he slackened the pace of his horse and approached the
opening in the wood cautiously. What he witnessed confirmed his worst fears. Herondine was there bound in
chains, his horse dead, and his career ended. Nay, before
he could recover from his surprise, the dust caused by the
departure of the party obscured the clear atmosphere of

the place, and in another instant all had disappeared. Furflew, in order to exhibit a commendable courage in a trying emergency, raised the carbine at his side as if about to fire, but desisted, as there was no enemy in sight. Indeed, he believed it prudent to keep quiet on the occasion, lest he might draw the Confederates after him, for he had turned his charger round and was retreating in good order. He reasoned with himself it would be wiser to report the facts of Herondine's capture to his friends than any good he could afford him by following up and exposing himself to death or sharing his fate.

Meanwhile the struggle on the battlefield was tremendous. The onslaught of the Confederates heretofore related drove the Federals off the plateau, while to regain this lost ground seemed to be the principal object of the latter during the last hours of the fight. Up from the valley and the depression of the Sudley road over the margin of the piece of tableland which held their enemies, McDowell's army charged repeatedly. In platoons, by sections, in companies, or battalions, regiments, and brigades, they rushed up before the Confederate batteries only to be driven back in confusion. They were obliged to fight with small arms on the run against a regular line of battle, with all its accessories, designed to withstand a charge of horse or foot.

There was no further flank movement, no artillery line to fall back on, no protected ground where they might rest during the night and renew the fight in the morning, and, finally, no concerted movement, resulting, of course, from continued defeat. Single regiments of brave men attempted to perform the work of a division, many of them yielding up their lives freely on the score of patriotism, yet knowing their action would not accomplish what was expected of it. The position lost on the Henry hill was retaken several times, but had to be given up on account of the splendid management of the Confederate troops.

Near the close of the battle Howard's brigade came in on the double-quick. McDowell, seeing it, collected his available troops, and with the newly-arrived reinforcements crossed the bluff, forced back the Confederates beyond the Henry and Robinson houses, and reoccupied the position held by his batteries earlier in the day; but where were the cannoneers, the guns, the horses, and the brave officers who had directed them? Dead, overturned, or in the hands of the enemy!

Beauregard observed the movement. He knew how successful he had been in the first assault he had made with his troops across the surface of the plateau. Fresh troops, hurried up by Johnston, now reminded him he could make a final one. General Kirby Smith's brigade, seventeen hundred strong, was directed by General Johnston to Beauregard's left. While marching to position, Smith fell severely wounded, his place being filled by Colonel Elzey. These new troops, together with the whole Confederate line, were ordered to move forward in one wild charge, and every factor and implement of war went down before them like grass in the face of a mower. The Federal army retired on Washington, the Confederates remaining masters of the field.

Furflew was but a short time separated from Herondine when he encountered a vast crowd of people moving in one direction, towards the national capital — civilians in vehicles and on foot, soldiers with and without arms, ambulances carrying the wounded, teamsters urging their horses or mules to their full speed, horsemen dashing across every conceivable obstruction in their anxiety to get under cover or out of reach of the enemy, for it was generally believed that the Confederate cavalry would come up at any moment and cut down every person in sight. To add discomfort to this distressing situation, the sky darkened and later it began to rain; and the variety of patriotic enthusiasm which a few hours before had animated the minds of thousands of good men now lay dead at the feet of hardship, disgust, and weariness.

Furflew, learning that the Federal army was on the retreat, wheeled his horse into line and remarked to himself how advantageous ventriloquism was compared with army life. Then, striking into a group of stragglers, he debated questions pertaining to the recent battle on his way home.

CHAPTER XVIII.

SAFE UNDER FIRE.

BESIDES what has been already related, it may be said that crowds of civilians sought prominent points overlooking the battlefield of Bull Run, eager to catch a glimpse of the action. On the Northern side the congregation appeared very conspicuous, whereas, on the other, the Southerners did not make so large a display. Some regarded the occasion as suitable for enjoyment in the manner that people are induced to attend a prize fight; others were imbued with a laudable concern for the main issue between the contending parties; while a large number became interested on account of the impending danger to their friends in the ranks of the armies. Two men were there, however, who seemed to have no well-defined purpose at heart for the event. They had been attracted to it by some unaccountable force such as controls persons when they heedlessly follow the bent of their inclinations on the expectation of reaping a rich reward of pleasure or profit.

The two men in question came from the south, pursuing a northwesterly direction with the evident intention of keeping the battlefield well to the right. Although similarly and tastefully dressed there was a wide difference in their appearance as individuals as well as in their social status. One was the owner of the carriage and spanking pair of horses which furnished them transportation, while the other held the reins like a coachman. On a closer scrutiny it was plain their identity could not be mistaken, for the volubility of the elder man and the easy self-confidence of his companion revealed them to be acquaintances of the reader; namely, Saracen Gay and his servant Flappins. The progress of the war having detracted patronage from their favorite pursuit, hypnotism, Flappins believed they could find amusement of some kind near the position of the army, either while witnessing the forward march or retreat of troops, the movement of supply trains, or the variety and grotesque appearance of camp followers speculating on some imaginary gain.

As a precautionary measure, Saracen Gay had sought and obtained information from reliable sources in regard to the conduct of the expected battle at Bull Run. He was assured the Confederates would take the initiative and constitute the attacking party; that the assault would be made on the right, and therefore he would be perfectly safe to travel and bivouac on the left of the lines, which would be quite a distance from the scene of the principal action.   Conceive his astonishment, however, and that of Flappins, when, on the morning of the battle, they found themselves actually in the center of the space bounded by both armies.   There was ample time for observation. They had come up on a well-appointed public road the evening before ; and, as the weather was warm and pleasant, Saracen Gay directed Flappins to turn the horses to the right into a pleasant pasture, where they could be secured for the night, while the two men would sleep in the carriage adroitly arranged so as to be comfortable.

In the morning they heard the roar of the cannon in the neighborhood of the stone bridge and chuckled with delight at the security of their position, Flappins in the meantime getting the vehicle ready for further movement. Then he drove his companion to a house which could be seen about half a mile distant, so as to partake of a comfortable breakfast.   Here they were entertained sumptuously, notwithstanding that it was a farmhouse and the lady owner of it an invalid.   Saracen Gay delighted his auditors with sketches of his life — amusing stories of incidents in which he participated — and dilated boastfully of his accomplishments and the prowess of his faithful attendant.

The morning hours quickly sped away.   It must have been after nine o'clock when Flappins appeared at the door returning from the horses, which he had gone to see some time previously.   His face was pale and his limbs trembled, although, as everybody knew, he was a man full of courage and energy.   Making a hook with his forefinger, he beckoned Saracen Gay to follow him.   In the vicinity of the house there was a knoll from which a view of the surrounding country could be obtained. Here the two men halted and stood transfixed at what they saw. Everywhere around at the distance of a few miles, more or less, appeared long lines of troops apparently in motion coming towards the place where they were standing. From the north, south, east, and west they seemed intent on closing into one great circular line from which there could be no escape. Rudely and erroneously as the two companions had been accustomed to conduct investigations, still intuitively they measured the distances in the perspective with the keenness of vision of connoisseurs. The prospect was inexplicable and terrific. They would be absorbed hopelessly, if not fatally, by the least touch of this crowd, for in their own explicit language they did not know which was which — Union or Confederate. Nay, when firing began, as it would very soon, all those in the line of fire must fall. It might commence at any moment; hence Flappins's anxiety and fear of consequences which would involve both his living and his life, for the career of Saracen Gay would come to an end as well as his own. After concluding a survey of his surroundings " the poor man of Christendom " said, with wonder depicted on his countenance :

" Ris, what brought us here, anyway? "

"The smell of a good breakfast," answered Flappins, promptly; " but," he continued, "that ain't out of it. We came here to escape being caught, and now we're caught without escape, whether we like it or not."

" Ris," resumed Saracen Gay, " can you explain this rather fearful situation to me without being tedious. Really, I do not understand. We must have lost our reckoning and struck the right instead of left. I'm mystified, if not

altogether confounded, by the turn things are taking.
What is in the wind, Ris? Are we the victims of a
mirage?"

Flappins smiled faintly as he volunteered an answer to
one of these questions.

"Saracen, there's death in the wind, and don't you forget it."

Then Saracen Gay grew pettish. The serious and threatening appearance of the prospect annihilated the mirthful
disposition within him, and he appealed to Flappins piteously, moving close to the man as if, like a child seeking
protection, he had been terrorized beyond endurance.

"You can do it, Ris," he said. "You won't let them
touch me. I was always safe in your company. Won't
you save me now? Won't you, Ris?"

Flappins felt the weight of responsibility pressing upon
him at that moment more than ever before as he replied:

"Oh, of course, Saracen, I could cut my way through
the ranks like this," and he swung his arms in the air as a
person using a sword, "while you might easily follow in
the opening; but I'm afraid they'd grab you before you got
through: so we'll get a safer plan."

Saying this, Flappins hastily returned to the house and
informed the family of the situation on the outside. He
made a suggestion, also, which, in the absence of anything
better, was concurred in by those present, there being little
time to spend in debate. This was what Flappins recommended: the invalid lady, with the two other inmates of the
house—a boy of eighteen and a middle-aged woman—
to take the carriage down through the adjacent valley and
seek good shelter in a ravine at the end of it, where large
trees formed both shade and protection, while Saracen Gay

and himself would go into the little brick cellar under the kitchen of the house, remaining concealed there until the battle ended.

"Mind you," continued Flappins, raising his finger to direct attention to the importance of the proposed arrangement, "if we didn't come here you never could have lit on such an outfit. The team is the best in the country by long odds, not to speak of the carriage; so jump in and get out."

As quickly as the occasion admitted, the women took seats in the carriage, and the boy, mounting the box seat, drove off; while Saracen Gay and Flappins descended into the little cellar, securing the entrance above them, a trapdoor, to prevent intrusion.

"I think," remarked the man to Saracen Gay, when safe within the cellar walls, "I have made a purty fair deal this time. You see I had to throw the turnout in to secure the cellar for ourselves. We're poor; but we can stand the loss, can't we?"

"Better than most people," answered Saracen Gay.

"I thought it much more profitable to save your life than carry your dead body home," rejoined Flappins, forgetting that this form of expression exhibited his selfishness instead of real friendship for his employer.

"You are truly wonderful," returned Saracen Gay pleasantly, not noticing the significance of the sentence; "but it is like you," he continued, "always doing something more than other men — in fact, surprising the world by your genius."

"Now, Saracen," resumed Flappins, "the beauty of the trade is this: the people in the carriage may get the fire from the guns into 'em, or dropped onto 'em, as the case may be, whereas we'll be *under* the fire, but never get hurt because we're in the ground.''

'' Ris, you're a rare un,'' said Saracen Gay, laughing hysterically ; for the evident security which the little place afforded him, backed by the man's assurances, began to revive his drooping spirits. A short time afterwards the real battle began.

Seated on a rude bench in the underground apartment heretofore described, with little gleams of light descending through the interstices of the trapdoor, Saracen Gay and Flappins listened intently to the multitudes of sounds composing the uproar in the vicinity of their hiding place during the action of that memorable day.

The infantry and artillery firing during the forenoon seemed interminable. The rattle, the boom, the crash, the explosion, intermingled with minor sounds, produced an awful combination, such as is not even heard coming from natural phenomena. To the listener's mind it appeared as if a planet had burst in the heavens and the fragments were carrying death and destruction to the earth In support of this idea, the winds wafted to their ears the shouts of derision and exultation of the contending parties, the hoarse, unintelligible words of command, and the groans of the wounded and the dying.

After hours spent in listening to this dreadful play, the sources of terror changed to something even more terrible. The earth trembled with the tread of bodies of men, troops of horses, and artillery wagons, all moving to some other objective point. Soon it became apparent that the combatants were coming nearer ; for footsteps were heard on the floors of the house above, and the belching of cannon made the walls of the cellar shake as if they were about to fall in and crush the occupants to death. During this trying time the men scarcely breathed. Flappins held Saracen Gay round the body with his strong arm to prevent nervous shock, although both were worked up to the highest point of nervousness on account of the uproar. They could hear bullets pierce the walls of the house, the crash of breaking glass, shells bursting in the air or on the roof, and men falling on the earth near the trapdoor never to rise.

It appeared singular that prearranged calculations such as Saracen Gay and Flappins had been accustomed to make should turn suddenly into dire calamity. Even in this manner did the men reflect; and Flappins especially thought that, after all, the people who accepted the carriage and horses had the better share of protection, but dare not mention it to his companion, as it would reflect against the character of his own judgment.

Several times during the day it was believed the last moment of their lives had come, so fearfully did the commotion increase, and the men would groan simultaneously as if each had received his deathblow; yet they lived through the siege unhurt, notwithstanding the insignificance of the earthworks behind which they were concealed. It may be said also that during most of the time here referred to Saracen Gay was powerless to move. He lay a helpless mass in the arms of Flappins, unable even to articulate words and only exhibiting signs of life by his quick breathing and an occasional pressure of his hand on Flappins's arm whenever a more than ordinary strife was heard above.

Relief from this unenviable condition was slow in coming, but it finally came. About four o'clock in the afternoon the heavy firing ceased. The lesser sounds of battle seemed to be moving into the distance ; the heavy marching of men and bumping of the earth's surface from disabled wagons were slowly drawn off; and it appeared certain to the minds of Saracen Gay and his attendant that the battle was over. Still, they moved not for fully half an hour after the noises they had been listening to had ceased altogether. No sensation or pleasure ever came to them with half the satisfaction of that rest, silence being on one side and security on the other. It was as if they had been carried on the wings of birds into dreamland for the enjoyment of the unattainable on earth. Flappins, making a great show of courage, disengaged himself from the grasp of his companion as he said :

" I'll revive you, Saracen. I ain't afraid any more than I would be of a scarecrow in grandpa's cornfield. See here ! " and throwing the trapdoor upwards and back- wards, he stood proudly before his employer in the light of the evening, the fresh air also coming plentifully through the aperture just made.

Saracen Gay looked at Flappins as one would view a magician. He did not speak, but the man knew if he had spoken he would have said : " What wonderful courage you have, Ris, and with such odds against you, too ! It is truly astonishing."

Flappins raised his finger playfully to indicate confine- ment to Saracen Gay's present position of rest ; while he, with the boldness peculiar to him, mounted the steps and disappeared on a tour of inspection, as well as to forage for something to eat.

After an absence of ten or twelve minutes, the person- ality of Risbon Flappins appeared transformed in a wonderful manner. His limbs trembled, the articles he held in his hands jostled against each other as if he had been stricken with palsy, and his face seemed elongated and ghostly. Bending over Saracen Gay, Flappins, without speaking, began to apply the contents of a bottle to the sick man's hands, face, and feet. Then he gave him a drink from the same receptacle, saying in a low voice:

"Saracen, what's good for the outside is equally so for the inside. This wine will benefit both places."

He also raised the bottle to his own lips, remarking in an undertone as if reasoning with himself: "My sakes! there ain't no use in thinking of Good Templars' pledges here, and don't you forget it."

When Flappins's treatment of Saracen Gay had the effect of restoring that gentleman to full consciousness and vigor, when the slanting rays of the sun had disappeared from the battlefield and the two armies had come apart leaving many a hero in the dust with his name and his fame soon to be buried with his remains, and when the beautiful twilight came down from the heavens like an angel on outspread wings, the men emerged from their hiding place and began an examination of the prospect before them. They stood a little while hand in hand like children. What was stern or combative in their natures had been subdued by the terrors imposed on their presence by the agents of the battle. It was not so much that their spirits had been whipped by mysterious powers as that their souls had been overshadowed by awe in the midst of phenomena whose existence was regarded heretofore by them as fabulous.

Flappins by a slight inclination forward induced Saracen Gay to follow. He led him into the house where in the

morning they had breakfasted with so much satisfaction.
What a change was here ! It appeared as if the section of
a cyclone had passed through it, rending the walls so as to
exhibit great, jagged apertures in the sides and through
the roof, twisting the studding out of shape, and splinter-
ing the weatherboards into kindling wood. The glass of
the windows was piled in fragments on the floor, some of
them having been carried onto the breakfast table, into
the pantry, and over the counterpanes of the beds, as if the
design of the bullets and the bursting shells had been to
scatter glass over every available nook and corner of the
house. Flappins, feeling the obligation resting upon him
of guiding his party through the present difficulties in a
very limited time, seeing Saracen Gay completely absorbed
in the contemplation of this fearful wreck, touched him
lightly on the shoulder, and, pointing to an inner room, said:
  " Look, Saracen ! "
The man addressed turned his gaze in the direction
indicated, and lo ! there lay on one of the rude beds the
dead body of a woman covered by a winding sheet, the
features being attenuated and somewhat contorted, but the
eyelids stood open as if to induce the orbs of vision to view
yet a little while longer the terrors imposed by man in
conjunction or in contrast with the beneficence of God.
On approaching the couch the men were startled on recognizing the invalid lady who had entertained them in the
morning; and Saracen Gay, forgetful of that sympathy which
human kind occasionally bestows on its benefactors, said
irreverently:
  " O Ris! bless my heart! where is the carriage ? "
  " And the horses?" promptly answered Flappins—" the
gayest team from here to themselves."

"I cannot imagine what has happened," continued Saracen Gay. "Did this dead person ever leave here, or was it that she simply died in her bed like everybody else, as was natural for her to do?"

"It puzzles me just to know the ins and outs of it," replied the man, "but it's a sure thing that she left on time, because I shoved her into the carriage myself and saw them drive her down the slope." After some reflection he continued, raising his finger before the face of Saracen Gay: "I'll bet a bit they found it too hot for her in the gulch and tried to run her back, but got left. Didn't we do well, though, to make the trade? I knew they'd catch thunder in that quarter, but, of course, couldn't give the thing away, as I had to look out for number one."

In such ungenerous words as these did Flappins dilate on his contract with the deceased lady whereby he secured the cellar for the protection of himself and Saracen Gay in exchange for the use of the carriage and horses which carried her to destruction.

Turning quickly from the scene, whose melancholy phases began to operate in a distressing manner on the mind of "the poor man of Christendom," Flappins led the way out of the house to a prospect still more appalling. It was in the first twilight that came over the battlefield, before the hospital corps of either party had come to carry off the wounded or any change had been instituted in the place as abandoned by the powers of war. The clouds of smoke and dust enveloping the retreating army could yet be seen in the distance, as well as those pursuing the victorious one, whose weary soldiers fell back to their camping grounds to recuperate from the fatigues of the day, excepting some bodies of cavalry under orders to harass

the stragglers of the enemy.   The silence peculiar to night
was steadily approaching, resembling the cessation of a
thunderstorm.   All above the field proper there was calmness, but on the semicircular horizon towards the north
there were heard sounds at intervals like signal guns or the
firing of a battery in honor of a president.   These, it may
be said, emanated from the brigades of infantry covering
the Federal retreat, and gradually grew less as the Union
soldiers moved away.

In the vicinity of the house just abandoned the dead
and wounded were as numerous on the ground, apparently,
as the first fall of autumn leaves when rustled by the vigorous wind of October.   As far as the eye could reach in the
imperfect light of that hour, the bodies of the slain were
scattered in an indiscriminate manner, showing the harsh
and unnatural design of the convulsion which instituted
this state of things.   Over the field at intermediate points
could be seen the limbs of disabled cannon projecting into
the air ; dead horses sharing the fate of their riders; guns,
sabers, pistols, bayonets, accouterments, and provisions
strewn about in large quantities; and dark, irregularly
shaped ruts where cannon balls or bursting shells had torn
into the surface of the earth.   Columns of black smoke
struggled to rise and diffuse themselves through the heavy
atmosphere, but remained visible like huge human shapes
conjured up by unseen powers to mourn over the dead, giving, not only a hideous appearance to the plain, but stirring
up a sulphurous odor, suggesting to the mind of the observer that their home was of the nature of the bottomless
pit.

Flappins, finding that with the deepening twilight there
came also signs of rain, bestirred himself in his search for

the carriage.   He concluded it could not be far from the house if the parties concerned about it in the morning had returned with the invalid lady, as was certain from what he had seen within.   This idea proved correct, for in a gulch at the back of the garden he discovered the much desired conveyance.   It was in a dilapidated condition, however, having been ditched in a systematic way, with one of the large wheels broken, the body perforated with bullets, the covering torn to shreds, and the varnish cracked, splintered, and in some places altogether worn off.   As a whole, the vehicle could scarcely be recognized, being gray with dust; and the horses had disappeared.   This was a poor prospect for escape from the terrors of the night, but Flappins was equal to the occasion.   He procured a strong lever, and with the assistance of Saracen Gay righted the carriage.

"You have often heard," said he, "about the inconvenience of the fifth wheel of a wagon; but I'm going to show you, Saracen, that it's worth betting on this time, and don't you forget it.   One of these wheels I see lying around here will fit the carriage to a dot; so, when I get her in, we can move."

"Nothing can beat you, Ris," said Saracen Gay confidently.   "I verily believe you can move the carriage without horses, like a giant."

Flappins appeared concerned at this remark, as it could be seen that there was neither a horse in sight nor a hope of procuring one, for every animal of the kind had long since been confiscated or pressed into service by army men; yet he answered good-humoredly:

"Never you mind, Saracen; if I don't send that carriage scooting into the road before daylight, just as if a cannon had struck her in the rear end, call me Jack Robinson."

Then he intimated to Saracen Gay that he should take a seat in the vehicle and make himself comfortable, while he, Flappins, would go into the darkness and procure the promised aid. By this time the wheel had been adjusted to the carriage, and, although heavier than the original, seemed to answer very well. At first "the poor man of Christendom" dissented vigorously from this plan, but under the persuasive reasoning of Flappins he finally consented to it. It seemed a terrible fate to be abandoned on the battlefield with the dead and dying, rooted practically to one spot; but Saracen Gay reflected that Flappins had never failed in any past enterprise, nor would he, in his belief, in future or in the present emergency. Besides, the man's language, always boastful, inspired confidence.

"I know where to find things, Saracen," he said. "Recollect what a trade I made with the —"

He did not finish the sentence, but, pointing with his thumb over his shoulder, referred to the invalid lady heretofore mentioned, now dead within the house. Then Flappins disappeared in the darkness.

Saracen Gay looked out upon the night with a more concentrated vision in search of objects than he had ever previously used. The darkness had grown thick and murky, owing to the obscuration of the sky by rain clouds. The forms he had seen in daylight were no longer visible; but in his mind they had become enlarged until they assumed immense proportions, and with them appeared to the fanciful imagination others having no real existence. He thought he saw huge shadows moving over the field with implements of war in their hands as if in search of something, and it was easy to conceive that perhaps they were looking for him! At this he trembled, gathered himself closely into a corner of the carriage, and listened for the return of Flappins, now an hour or more absent.

Instead of being greeted by the welcome sounds of his voice, however, he heard others that rather increased his trepidation. At first they had been confined to the vicinity of the place where he was located, but as the silence of the night deepened and he listened more intently than heretofore, they arose at intervals from point to point until the entire district as well as the atmosphere above it seemed involved. To him, who was no interpreter of signs or sounds, these latter passed unnoticed in the beginning of his watch ; but their persistence at length roused him to the reality of that from which they proceeded. When the truth flashed upon his thoughts, he was horror-stricken. These disturbances in the night were the groans of the wounded, whose activity while in health and vigor had been neutralized by the accidents of war, and now, maimed and helpless, lay under the inclemency of the weather like sheep without a shepherd, abandoned to the storm on the bleak mountain side.

When the full extent of the disaster here indicated came to the mind of Saracen Gay, he wept. Nay, more ; he began to reason for himself, and came to tolerably correct conclusions under the necessities of the situation. Besides, there was another change in the scene. Flickering lights appeared in several places. These evidently were lanterns carried by men searching for soldiers not yet dead — relief corps come to carry the wounded to the hospitals.

" Is this all ? " he asked mentally, as he peered into the gloom, still suspicious of danger or difficulty.

" No." The answer came from the infinite as if the dark depths of the void understood his question, although delivered in secret to himself, and vouchsafed a reply such as harmonized with its doleful character.

Through the margin of the little light around him, on one of the ridges where many a patriot fell he saw two men busily engaged in some mysterious enterprise who carried no lights. He followed the forms with great interest. They bent low frequently, then as often assumed the upright position and shuffled from place to place noiselessly and as if afraid of being detected.

"What do these movements mean?" he asked himself.

Would the solution of the question come to him as others did? Yes. The dark figures he saw were men engaged in despoiling the dead. He trembled for his own safety as the truth followed the inquiry. Should they come his way and find him unprotected, they would kill him instantly. He could expect no mercy from such men. If any person had seen his countenance at that moment there could be read upon it wonder, terror, and disgust. He cowered in his little seat, drawing his large overcoat around him, like one about to receive his deathblow. The rain pattered on the parts of the carriage which had escaped destruction, one of which hung above his head and afforded him a little shelter; the murky night became blacker and more profound; and the human ghouls had actually turned and were coming towards him, as Saracen Gay concluded that this was the most fearful moment of his life. Then, like a criminal on the scaffold, he waited with breathless expectation either a reprieve by the return of Flappins, or a miserable death.

CHAPTER XIX.

WOUNDED ON BOTH SIDES.

THERE was a sudden halt manifested in the progress of the two men approaching Saracen Gay, due to a peculiar noise quite audible to both parties. This noise first came from the depths of the valley beneath, gradually ascended the side of the bluff, and cheerily sounded near the ears of "the poor man of Christendom." It was a repetition of the word "whoa!" While the ghouls disappeared in the darkness, Saracen Gay recognized the voice of Flappins, but wondered at the strangeness of the word. Presently the man addressed him.

"I've made a raise, Saracen — the best there was."

Saracen Gay looked through the darkness and beheld the outline of a large animal near where Flappins stood.

"Do my eyes deceive me, Ris, or is this really a section of Bull Run Mountain you have brought up here?"

"It is the bull without the run," replied Flappins jestingly. "He'll carry us through in a walk; and this will be an advantage, because everybody else is running so fast that we will have the road all to ourselves. Besides, Saracen, he can travel through all kinds of weather without a stop, and won't be hurt by the transaction."

"Is it an elephant, Ris?"

"No, Saracen, it ain't. It's an overgrown steer — an ox."

Saracen Gay groaned on hearing this piece of information.

"Is it reasonable to suppose this fellow will do the work of our horses?" asked Saracen Gay.

"Of course he will," answered the man.

"How wonderful! And do you think, Ris, he'll go off like a cannon ball?"

"Ah, Saracen, you have a great memory," said Flappins, as he remembered having promised to procure a conveyance that would carry them over the route with the celerity of the article described; "but," he continued, taking up the thread of his companion's discourse, "he'll be wise to go slow this time. We'll let him have his way, Saracen; he guesses more about the situation than you and I put together if we worked at it for a month."

"Your knowledge of animals is something surprising, Ris," said Saracen Gay in a complimentary tone of voice; —to which the man responded:

"You bet. I know what he knows besides what I know myself, which is considerable; therefore, while he leads and I drive you cannot be beat."

This assurance pleased "the poor man of Christendom" very much, notwithstanding its illogical conclusion. His drooping spirit revived somewhat, also, while Flappins hitched the ox to the carriage and adjusted a covering above it consisting of three or four rubber blankets which he had previously collected for that purpose, as these articles were plentifully scattered over the field.

"You never found out how I dropped onto the ox, Saracen," said Flappins, pleasantly, wondering why "the poor man" had not questioned him on this point; "then I'll tell you. The farmer that owned this ox is a cousin of my aunt's husband's mother. He lives about a mile from the Gainesville road — 'tain't far from here — and, meeting him a few days ago at market, he told me he dreaded raids on his stock by marauders in this war. On inquiring about the size of his herd, he said it wasn't much — only one head of oxen, which was valuable, all the same. He hired the ox out to carry the dead to the cemetery. In the country district where he lives there is no such a thing as a hearse, and as his animal was the slowest creature in the vicinity it was thought the best for the purpose, so as to keep the interment of the dear departed up to the last moment. He made money, Saracen, and don't you forget it; but, behold you, as my grandmother Flappins used to say, the way things turn out is a caution. I asked him how he was going to manage, not knowing that the information would ever be of any service to me afterwards; and shading his face with his hand so that no third party could hear what was said, he told me in case of danger he'd hide the ox in the big cellar under the stable, which is banked up with dry manure as if everything was just level with the ground. Will you believe it, Saracen, that that there man had tears in his eyes when he thought how safe his ox would be? Well, when we got euchred; when I thought that your life depended upon mine, and that the difficulty of our situation here must be relieved at any cost, although, of course, we're poor; when I saw no way out excepting through this ox, for, as you know, every horse, mule, and ass in the country is in service; taking all the risks upon myself in good part, as well as the inconvenience to the dead, not to speak of my relation's tears, I went for him baldheaded, and here he is!"

Saracen Gay remained silent for several minutes, lost in wonder at the daring feat described in this recital, for he did not understand whether it was meritorious in him to praise or censure the man for his conduct in the case. He trembled at the reflection of being borne forward by the very animal heretofore employed to carry the deceased

of the ultra Gainesville road people to their last resting
place, besides running the risk of being indicted for having
stolen property in his possession; but, to offset these terrors, he saw a means of escaping from premature death and
a return to the pleasant times such as he had enjoyed before
the war.   Hence he poured forth a series of sentences in
praise of Flappins that fairly made that man laugh, notwithstanding the dangers surrounding their situation.   In
the meantime, every detail for the journey having been
attended to, Flappins, standing erect near the animal's
head and having a long pole in his hand, touched him
with it on the ribs as a gentle reminder that they were to
advance, shouting at the same time, "Whoa!" in the style
he had heard others use it, so as to make the ox understand they were at a burial instead of a retreat.   Then were
heard sounds characteristic of a start — the creaking of
the wooden collar around the beast's neck, a straining of
the impromptu traces, a resistance of the carriage in the
soft ground, which was overcome in an instant, the lurching of the vehicle to gain an equilibrium, and the voice
of Saracen Gay, jubilant over the successful movement
towards safety and freedom.   Then, with a difficult and
hazardous trail before them, the party moved through the
night.

It was here for the first time that Saracen Gay reflected
seriously on the value of Flappins' services to him, and
learned the meaning of the word "faithfulness" as applied
to workers.   All through that dreary night the man stood
at his post, now advancing before the ox to ascertain the
character of the ground, again removing heaps of slain
from their passage or guiding the beast around them so as
to economize time, and at intervals cheering Saracen Gay

by words of hope. The rain poured upon him, but it did not dampen his ardor. The gloom of the night obliterated all traces of a definite route; but his knowledge of the country, his powerful animal instinct, and his perseverance carried him through it steadily with little interruption. And what gave Saracen Gay more satisfaction than any other feature of the journey was the pleasant mood of Flappins as he performed every act connected with it, as if the occasion were a mere ordinary one.

The direction pursued was northward instead of south, for Flappins supposed that both armies had gone that way with the intention of remaining; and while his first experience in following an army had resulted in woeful distress, he hoped to do better next time. He conceived the idea of going to Washington to hear all about the war and see the great men concerned in it operating on the other side. Of course, the mental condition of Saracen Gay, when fully explained as heretofore, would protect them from the interference of the authorities, for it was well known that not only invalids but many radical Southern sympathizers resided in the national capital during the war without molestation.

Besides the obstructions and hardships lying in wait for the two indefatigable pleasure seekers here in view, nothing appeared to them so distressing as their inability to relieve the wounded. Frequently Saracen Gay appealed to Flappins in most earnest tones to stop and render all the assistance in their power, but as often was he met by the remark that it was impossible

"Never before did I refuse you, Saracen," said Flappins on one occasion, "but what would become of you if my strength gave out? I ain't able to do two things at once.

It goes without saying and it goes to my heart as well as yours to hear this awful state of things ; but I started in to save your life, and I'm going through with it before I take my hands off of you."

These assurances of earnestness and attachment kept Saracen Gay within manageable bounds through the most trying ordeal ever experienced by his attendant. When the dread terrors of the night seemed interminable,— when Saracen Gay expressed the belief several times that they must succumb to the extraordinary difficulties which beset them,— when the air was rent by the bellowing of the ox as if he instinctively apprehended the distress prevailing in the neighborhood,— the rain ceased suddenly and traces of the dawn began to appear in the east. Then Flappins called a halt for the purpose of providing rest and refreshment for his party. Accustomed to travel, and having an unlimited amount of resources at his command, the man found it an easy matter to provide for their wants. A compartment under the carriage, containing provisions and utensils, fortunately remained unbroken ; but, apart from this, Flappins was generally known and respected everywhere, and his demands for assistance willingly met. During the preparations for breakfast a gray color appeared in the atmosphere, as if some ingredients had been insinuated into it which had the effect of dissolving the darkness. This gray tint rapidly gave place to one clearer and more pronounced ; objects became visible ; the vision was permitted to extend itself over a vast territory ; and the first day after the battle had come.

Saracen Gay disengaged himself from the wraps provided for him during the night, and stepped lightly into the temporary camp selected by Flappins. On ·close calculation, they had traveled about two miles. The principal part of the field was behind them ; but sufficient evidence of the conflict was still apparent on the outskirts, which they had reached.

" The poor man of Christendom " turned away from the scene, whose features had heretofore given him such dreadful distress, and examined one by one the several divisions of his own party, Flappins did not by any means appear at his best. The vanity of the man had been somewhat chastened by accident and severity, causing him to speak less than before, but to attend to the business in hand with greater attention. His face had assumed a deep florid color, both because of the amount of physical exertion performed on the occasion and the effect of some good whisky which he occasionally imbibed. His eye had not the fire of yore, nor his tongue the flippancy peculiar to it before the war. He was erect, but his step lacked firmness and his arms the definite positiveness one exhibits when conscious of possessing a full complement of physical power. The carriage presented a woebegone and dilapidated appearance. Despoiled of its beauty, curtailed in its proportional lines, tattered, bent, patched, grim with the mud of red earth, and stooping forward like a person in the last stage of life, it made the observer imagine its days of usefulness were forever at an end ; but when Saracen Gay looked at the ox, his heart bounded with joy. Oh, what a wonderful beast he was! Above the usual height of animals of his class, he appeared to have reached extraordinary dimensions in the vision of Saracen Gay. His limbs like pillars supporting a huge body, it did not appear as if the labor performed by him during the night disturbed either the serenity of his life or the power at his command. While he stood immovable at the will of his keeper, the peaceful aspect in him and around him seemed a spirit taken from some imaginary shore where the golden sands of the beach meet the purple glow of the evening to link in one continuous chain the glories of an oriental day with the somber grandeur of the night. In unison with this idea, his eye looked out on the prospect with the calmness of a stoic, and his breathing was soft and noiseless like the west wind when its passage through the woods neither bends a bough nor disturbs a leaf.

"Ris," said Saracen Gay, addressing Flappins, "is the beast looking at anything in particular? He seems to be taking it all in.   Might not he be calculating on the number of the wounded?"

"He might, for all the good it will do him," answered the man; "but let me tell you a thing or two, Saracen: he's looking out for fodder; that's all."

"Everything is fodder to the beast," returned Saracen Gay reflectively; — to which Flappins replied:

"It's purty much that way all over."

Reminded of the necessity of securing provender for his uncouth helper, Flappins left camp by an easy march and directed his steps towards a disabled wagon which appeared to contain hay. As the objects mentioned were only a short distance from the starting point, Saracen Gay stepped forward also to accompany him.   When about to seize the provender the friends were startled on discovering two men on the off side of the wagon lying with their faces downward and their accouterments strewn indiscriminately around where they lay.

"We're in it, Saracen," said Flappins, expressing in this way his dissatisfaction at the fact of being obliged to turn away from his legitimate duties for others which did not belong to him.

"They are soldiers," observed Saracen Gay, seeing uniforms; but as he was not then acquainted with their colors and character, he did not know to which government they belonged.

Flappins, taking hold of the larger man, turned him over so as to exhibit his features. It could be seen immediately by the rigid appearance of the body that the man was dead ; and, with an ominous exchange of glances, accompanied by corresponding shakes of the head, Flappins turned his attention to the second case. This proved to be quite a little man, fortunately not dead, but disabled by wounds. When raised from the ground, he was limp and groaned piteously. Flappins soon placed him in an easy position, and, making an examination for wounds such as she had been accustomed to do for horses disabled by accident, found that he had been shot in several places, but not fatally.

"Carry him into camp, Ris; there is room for one, and by saving his life you might perhaps compensate the world for the death of the woman," said Saracen Gay.

Flappins smiled grimly at this allusion, and, feeling how just it was, went to work with a will to transport the wounded soldier to their camping ground and finish up the business of the morning. After two hours' hard labor the party was ready for a new start. The little man rescued from the battlefield was resting comfortably in the carriage beside Saracen Gay. Flappins had also a seat on the front part of the vehicle, but, with his accustomed energy, preferred to stand near the head of the ox as guide and interpreter. In order to quiet suspicion and give the public an

idea of the character of the party, Flappins, at the suggestion of Saracen Gay, had drawn in large letters this notice,
which was posted in front so as to be readily seen : " For
the Wounded.   Full."   Flappins on his own responsibility
added the last word as a reminder that further applications
for relief would not be entertained.   When they reached
the highroad and movement in the direction of Washington seemed fairly progressive, Saracen Gay began to converse with his wounded charge.

" On which side were you wounded ? " he began, endeavoring by this question to ascertain whether he belonged to
the Northern or Southern army.

" On both sides," replied the soldier, who, not compre-
hending the significance of Saracen Gay's words, located
the seat of his wounds on the right and left sides respectively.

" Ris, can you explain this curious thing — how a man
may fight for two opposing parties at once ? " inquired " the
poor man of Christendom."

Flappins, who did not fully understand the point at
issue, answered confidently so as to have no further dispute
on it :

" It's as easy as toeing a chalk line, Saracen.   He can
kick at one and shoot at the other.   Therefore, when the
kick recoils on the one hand and the shot on the other, he's
wounded on both sides.   Do you see ? "

" Oh, Ris," resumed Saracen Gay, " what a great ex-
pounder of truth you are !   I could never understand anything if you did not give an explanation."

As it seemed a duty incumbent on him in return for benefits received, the little soldier began voluntarily to recite
a short account of himself.

"I was a three-months man," he said, "and my time is out today. I guess the war is over for me. I fought enough — myself and my comrade. I'll go home and think twice before I leave it a second time. Do you know what I did?" he continued excitedly. "I sold my place for about half of what it was worth in order to be with the boys in the war. Every one seemed to be going; families were broken up; old residenters moved away, nobody knew where; and a holy terror came upon the balance that kept them on the watch as if the end of the world was near at hand. I lived at Council Bluffs on the crossroads and was doing well with the overland travel. I sold them trifles for good money; it is really so": and the little man laughed as he used to do formerly when known to the reader as Crow Whifton.

"My comrade," he continued, "was Flanks Honeybone, the night watchman at Omaha. He was fond of taking a "spin" through the town before going on the watch, but this last spin he took in the war was too much for him. Do you know? he was the best-natured man there was — brave, too, and a good soldier. We were in the same company, and both fell wounded together. Will you believe it? that man, my comrade, carried me off as if there was nothing the matter with him. Seeing the wagon, we got shelter beside it; but Honeybone died in the night, while I, the weaker of the two, lived. He raved a little before he died. He said, towards the last, ' Whif, old chum, here's luck,' as if we were again in Omaha and he was going to drink his favorite cocktail. It is really so."

Finding by the gravity and attention of his listeners that he had interested them deeply, he continued:

" The way I sold my place was odd.   I gave it into the
hands of agents to sell for me.   I spoke to my friends and
notified my acquaintances ; but they could not make it go,
because real estate was at bed rock.   I did not know what
to do or which way to turn, except to turn out and abandon my property, when one day I met a talkative woman in
Omaha.   The whole community despised her, and I followed suit, because.there was not a thing she heard but she
retailed around until every one, gentle or simple, heard it.
Well, sir, that woman just found out that I wanted to sell my
property at the crossroads, and she made such a sensational
matter out of it and of it that in twenty-four hours after she
went on the stump I got a purchaser !   It is really so."

Saracen Gay and Flappins joined with Whifton in the
laugh which his story called forth.   After some further
conversation "the poor man of Christendom" beckoned
his man to come to his side of the carriage so as to have an
exchange of opinions on the present situation.   They
spoke in low tones so as not to be heard by the invalid.

"Northern man, Ris."

"I guess so, Saracen."

"Kind of good fellow.   I bet we could get him to
catch on to hypnotism, although I would not reckon on
him as a ventriloquist."

"He has the eye of a hypnotizer, Saracen.   You can
reckon on that, anyway."

"Tell me, Ris, how will it do with us to carry him into
Washington ?"

"It is the best on the cards if we were looking out for a
good thing twenty years."

"Really, Ris, you surprise me.   How do you make it
out ?"

" It will appear we have a moving hospital for Northern soldiers."

" Yes, Ris, but how about the South — our own government, you know? Won't they think it rather strange to see us figure in such company? "

" Naw," answered Flappins with some hesitancy, for he was considering in what manner he could meet this rather direct question. " ' The poor man of Christendom ' is never bound by rules. He must go where he has a mind to and do what he thinks best. If the South gets rattled, Saracen, we'll take their bonds to please 'em."

" Buy 'em up, eh? Ah, Ris, you are an estimable fellow, full of resources, and so reasonable that you can defeat all opponents."

Making a motion of approbation to Saracen Gay, Flappins withdrew to his post, and the party settled down to the understanding that they were on a difficult and tedious journey. It would be inappropriate here to describe in detail every incident, dialogue, jest, and sally emanating from Saracen Gay and his party during the period above mentioned, or to dwell long on the slow but steady pace of the ox and the indomitable energy of Flappins, whose careful attention to the wants of those depending on him made them comfortable and contented. After a march of seven days they appeared on Pennsylvania Avenue in Washington, the greatest curiosity offered the public of that time and place. Surrounded by a vast crowd, Saracen Gay was secretly delighted with the sensation they had thus created. He said in his simple way to Flappins:

" Ris, they are hypnotized, every one of them. What a great success we are ! "

To which the man replied :

"We struck it rich this time, and don't you forget it. I would rather be Ris Flappins today than the emperor of China tomorrow."

A greater surprise, however, was reserved for Saracen Gay and Flappins. When at the height of the popular ovation accorded them, for such their reception seemed to be, a man pushed through the crowd and stood before "the poor man of Christendom" as if soliciting recognition.

Immediately Saracen Gay, extending both hands, cried out in evident self-satisfaction :

"Professor Furflew! our long-lost friend and professional brother! What luck to meet you here where your art is so manifest that Washington goes wild over it! Ris, look here."

Flappins turned and beheld Furflew smiling before "the poor man of Christendom" with all the zest of an old friend made happy by this accidental meeting. He seemed to have improved very much, and when he spoke to them there was an acquired accent, or tone, in his language which told of a prosperous position. It would be idle to attempt a description of Flappins' surprise and joy on again beholding the man from whom he had gathered so much fund and material for amusement. He actually embraced him and otherwise gave evidence of his sincere satisfaction and the pleasure he derived from his society. After mutual exchange of experiences since parting in the South the case of Whifton was submitted for settlement. Furflew volunteered to procure a team and take him to a general hospital, while Flappins would secure apartments for Saracen Gay and himself at a comfortable hotel until fully recuperated, having his carriage repaired at the same time. Thus in half an hour after they met they parted, the necessities of the occasion requiring it; but Furflew promised a good time in the future, when business engagements permitted him to rejoin them.

When Flappins found a place suited to his requirements and Saracen Gay was again in genial quarters, there was yet something to be settled; namely, the disposition of the ox. He was no longer required. Having carried them through a precarious period and a dangerous journey, they must now turn him off because neither his personality nor his manners were suitable for the society they were about to enter. It was questionable if any person would accept him as a present, or gift, and it would be impossible to return him to the original owner. That night while Flappins was returning from a walk in the purlieus of the city, he heard two butchers talking about the supply of meat in the market. One of them related to the other how he was sometimes at a loss to supply the demands of his customers because, on one fashionable row especially, everybody wanted the same kind of meat at the same time. This he accounted for by saying that there were two ladies at the end of the row who led the others first by fashion, next in methods of housekeeping, then again by fads, and finally in everything.

" When they say 'tripe,' it's tripe all along the line," he said. "Today," he continued, "it was bacon and liver, but tomorrow, mark you, they ask for soup bone. I hain't got it; that's all."

Flappins drew his hand over his mouth like an orator about to address an audience. His head was high in the air, as if some new enterprise had bewitched him into an unusual strain of vain thought. He made a motion with

his hand to signify that every person coming at that
moment to interfere with him or otherwise must be kept
back, and, stepping lightly up to the butcher who had just
spoken, made some proposition to him which could not
be overheard. The man looked up sharply at Flappins, turned his head so as to revolve the problem a few
minutes in it, then bent his gaze on the ground and answered:

"I'll see him."

An hour afterwards the faithful ox which had carried
Saracen Gay and his party to Washington was conducted
by the butcher to his slaughterhouse. What happened to
him there need not be mentioned openly; but, by infer-
ence from the conversation of Flappins with the butcher
aforesaid, his fate was one to be deplored. Saracen Gay,
who was tender-hearted, would never have sanctioned this
summary disposal of the ox, especially as he had probably
saved his life; and even with Flappins, matter-of-fact man
as he was, the recollection of the transaction haunted him
during the night until he groaned with anguish; but he
managed to ease his conscience by remembering how
uncertain all things are in a world of circumstances con-
tinually passing away — and why not the ox? When
questioned next day as to his intentions regarding the
beast, his replies were more or less evasive.

"I found a fashionable quarter for him, Saracen, where
the good he does will be appreciated. Gentility knows
what to do with a fellow of that kind. It don't stop at
half measures, you bet. He'll be taken care of, and,
besides, he is off our hands."

"And how are you going to treat your relative for his
loss?" inquired Saracen Gay.

"I'll send the price paid me for him as restitution money, but never tell who did the stealing. Nor," he added to himself mentally, "will it ever leak out, if I know myself, that he supplied some of the high-toned people of Washington with soup bone.

CHAPTER XX.

THE IDEAL AND THE REAL.

FURFLEW and Whifton, brought together through the instrumentality of Saracen Gay, soon became fast friends. It was found at the hospital to which Whifton had been conveyed that his wounds were not serious. During the first week of his detention under medical treatment Furflew came to see him daily, thus affording each an opportunity of relating a portion of his history to the other as a means of entertainment while the visit lasted. It may be readily imagined, therefore, how soon the fate of Herondine became known to Whifton; for to Furflew, who related it, the capture of his chief and his own perilous escape were the most thrilling incidents of his career. Whifton appeared unusually agitated on hearing the account. He questioned his companion closely about the arrest, and volunteered the opinion that he knew the aggressors, or those concerned in it on the opposite side. These opinions led him into a description of the events that transpired about the time of Herondine's appearance in Omaha, omitting, of course, such facts as related to his own copartnership with Hamilton Hitch and the affection for Grace Finnestare.

But there was more than these called up in Whifton's mind by Furflew's information. The image of his ideal love burst again on his imagination with her classic beauty magnified and the sweetness which characterized her life modulated so as to enter his soul like sunbeams on a dreary waste. He pictured her weeping while in dire distress over her husband's dangerous position, and every fiber of his heart responded sympathetically, as if the touch of a divine power had awakened them into action. His meditations, like the vision of a dream, may not have covered any extended period of time in the presence of Furflew, but the few moments spent with his love in this manner were as full of pleasure as years of ordinary bliss to other mortals. The fancy which had first amused him grew in his mind with time until now it filled the whole current of his life with blissful satisfaction. His passion had not the sting of unrequited love, because, fortunately for him, he never permitted reality to interrupt the tenor of his daydream or sought practical love-making with the object of his affection. Therefore there was no climax where disappointment came in with fulfillment, but a continuous feeling of happy thought that nourished his life like the sun the flower in places inaccessible to man. He had set the gauge for the love of his heart, knowing it to be best, and held to its dictates. No doubt there was some particular time or place or circumstance that taught him this extraordinary caution — some instant, when standing near Grace Finnestare or beholding her conversing with an imaginary rival, when his heart threatened to break on account of the wounding of his feelings through the instrumentality of the situation. Hence he had selected the ideal as being far more agreeable to him than the real, however much the latter suited other people. He would forever love his love at a distance. On the present occasion he was anxious to compare this condition of his affections with that of his companion Furflew, who had incidentally mentioned he was a married man.

"The strange way that I'm fixed," said Whifton, "is this: I'm married and not married. It is really so."

"Gracious! how odd!" rejoined Furflew. "Spliced, eh? and disjinted at the same time!"

"To bring it up to the higher grades of language," continued Whifton, "I hold the ideal but not the tangible."

Furflew burst into loud laughter at the thoughts this language evoked, although he did not understand its real significance. It was its odd character that made him laugh.

Whifton resumed:

"I love a woman I do not want to marry or even approach."

Furflew became more serious on understanding the mental condition of his friend, and inquired:

"Why do you love at all?"

"It is comfortable and salubrious," answered Whifton. "The human heart must love something. I have selected a beautiful lady for my choice. What matters it whether she is near me or at a distance, married or single, if I keep the secret within my own heart. Thousands worship idols; others adore spirits that have no existence. I improve on both; I have an idol and a spirit combined in one. A man follows his spiritual nature, or the animal, and sometimes struggles to keep after both. From being a beast he aspires to be a god. Why not put on the garb of a god at the start, and hold to it. I only nursed the thought of my love until it grew to be a companion. It was united to me. This was the marriage part. Afterwards my life was like a summer's day. I was delighted with that which had all blissful sensations and no recriminations. Through all kinds of weather the lovely form presented to my mind was the same,— soothing, lovable, and godlike. In dreams she visited me. In the imagination we roamed over fragrant fields, through gardens of flowers, and even went into the clouds following the path of the sun."

"Oh!" exclaimed Furflew, "what a gay old time you had!"

"I was content," continued Whifton,—"as happy as if it were really so. Moreover, I was good. It saved me from the gross world. It lengthened my period of hope, like a man in distress thinking of home so as to collect a moiety of comfort by that means. The longer I remained faithful to my love, the better it was for me; and a most singular thing about it was this: it kept old maids and sporting widows from throwing dust in my eyes."

Furflew laughed hysterically at the success indicated in this speech.

"You had an open switch somewhere that threw them off the regular track," he said humorously. "It was good enough for 'em. See here, Whif, I'm blessed if I can make out anything in yours but nothing. I ain't posted in spiritualism or noculation, and don't go a cent on things that can't be seen with the naked eye; but I'll give you a dead pointer all the same: that there plan of yours to keep the flies off of you and make you a single man the balance of your life is worth seventeen marriages all told, best or worst."

Here Furflew began a narrative of his experience as a married man that held Whifton spellbound for an hour or more by its harrowing features and dreadful endurance.

Furflew's story reiterated the account of the hideous deformity or evil associated with the human family of unhappy marriages due principally to incompatibility of temper and the variety of opinions of individuals brought together as husbands and wives.   Whifton lent his ear to its details as if listening to the voice of an oracle in the recesses of the earth, whose significance included some startling revelation.   What he had heard, therefore, about two hearts becoming one, in a large number of cases was a myth.   All that had been said through the ages of time concerning the blissful state of wedlock was not true, but merely the formal declaration of opinions and recommen- dations designed to uphold a system which was supposed to be necessary for the preservation of the human race.   Of course it would be idle as well as unjust to deduce these conclusions from one case, but Whifton called to his aid the observation of his entire life down to the statement made by Furflew and every item noted corresponded with his reflections.   The civil law had been employed to sanc- tion this system.   Heaven and earth and the powers thereof were invoked as witnesses of the contract binding husband and wife together for a lifetime whether their after conduct to each other justified such association or not.   Alas for the ignorance of human invention and domination ! the multitudes that have gone to the grave heartbroken, disap- pointed, cheerless, hopeless, despairing of finding solace anywhere, victims of an ironbound rule which held them in abject misery, and viewing the approach of death with supreme satisfaction, bear testimony to the fallacious basis on which the institution was founded.   It is not sufficient to proclaim, " What God has joined together let no man put asunder," because division, not unity, is the higher law. Personality — individuality — is the design of the Supreme Power. Freedom from crime, freedom from bondage in any shape or form, is the natural inheritance of all persons qualified to observe the dictates of law. So soon, therefore, as any individual usurps the legitimate freedom or peace or comfort of another, the terms of the contract between them are no longer binding, judging from a logical standpoint. No rule regarding or enforcing the continuous unity of persons by marriage, their dispositions, feelings, etc., can apply to more than a moiety of mankind, because they cannot be induced to agree. Therefore the married state should be classified, or consist of degrees, the highest being the one espoused by those who select to live together through a lifetime; but the civil law should legalize contracts of marriage for stated periods and make their issue legitimate. In laying down rules for the regulation or government of the people, men err most in trying to obtain too much from the operation of a single law, where such regulation should have been controlled by many.

Furflew's experience was an aggravated one. He was unfortunate in becoming the fourth husband of a woman who had long learned to be self-willed and adhere strictly to the bent of her own ideas, never tolerating the opinions of anyone else. Therefore when Furflew came to live with her, incompatibility at once became apparent between them. She found his methods faulty, ridiculed his reasonings, spurned the suggestions he made, and derided his efforts as those of a fool. While Furflew eulogized ventriloquism, his wife scoffed at it as the work of a mountebank; nay, the secrets of his profession, such as it was, were revealed for the entertainment of her visitors, and his future designs exposed broadcast to the criticism of a sneering world. Every aspiration he had previously entertained concerning wedded bliss, every felicitous dream of comfort and easy circumstances and the decline of an honorable life soothed by the loving words of a gentle companion, fled precipitately from his mind like dead leaves before the angry blasts of winter. From being contemptuous she turned to scolding Whatever genius he possessed was neutralized by the cross fire of her words, his ambition crushed, his hopes dissipated; and life itself became a burden. For a long time his acts were circumscribed to suit her notions, so as to establish some kind of peace, but his endeavors in this direction only seemed to aggravate the virulence of her temper. If he moved in her presence, it was accounted a crime, or rather a trespass on her dignity; if he spoke, it was said to be presumption. Hence he became motionless in the one case and dumb in the other. He resembled a person destined soon to occupy a tomb. This became more apparent as he sat for hours statuelike with folded hands and eyes fixed on vacancy. He could no longer meet men with a smile. When he visited public resorts, he sneaked through back lanes and dark alleys, the slums of the town where the scenery and surroundings harmonized with his thoughts. Although the beauty of external nature hurt him not, yet he could not behold it with delight. His vision even had become vitiated, his appreciation warped, and his love of the beautiful overwhelmed in the vortex of her vituperation.

Furflew's description of his troubles was not choice. The flow of his expletives and vile epithets resembled a torrent made furious by a rainstorm. He raved as if in a fever, because heretofore the memory of his married life had been purposely sealed up so as to permit him to enjoy

ordinary existence. When the contemplation of it did
come, however, with Whifton as listener and sympathizer,
all the dormant anger of his nature was set loose to play
for the time being in one terrific scene of which he was
the presiding demon. He foamed at the mouth; and the
wild glare in his eyes turned red in the tempest of his
passion, like a warning light in the darkness on a dangerous coast. Sometimes he became amusing when dilating
on her carelessness and eccentricities. The gifts he had
given her on their wedding day were misused mercilessly.
The silver fish knife she employed as a poker; the spoons
found their way into the ash barrel; and his picture, of
which he was proud, became the cover of a boiler that
forced the outline of his personality to vanish with the outgoing steam. Everywhere in their home there was evidence of the destructiveness above outlined. The door
handles were broken off, the window curtains torn, old
clothes scattered over the chairs; there were not half a
dozen unbroken teacups in the house; the carving knife
was permitted to rust in the sink; the dust to accumulate
on the walls; and even the bars of the iron grate in the
stove were twisted out of place as if some force as strong as
dynamite had been employed in the work. Notwithstanding her age and experience, Mrs. Furflew flirted; indeed,
she seemed to think it as necessary towards maintaining a
cheerful disposition as pomatum for the hair; and, singular
as it may appear, she rarely selected a superior-looking
individual, but any man in sight. · In economy she was
nowhere, always selecting the less for the greater, losing
heavily at every purchase. She loved society, loved to be
the leading figure on parade under the lamps of a drawing-
room and the most conspicuous talker in a crowd of women,

ruling others out of place better qualified than she for the work, and far more becoming. Sometimes affectation appeared in her language to an alarming extent, causing Furflew, if present, to look up as if he had heard the report of a decline in stocks or the warning of a rattlesnake. It was then he fully understood what his mother had once told him about marriage. Hearing him speak of wedlock as a condition he would wish to espouse, she said :

" And so, my son, you desire to begin the troubles of the world ? "

" To *begin* the troubles of the world ! " repeated Furflew in astonishment. " I thought I would be about over 'em when I got married."

" O no, my dear," responded the mother; " troubles never really appear until you have a wife."

Still he ventured, and purchased his experience like a little man ; but, behold, he was beginning to think he had had enough of it.

Mrs. Furflew hated to move anything out of her way, such as an article of furniture or other material. If a chair, for instance, happened to stand in an open doorway, she would prefer to squeeze herself through the narrowed passage a dozen times rather than remove the obstruction. In like manner did she treat pans, buckets, spoons, or gloves left on the floor. Instead of picking them up, she would march in a circle around them or describe an angle of forty-five degrees through the apartment, thus causing her much inconvenience and loss of time.

The last occasion Furflew had of witnessing an exhibition of this kind was on a Sunday afternoon while his wife was dressed in her best clothes. Furflew observed the rolling-pin lying on the floor in his wife's way a short distance from the kitchen stove. Notwithstanding its dangerous propensity to roll if pressed from above, the woman heeded not its presence, but as usual avoided it as much as possible by the circuitous or angular passage. On the occasion here noted her movements were rapid. No doubt the glamour of dress animated her and produced an unusual buoyancy of spirits which accelerated her locomotion. Furflew knew in his heart she would not resort to the better alternative of removing the rolling-pin to its proper place, and began to speculate on what was likely to happen as a result of her carelessness. Twice she touched the end of it with the tip of her boot, causing the culinary article to spin out each time nearer the direct line of her movements. Furflew saw the danger increasing, but instead of withdrawing the source of it or giving his wife a word of warning, he pretended to be engaged otherwise, knowing full well his recommendation would be scoffed at as so much miserable drivel unworthy of notice; but his interest in the scene continued to be deep and absorbing. The rolling-pin seemed to invite pressure. It would turn gently when touched, as if for convenience sake, expecting the foot of the woman to follow its movement, then stop in an attractive position wooing expectation. At last the opportunity came. Mrs. Furflew, in one of her sudden visits to the stove, tried the soup. It had been boiling some time and gave out a delicious odor quite in keeping with mutton bone, celery, and minced cabbage leaf. Just as she turned from the stove and was recrossing the floor, she applied a table-spoonful of the hot soup to her lips. In an instant she felt she had committed an indiscretion. Nay, more; the nervous shock produced by the scalding liquid in her mouth contracted her right leg for an instant, then forced her foot to the floor. Alas! the spasmodic effort only precipitated new disasters. The sole of her boot came directly on the rolling-pin. She leaned heavily on its smooth but unstable surface, and away she went! There was a shriek, a rustle of clothing along the floor like the sound of a gust of wind, a gurgling noise in the woman's throat, a crack of the left knee (this member having remained stationary while the other one was carried with the implement above named), a bending or swaying of the person as when a mountain topples, then a fall that shook the house, and Mrs. Furflew measured her length on the floor.

It was a supreme moment, and Furflew caught its inspiration. He arose from his seat, then burst into laughter long and loud. He could not control the desire to be merry, although he knew the exhibition of it in the manner here mentioned would bring his matrimonial career to an end if it did not break every bone in his body. Therefore he exulted as one about to sail on a beautiful sea bound for a happy destiny on some foreign shore. Nay, when the wife glared at him while yet down, thus bringing his audacity to task, he laughed the more intensely; but when his merriment ended he fled from his home never to return. The time was propitious for flight, and the man embraced the opportunity, doubtless having previously determined on such action. The ties that bound him he severed without remorse, regardless of civil law or usage, because he thought a higher one having greater regard for his individual happiness took precedence of the others and bent his will to its demands. Like the first man, the world was all before him. He would again freely cultivate the genius which he felt was his, and make merry over it without being subject to a scolding. His ventriloquism would flourish as of yore; sleight of hand also would bring him some compensation, and trick of the loop fascinate its quota of gamesters at public fairs and on the race track.

This, in substance, was the burden of the complaint made by Furflew in the hearing of Whifton. It brought the little man to reflect seriously on the several phases of married life and contrast them with his own condition, doubtless enabling him to come to the conclusion that he had selected the better part.

"I would like to ask you one question, Professor," said Whifton, "just out of curiosity and good nature. What dish, for instance, was most served to you the winters you lived with that woman?"

"Cold tongue," promptly replied Furflew, while a smile played around his lips as if he were perpetrating a joke.

"Pooh!" resumed his companion, "it is a favorite joint with me when I'm at home."

"Ah, comrade," returned Furflew, "yours was taken naturally from the head of a steer, while mine was flayed off the tongue of a serpent. Don't you see the difference?"

Whifton nodded assent with a laugh, and the subject dropped. It was felt that the requirements of the present and future were demanding the unreserved attention of the men, the services of both being needed; and, from the language expressed by each, it was certain the work before them bore an arduous character. Furflew, having lost the leadership of Herondine, was now under orders to report for duty at Saint Louis with the secret service men at that point, thus removing him to a new field of operations. In regard to his former chief, the authorities in Washington would do all in their power to rescue him from the clutches of his enemies, probably by exchange for a Southern prisoner, like those captured in battle. The man also explained to Whifton that he had furnished Herondine's family in New York a full account of his capture and carrying off from the field, thus practically disposing of the case so far as he, Furflew, was concerned, although regretting exceedingly Herondine's absence and misfortune.

In a few days after these interviews had taken place, Furflew withdrew to make his final preparations for departure, and Whifton was left companionless. His further detention in the hospital, however, was inconsiderable, occupying only about seven or eight days. During this time it was noticed that Whifton meditated deeply on some subject of great importance in his own estimation. On his countenance there could be discerned sadness mingled with the gravity of investigation. His little breast would frequently protrude itself while he gazed into vacancy as if there had come into his calculations a noble plan or design worthy of a taller man. Subsequent to his leaving the hospital he was seen about the offices where discharged soldiers received a settlement of their accounts or final statements. He was also seen to enter the White House, probably to solicit some privilege in the gift of the President. Then he disappeared.

CHAPTER XXI.

THE AFFINITY OF EVIL.

THE career of Hamilton Hitch in the South continued to tend upwards. From the detective agency, where he had rendered valuable service, he succeeded to a judgeship. The court over which he was appointed to preside, however, did not appear to be one of the superior kind, or, for the matter of that, regular in any sense of the word, but an innovation or a creation designed to meet the necessities of the times — in fact, what might be called a court of exigency. War had carried with it a class of offenders peculiar to itself, requiring ulterior means of conviction or punishment. These offenders were the spies of the enemy. Their energy, intrepidity, and dangerous capacity for discovering plots and plans for the information of their friends made them objects of detestation to their foes. Indeed, the spies employed by both sides were deemed worthy of receiving the swiftest and most unmitigating vengeance possible in the hands of their captors. Many of them were hanged in the open field without trial, while occasionally individuals of the profession met death in this way on mere suspicion. As the period of the war began to extend itself, the punishment meted out to spies was systematized. Men were too much engaged with their duties as soldiers to stop to consider the guilt or innocence of a supposed spy, and hence a large number of these so-called criminals were sent to central points and given the semblance of a trial. Thus the courts of exigency sprang into existence almost instantaneously, like drinking booths on a race course or flambeaus around the entrance to a circus.

It was somewhere in the suburbs of Richmond that one of these courts was established about the time above described. For obvious reasons the name of the situation is omitted, as, to tell the truth, the great majority of the population of the city knew nothing whatever of its existence, if it really had one. At first it was thought impossible to secure the services of a man with sufficient nerve to occupy the bench of this court, for, be it remembered, it had been set apart for a special purpose such as must necessarily shock the senses of most people; but when Hamilton Hitch was studied up and became fully known, the difficult problem was solved. The necessity of hanging brave men otherwise guiltless of crime was a stupendous evil; but, virulent as it appeared to be, it had an affinity in Hamilton Hitch. When the proposition was made to him he smiled an acquiescence that left no doubt of the result. Even the desperate men associated with him in the undertaking felt instinctively they had secured the right man. Nor did he disappoint their expectations in the least degree when he assumed control of the situation. Many a turbulent character with a heart as strong as that of a lion blanched on hearing his decisions. Many a proud soul condemned to death by him on the most trifling evidence wondered that creative powers should ever attempt the production of such a beast. No man placed on trial as a spy in his court ever escaped. Before the sun which witnessed his condemnation marked again the meridian line, he was a corpse. So steadfastly did the new judge adhere to the death roll that the attendants of the court gave him the sobriquets of "Neverfail" and "Black Ham." Within the lines of his jurisdiction his power was absolute. He may or may not have kept a record of the business of his court ; but generally sober-minded men shut their eyes and closed their ears to it lest its hideous nature should deprive them of sleep or produce some disease of the brain. Sometimes a dreamer awoke at the midnight hour to hear the heavy rumbling of a vehicle in the street leading to the suburbs, little suspecting that it contained prisoners—spies

destined to appear before "Judge Neverfail." It was their
last journey; and the ominous sounds coupled with the
time and place were indicative of some cruel disaster
seething in the depths of night.

In proportion to the success of the Southern arms the
boldness and unscrupulous methods of Hamilton Hitch
increased, as if he felt unlimited power coming to him from
the genius of evil which he had ever obeyed so as to enable
him to slay without mercy as many others opposed to him
and his set as came within the boundaries of his jurisdiction.   The place assigned to him, in which were situated
a so-called court and offices, seemed to harmonize with the
spirit of the man.   It was near the grounds where gulches,
ravines, and ruts abounded, and the charred stems of partly
fallen trees.   The buildings were low wooden structures,
erected prospectively for stables for cavalry but subse-
quently divided into apartments suited to their present
purposes.   The dimensions of the court were not more
than fifty feet long by forty feet wide, with a strong wooden
bench at one end and a few old seats in the center and at
the sides.   It had a low ceiling.   The wooden lining above
and on the walls remained unpainted, and the dim light
coming through a few small windows gave a sepulchral
aspect to the place that at first sight made itself felt.   The
court was not calculated to accommodate many people, and
the sessions were not long.   Besides the rooms occupied by
attendants and guards there was a row of cells for prisoners
designated the jail.   Behind these cells was a yard enclosed
by a high fence.   The space here referred to was not extensive, and had little ornamentation.   It had been paved with
cobblestones, swept cleanly, and sanded.   Just where the
sun newly risen usually danced its beams of light for a few

moments as if to gladden the hearts of men there stood an ominous-looking structure consisting of rough lumber, unpainted and weatherbeaten. It resembled to some extent the framework of a windmill, having strong upright posts, crossbeams, and platform. There were some dark-looking entrances to this questionable monument, one above and two beneath the platform, evidently coming from the adjoining cells. The chilly aspect of this silent piece of work with its terrible accessories soon revealed its name to the astonished mind. It was a gallows. One of the passages beneath the gallows was long and circuitous, ending in an adjacent piece of ground, where also some human careers terminated. They called it irreverently "the lock-up for the dead," "Prisoners' Rest," "the cemetery." Owing to the fact that troops congregated in the vicinity of the place, having barracks there, and that wagons carrying supplies were constantly moving to or from it, people imagined the low, shambling buildings above described constituted part of those necessary for military purposes then in use.

Judge Hamilton Hitch resided in the outskirts of the city about ten minutes walk from his court room. He boarded and roomed in a house where he was the sole guest, the other occupants being the owners — a man and wife who had accumulated some wealth through the industry of the former at hod carrying. Their domicile was large, prepossessing in appearance, and handsomely furnished; and to secure the exclusive use of it with the exception of two living rooms in the rear, the Judge paid extra rent. He was now a great man, conscious of the fact, and lived up to it. He dressed and walked like a person of distinction, assuming the elastic step so often seen among senators, judges, deans, and little doctors. Generally he was not seen in public, never at special gatherings of the social world, and very rarely at the theater. The trick of pushing through society in order to become notorious or to gain conspicuousness was in his estimation the natural concomitant of a fool.

After the battle of Bull Run, when Danderton returned to Richmond and reported the capture of Herondine, Hamilton Hitch seemed more shocked than pleased. The event appeared so great that his joy overreached itself and hurt his sensibilities. Some unknown power of which he had no cognizance struck his heart in a mysterious manner and made him tremble. Nay, he was assailed by a fit of weakness, and perspiration poured through the pores of his body. Still, he smiled his satisfaction and began at once the contemplation of the case, so as to become acquainted with each detail from the arraignment of Herondine in court to that of his execution.

"You can make him out a spy?" he said to Danderton while they were discussing the subject.

"Nothing easier, Judge. You yourself came near on to him in Charleston. If that Whirlston woman had not interfered, you would have nabbed him to a certainty."

"I remember the circumstance," remarked the father; "but," he added, "are you sure he was there?"

"Almost positive. Do you know it was he and Mrs. Whirlston I met one night coming from church? After they passed me I thought the figure of the man familiar, yet could not place it on account of the dress and the company. Nothing seemed more improbable than that Herondine, the husband of Grace Finnestare, would be in Charleston masquerading alone and at night with an attractive widow; but afterward, when I received a dispatch from one of ours at Washington telling me that he was in the detective service and had gone south, the thing was plain enough. It was then you tried your hand and lost the game also."

Judge Hitch smiled sarcastically at the allusion to his failure on the occasion noticed by Danderton. Some of the bitterness of speech characteristic of him when speaking of women was now displayed as he answered the comment.

"It would have made a dog howl to see her trying to prevent me entering her house in search of Herondine. Her shoulders moved as if touched by magnetism, her lips trembled, the natural look of the eye changed to ferocity, and I believe she would have scratched my face if I did not wait patiently the proper time. I knew her efforts were a mere bubble such as women put forth when they brag about anything, and when I threatened her with the law she squirmed: but it was too late; the man was gone. I would have given a cool thousand had I caught the two together."

"My sakes!" exclaimed Danderton excitedly, "it would have been a grand catch — a haul good enough to laugh over. Think what news it would be for his proud wife and the people of her set."

"I figured on something of that kind," returned the father, insinuating that he not only calculated on the capture of the man but also the blasting of his reputation by the circulation of false news after Herondine's imprisonment.

"What would you have done, pap, if you had had your way with that woman?" asked Danderton carelessly, referring to Mrs. Whirlston's opposition and the punishment it entailed.

The Judge answered something in a low voice, accompanying the words by a grimace and a hiss; then in a louder tone remarked :

"I'd send her to prison for ten years and have her live on bread and water six out of every seven days of that time. As it was, she had a narrow escape. After you left Charleston, General Beauregard interceded in her behalf because he believed she was misled by false appearances and false statements and therefore should not be prosecuted. Besides, there was no direct proof given by the detectives that the person she boarded at her house was Herondine. We were obliged, therefore, to let the case drop."

Danderton then related his experience with Furflew.

"I knew him," he said, "as a deserter named Curler, and, moreover, I strongly suspected him of being a fellow of Herondine's. I was never so much surprised in my life as when I was interrupted in the act of arresting him by Saracen Gay and his man. I believe, Judge, the South has too many fools of Saracen Gay's kind who are permitted to do just as they have a mind to."

"There are worse idiots than these," responded the Judge reflectively. "Certain persons seeking power and place are already causing dissensions among our leaders that will go far in undermining the stability of the Confederacy."

"Ah!" said Danderton, returning to his own subject, "you should have seen that ventriloquist scamp. His coolness was astonishing. As I approached the stage, he knew me and yet never wilted. I came within arm's length of him, when he received assistance and escaped. I reported the matter to the authorities, but I was informed by a private communication that if I valued my position I would not make any complaints against men of Saracen Gay's class. That was a pointer rendering me service. I made no further report; but I was determined to track Herondine to the end of the earth, if necessary, and capture him. I began by carefully examining every piece of news that reached the bureau from the North. I followed Bonham's command into northern Virginia until I came in view of Washington, as I knew it to be Herondine's headquarters. I had a vague idea that possibly he might cross the Potomac and incautiously come within my reach. He was never absent from my thoughts. Finally I received information that he would be attached to McDowell's army of invasion; and I then suspected that he would be found somewhere near the general on the day of the first battle, either to watch for spies of the South or to render some important service. This was joyful speculation to me. I had a dozen squads of men on the watch the day Bull Run was fought, some of them coming close up to the flanks of the enemy. Through a field glass I discovered Herondine on the run. He made a good showing. I knew him by the shape of his body and the set of his head. I rode rapidly to the edge of the wood, telling my men to follow so as to intercept him. When he appeared, I grew excited; but seizing a musket, I leveled it at him lest he might escape. Twice during an instant was my mind bent on killing him, but each time something stopped me. Finally I shot his horse and brought him down, when my men rushed out and secured him."

"It seems odd you did not shoot him," remarked the Judge, who had listened gravely to the foregoing narrative of his son.

" We cannot account for these trifles on which great events seem to hinge," returned Danderton. " I always found them present at the most important moments, whatever work I was engaged at ; but, pap, did I not do well in this transaction by bringing down so fine a bird as Herondine ? "

" You went beyond yourself," replied the Judge. " Your perseverance was wonderful. I know of no one in the department deserving so much as you. My efforts, even, did not come within half value of yours. I shall make a report to the government about your services, and we will secure for you a high position."

The Judge would have proceeded in this strain had not Danderton raised his hand as a sign that he desired to make some modifying conditions before accepting all within the glowing prospect whose description the father had then commenced.

" I wished to bring Herondine alive in here, pap, hoping that his wife would follow," he said.

This assertion of the son was given out in a timid voice, as if he expected and feared the disapproval of the father.

" What ! " ejaculated the Judge in a tone of astonishment, while his face grew pale and his limbs trembled.

" It is the old thing, father," returned Danderton.

" D—— the luck ! " exclaimed Hamilton Hitch hoarsely. " You are still infatuated with that woman. I had an idea that the killing of Herondine was all you wanted, whereas it now appears you only want his wife."

" It never appeared otherwise, Judge."

" I was mistaken, then. You are excellent in everything, but a fool in this. All the benefits arising from my solicitude for your welfare will be destroyed by this one act. No words can express my contempt for your conduct in

harboring such thoughts; not that I disapprove of it because
she is a wife, or the thing, a woman, but because you cannot
succeed.   Will you mark that ruin and failure must follow
the undertaking?   You have within reach as fine a prospect
as any man on earth could wish for; yet, instead of preparing to enjoy it, you take into your mind a hope that
cannot be realized — one that may finally throw you bodily
into the cell of a lunatic asylum.   While we plotted Herondine's death, you were cheek by jowl with me; but now
that he is within our power and I am ready to slay him,
you cry 'Stop,' guided by some cowardice that you even
cannot explain.''

With a scowl upon his features, Danderton bent toward
his father while he retorted :

"It is not cowardice.''

"What is it, then?''

"The beauty of the woman, to be sure.   What else can
make a man a fool?   I own up to it.   I would be anything
to possess this woman.   I do not even fear death should it
lie in my way.   I am as anxious as you to see Herondine
die; but I wish to shuffle him a little beforehand, like the
knave of trumps in a pack of cards, in expectation of win-
ning something.''

The Judge bent his head in meditation, evidently disturbed by what he heard.   Nay, he struck his hands
pettishly against the arm rails of the chair on which he was
seated and exhibited other signs of mental distress.

"O Danderton, who can account for this folly that pur-
sues you?   I would rather see a wild beast on your track
any day than this cursed condition.   If you reason with
yourself an instant you will find there is no hope for you
with the woman.   On a former occasion, if you remember,

I pointed out how dangerous it was to fool with such tools as these."

"Have patience with me, father," resumed the son calmly. "I am but a child when dealing with affections of the heart. Perhaps I am no worse than men who hanker after and practice vice daily without being noticed. I have to choose what I like whether it is agreeable to other people or not. So far as I can see, this is the general custom among all classes. I want my experiments, and then let experience teach me. If I suffer I shall bear the blame. If I change my ideas by the gaining of knowledge, it will prove the cure of my faults to be such as may be depended on in future in similar cases. Remember we are fighting on the same line."

"Well, what further plans have you? How long do you intend to shuffle Herondine?"

"In a few days we shall be ready for his trial. I will be informed as soon as his friends pass through our lines. When they arrive I shall interview them: if there be hope for me with the wife, we could run Herondine home; but if not, let him die here. Isn't that fair?"

Without making a direct answer to the foregoing question, Judge Hitch resumed:

"Let us say, then, that this will be your last trial also. I am willing that you should gain all the experience possible, and therefore carry out your program to the end. If Herondine has nothing else to save his life than the running off of his wife with you, then the Lord help him in the emergency, for he will need it from some source."

"If she backs out I shall see his coffin lowered into the grave," added Danderton, as he arose to depart for his quarters in the city; and presently the Judge was left alone.

CHAPTER XXII.

BEFORE THE COURT OF EXIGENCY.

HERONDINE was imprisoned in one of the cells attached to the court of Hamilton Hitch, making it understood that he would meet the fate of a common spy. He soon realized there was no romance in the situation — no elaborately furnished apartments for his accommodation, or beautiful lady stealing through the guarded doors to offer him consolation during the dreadful hours of suspense which intervened between his capture and his trial. Everything around him partook of sternness and plainness, such as had been witnessed by those who went before him charged with a similar offense—a rude bench of wood for a seat, a mattress of straw of the meanest material, and an army blanket for covering, constituted his bed. The void filled the rest of the cell, whose dull walls, grim with uncleanliness, seemed to foreshadow the certainty of speedy death to the occupant.

After a delay for which Herondine could not account, but which the reader will understand was due to Danderton's request, the New Yorker was brought to trial. He was conducted by one of the guards through the doors and passages lying between his cell and the court room, which were all carefully watched by armed men. In the whole crowd there did not appear a sympathetic face. The sinister gaze characteristic of heartlessness met him on all sides. The hour was ten o'clock in the forenoon; the day was a glorious one, full of sunshine, through which could also be seen picturesque scenery extending far into the distance; and the balmy air from without, coming to meet him as if in friendliness, made his heart swell with emotion.   Notwithstanding the weight of his chains, Herondine's person appeared upright.   The shackles on his wrists were light, but those around his ankles, as well as the chain connecting the two sets, were quite heavy.   It required an effort of each foot to lift the weight upon it before proceeding forward.   Then the links of the chains rattled, and some of them gave a dull thud upon the floor as the man moved, causing even the callous-minded men along the route to turn and gaze upon him inquiringly to ascertain if he stood the ordeal in a courageous manner. Apart from his natural stateliness and soldierlike bearing, Herondine looked terribly shaken.   One would imagine he was a convalescent recovering from some malignant disease.   His features were overspread with a glassy paleness peculiar to a class of invalids ; his eyes had lost much of their animation ; he breathed quickly so as to be heard, as if laboring under great mental distress ; and the backs of his hands were unnaturally white, indicating to some extent the severity of his suffering.   The clanking of his chains was heard in the court room some time before he entered it, and every voice became silent as the dreadful noise announced to the listeners' ears that Herondine was on his way to trial.

What Herondine's thoughts were at that moment no one knew.   It was supposed that, having anticipated the worst, he was prepared for it and had schooled himself to believe that the climax of his mental suffering had come; for, be it remembered, such acceptance of fatality is as distressing as, if not more so than, the act of death itself: but there was a phase of his case awaiting him he did not expect which made him tremble in every limb as if he had been shot. As he entered the court, his heart almost ceased to beat on seeing in a corner near the bench his wife and his two aunts, already weeping for his fate. He stopped an instant, throwing up his hands as well as he could, as a sign of utter astonishment and bereavement; while Grace Herondine, seeing him, gave a wild shriek of despair and fell fainting into the arms of Aunt Frill. As the only witnesses of this scene were the Judge and the guards accustomed to duty under trying circumstances, there was no disturbance in court. It was accepted as natural, but the Judge made a sign which brought up a man to remind Aunt Frill that if any such exhibition were repeated, they — the ladies — must quit the place without hope of readmission.

Then the prisoner was placed in front of the bench surrounded by armed men; the sentinels were set at the doors and in the corridors; the ladies, after Grace Herondine's return to consciousness, resumed their seats in the strangers' corner; the officials of the Judge appeared to be in place; the crier and the prosecutor and everything in the apartment indicated the progress of the business in hand. When the prisoner raised his head and beheld the Judge, he trembled — not as a coward, but as one reminded of some terrible feature of human life that seemed inexplicable. Here was a condition the reverse of what he had previously heard; namely, the criminal was on the bench deputed to exercise the powers of a judge, while the good man stood in the dock with the certainty of dying a violent death. How strange that this should occur after centuries of law-making, preaching, and watchfulness on the part of those having the good of society at heart! Was it possible that even circumstances leading up to such a spectacle could shape themselves and mature in full view of the morality of heaven and earth? Yes. Evil was uppermost for the time being; let those explain it who can.

Hamilton Hitch looked on the prisoner with a pompous air, such as an ignorant man sometimes assumes when he is purse-proud or bespattered by promotion due to seniority. His own triumph over Herondine, as well as the late success of the Confederate arms, could be detected on his features. There was no smile perceptible, but merely some shade of animation that marked more distinctly the eternal scowl which had always been upon them. Nowhere, perhaps, within or without that court room, could there be seen an object so fearfully interesting as the person of this judge. When the light from a side window thrown open to admit more air fell upon him, every eye beheld one thoroughly merciless and treacherous. The outline of the figure bore some relationship to that of a hog after a drowsy sleep. He sat motionless without attempting to speak, remembering, no doubt, Danderton's instructions to him regarding the best method of coming into public favor—keep his mouth shut and the people would imagine he was a profound scholar or a wise statesman. In his present position he did it to inspire terror and make believe there was dignity in this statuelike behavior. His present situation might be accounted better, but his person worse, than previously. The thick neck was still prominent, but the head looked more or less shriveled, as if Time had twisted it designedly in a shocking manner so as to make the man detestable in appearance before bringing him to death. The middle part of his face protruded, doglike, making the facial angle very acute; and the top of his head appeared to have narrowed from some cause directed against sound intelligence. Even his hair was changing irregularly, the lower part being full gray, while that which clothed the upper parts of the cranium was white and crispy with little pointed tufts here and there, making, on the whole, a shocking picture when suddenly beheld Nature had withdrawn a portion of his strength and stricken adversely his individual members, but the power of evil had supplied him with additional presumption His eyes had retreated in their sockets, yet now they possessed a fiercer glare than formerly, and, from being swinish, they seemed like those of a wolf. Seated firmly behind the bench alone, with the special characteristics conspicuous as above mentioned, he bore some resemblance to an old bulldog waiting for a chance to bite.

The prosecutor, seeing everything in readiness, arose to make a statement. On scrutinizing his countenance, Herondine said mentally, "Should I escape the vengeance of the father, the son would complete the work of my destruction." He saw in the prosecutor his old enemy, Danderton Hitch.

"I accuse the prisoner at the bar, your honor," said Danderton, "of being a common spy."

Before any one could reply to this proposition Aunt Frill jumped to her feet, and, stretching forth her right hand, said boldly :

"It ain't true, Jedge. Alton B. is my nephew, born and raised, I might say, under my protection, to which Aunt Funton is here to testify, likewise his wife, Grace Finnestare that was. It ain't true nohow, Jedge. It never was in him nor in his family; moreover, he didn't need to spy on any one, good, bad, or indifferent. He ain't in it."

Aunt Frill's appearance arrested the attention of every person in court. Frail in body, with attenuated hands and face, her hair white as snow, her cheeks wrinkled, a ghastly pallor overspreading her countenance, and this language, half irrelevant, half amusing, made her appear deranged. Add to these features of the case her black clothing with flounces of heavy black crape, and there was a picture that any one might stare at in wonder. Her voice was clear, however — not harsh in its sounds, but musiclike — probably occasioned by the influence of the good spirit behind it.

"You must not interrupt the business of this court," said the Judge to Aunt Frill. "You were admitted to witness the trial, but not to plead for the prisoner."

To which Aunt Frill replied:

"I have a pass, Jedge, from President Lincoln himself— bless his good heart. It's for our whole party, mind you. When I heard of Alton B.'s trouble, I went to President Lincoln, and, introducing myself, said to him, 'Mr. President, I was for Douglas at the late election, but am fully satisfied that you got in. Will you give me a pass to go south? My nephew has been captured and I want to see him.' Will you believe it, Jedge, that man smiled, and, taking a sheet of paper, wrote the pass without another word; only, when I mentioned that my nephew was confined in Richmond, the President said pleasantly, 'I've ordered the army to go on there; so you'll have lots of company.'"

At the conclusion of this speech some of the guards laughed, but Danderton, arrogantly addressing the lady, resumed:

"I desire to remind you, madam, that President Lincoln has no jurisdiction here."

"No? the more's the pity, then, I assure ye," said Aunt Frill loftily. "He is the President for all that. What you have here is like the contents of my grandmother's pocket —a mixture of small things that, come to examine them, worn't no good for one thing nor the other."

Danderton looked at the Judge as if to appeal to him to correct this abuse of Aunt Frill's tongue.

"We cannot listen to such language," said Hamilton Hitch. "If it be repeated, you must leave the court." Then, turning to Danderton, he continued, "Prosecutor, go on."

In the meantime, Grace Herondine and Aunt Funton persuaded their companion to resume her seat and keep silent.

Danderton's statement to the court referred to the presence of Herondine in Charleston and Montgomery, but it failed to prove that the man was actually in these places. To cover this deficiency in his testimony he swore that it had positively been proven to him that the prisoner was in these places severally as a spy. Upon the Judge accepting this evidence as proving the charges against Herondine, Aunt Frill groaned and the other ladies began to weep, feeling that their case was hopeless. The report of the capture, however, was Danderton's great means of convicting the prisoner.

"Herondine was caught in the act," concluded he—"a thing that cannot be denied, for I witnessed it and found the documents upon him which the court has in its possession."

There was deep silence in the apartment when Danderton resumed his seat. Incidentally the Judge turned his face towards Herondine's friends as if to indicate how conclu-

sive was this last statement of Danderton's; and Aunt
Frill, believing the motion to be a challenge to respond,
arose and said:

"On the strength of his own words, Jedge, this man who
swears against my nephew is a liar. Alton B. was an aid-
de-camp, not a spy. Grant that he was carrying letters
from the commanding officer of his party — wouldn't you
do it? That was not spying out things. On this ground,
Jedge, he is entitled to be held for exchange."

Then Grace Herondine stood up and spoke. She said :
"Aunt Frill is correct, Judge. My husband, the prisoner, was an aid to General McDowell, and cannot be held
or convicted as a spy."

Every ear in court heard the music of Grace Herondine's
voice. Every eye looked at her admiringly, and then
turned to behold the Judge.

"The charges against the prisoner have been fully
proven," said the Judge. "It is clear to the court he is
guilty and deserving the punishment inflicted on others in
similar circumstances."

Hearing this unexpected declaration, Aunt Frill stood
forth in behalf of Herondine as few women ever did
before. While tears coursed down her wrinkled cheeks and
her breathing came thick and fast, she continued :

"I have his ransom here, Jedge. These papers are the
deeds of my property. There are, moreover, bills, bonds,
mortgages, assignments, acquitments, ejectments, releases,
collaterals, and certificates of deposit — in fact, everything
I possess. I offer them as the price of his liberty."

Aunt Funton followed Aunt Frill, making a similar offer
of the property held in her own right, but the Judge made
a motion of dissent with his hand and said :

" We do not accept ransoms for persons who are enemies of the Confederacy. The law is straight, and we see no reason why any divergence should be made from it. However, there was something else, Prosecutor. Did you —"

He referred to the conversation with Danderton the previous night regarding proposals to be made to Grace Herondine. Danderton understood, and replied:

" I made the effort, but failed in my purpose. Let him die."

Many of the guards appeared deeply interested in the magnanimous conduct of the two aunts; but the climax of the proceedings set in when Herondine's wife, stung by Danderton's allusion, addressed the court. The tears had dried in her eyes through the effects of her deep emotion. She was in the realm beyond tears where souls are appalled by dreadful catastrophe or impending destruction. In such positions many exhibit good or bad traits unknowingly. What the witnesses saw associated with her were the rare beauty of her youth whipped by chastisement into grandeur like the fire of a meteor in motion, and the uprightness of an individual conscious of possessing a noble nature with determination to maintain it. She said:

" If it be inevitable for my husband, the prisoner, to die by your judgment, we have sufficient fortitude to withstand the calamity — he in heaven and I on earth. There was no criminality in his life; therefore, we shall only have to regret separation, that which comes to every one sooner or later. It is you will have to bear the remorse of killing an innocent man. The iron hand of unseen chastisement, that never ceases to operate, will fall upon you and on yours until justice is satisfied you have had enough. We came to plead, to offer ransom for his life, to beg for mercy, but the only

condition you seem to imagine necessary and effective is
for me to renounce my husband and marry your son. O
man ! will you never understand that allegiance to my husband is worth more to me than the wealth of the world and
life itself?   How could you and your unfortunate boy think
for an instant that I, a Northern lady, would descend to
such low-bred methods on any account whatever ?   My husband will meet death willingly to save his wife from dis-
hónor, and I say for myself that the fair fame of the country
and society I represent shall never be sullied by any act of
mine."

She resumed her seat amid deep silence, although some
of the men present would have applauded if they dared.
Herondine appeared refreshed by the power of his wife's
words.   He straightened himself briskly, and would have
spoken if the Judge had not begun to deliver the final
decision of the court.

"Stand forward, Sternbeard, captain of the outside
guard," said the Judge ; "and you, Greenlaugh, captain of
the inside guard," he continued, while two men in uniform
obeyed the summons and stood near the prisoner.   "The
decision of the court is that this man Herondine be executed in the usual manner tomorrow at sunrise and buried
an hour later; that you witness these acts according to
custom and law ; — and may the wise dispensations of
Providence guard and promote the Confederacy.   Amen ! "

At the conclusion of this speech the Judge suddenly left
the bench ; the loud orders of the captains resounded
through the apartment ; a number of the guards surrounded
Herondine to prevent escape and to set the death watch ;
and the man who had previously admonished Aunt Frill
suddenly came up and hustled the ladies out the side

entrance, giving them to understand that they could see Herondine that way — but lo! the door was bolted behind them, and they found themselves in the street alone.

Dismay and horror were depicted on each countenance. They could not speak, but wept silently. Aunt Frill, accompanied by Aunt Funton and Grace Herondine, moved away to regain their temporary residence and discuss the next best means of saving their friend. As stated in court, they had come into Richmond with a pass from President Lincoln and some vague hopes of being able to pay a ransom for Herondine's life. They roomed and boarded in a private residence owned by a Southern man whose wife had been born and raised in the North and was known previously to Herondine's party. Hence they found her willing to give them good treatment as well as advice. This woman told Aunt Frill privately that party feeling ran very high just then; that people were afraid to question the methods of the government, especially any institution like this court where Herondine had been tried — although, for herself, she did not know much about it; and that the wisest thing to do was for the party to return home out of danger and trust to luck for the balance of what they expected.

This recommendation did not give much encouragement; and as the problem of relief seemed exceedingly difficult to solve, much of the day, after the return from court, was spent in bemoaning and lamenting their hard fate. In reviewing what had been done up to that time, it was easy to apprehend defeat and disaster. They had indignantly refused to entertain Danderton's proposition made to Grace Herondine on entering Richmond. On that occasion Danderton represented himself as the spokesman of the Southern government, invested with authority to give

them permission to witness Herondine's trial, but insinuated he would effect the prisoner's release on his own
account if Grace consented to remain with him in Richmond while Herondine returned home.   This phase of the
case appeared the worst of all, for the ladies knew that their
repudiation of Danderton's proposal would entail his eternal enmity and ultimately seal the death of Herondine.
Yet Aunt Frill's restlessness soon shaped another course.
Armed with the addresses of several members of the government, she issued from her rooms when the shades of
evening were stealing solemnly over Richmond, intent on
interviewing each and every one of them so as to save
Herondine's life.   Aunt Frill displayed wonderful energy.
The fire of her eye had rekindled as in youth through the
medium of her deep concern ; and the sounds of her voice
were sharpened, as if the acrimony of her distress had
destroyed the rich melody by which they had previously
been characterized.   In the twilight she passed like a
shadow, or some memory of the long ago, or the conspicuous figure in a complicated dream, whose weight left an
impression not soon forgotten.   She made calls late into
the night.   There were many who listened to her statement
but averred they had no power to interfere, as the case was
outside their jurisdiction.   Others cheered her with the
hope that Herondine would be exchanged as a prisoner of
war ; but when she added that he was accused of being a
spy, they shook their heads and appeared to think of him
altogether in another light.   When she rejoined her companions, there was much to speak of but little to hope for.

Herondine was conveyed to his cell fully alive to the fact
that his death was near at hand.   He reflected a little on
the possibility of his friends gaining a stay of proceedings

or a rehearing of his case before another court, or, perhaps, recognition as a prisoner of war; but, when his mind turned to review the unscrupulous character of Hamilton Hitch and of Danderton, he finally concluded there was no hope for him.

Danderton, soon after the trial, visited his father in his private apartments. The conversation between them referred wholly to Herondine and his wife. The son appeared more exultant than the father, because the passions which governed him were more vigorous, and as an individual he was more interested in the fate of the prisoner. As a matter of fact, Hamilton Hitch always felt distressed when considering Danderton's affection for Grace Herondine, for he foresaw the futile results arising therefrom; otherwise, the execution of Herondine would be little more to him than that of any other person in a similar situation.

"Look," said Danderton, raising his finger as if to point his words. "I feel as if I could kill the woman if I had the opportunity. Don't you, pap?"

"I never liked her, to begin with," said the Judge; "but that matter is altogether your own. I prefer hanging the man. It adds freshness to my life, especially when I can get under one of that good sort so much thought of, and raise him into the gallows. It's a sweet job, Danderton."

Danderton was too much concerned with his own thoughts to smile at this diabolical pleasantry.

"One thing more, pap, before we part," he continued. "I am ordered to appear before the chief immediately for some new and important duty. I cannot, therefore, be present at Herondine's execution; but will you personally see his coffin lowered into the grave? I vowed to witness it myself; but as I cannot do so, on account of this extra pressure on my time, I will get you to be my substitute."

After a little reflection the Judge answered:

"I swear, Danderton, I shall see his coffin go down into the grave as sure as the sun rises tomorrow morning, with the hope that it will be the last act between us and those detestable Herondines. Now be satisfied, and take care of yourself."

After giving a suitable adieu to his father, Danderton departed for his new field of operations, while Hamilton Hitch turned in upon his own conscience to gloat over the evil at his command and the number of the unfortunates upon whom it fell.

CHAPTER XXIII.

THE INNER LIFE OF A BAD MAN.

ONE might imagine that, coming into power and meeting independence as heretofore described, Hamilton Hitch would reject ideas such as directed him in former times when he was a dangerous thief. This was not the fact, however. He never even dreamt of reformation, but, on the contrary, studied, as he advanced, the most subtle methods by which he could propagate his nefarious designs against his fellow-man in the line above indicated. His ruling passion, or the inner life which absorbed his whole soul, was theft. No reward or emolument, bribe, or hope of fame could turn his mind from its fascinations for one single hour. He did not commit petty thefts as on former occasions, nor engage in others of a more dangerous character designated grand larceny; but he designed new means for their execution by others, arranged an organization of thieves, and contemplated future progress for its members when he would have them bound by crime and directed by craft. He brought thievery down to a scientific basis. What he had seen of human life justified him, perhaps, in doing this — measured according to the peculiar formation of his mind and the drift of his philosophy. Everywhere he turned he found thieves or those who would be thieves had chance given them a fair opportunity. The field was extensive, the mission great. He would organize a society of thieves; teach them principles of cohesion, faithfulness, and many others found prominent in the moral code; and to the people of this organization he would be a Christ, carrying conviction to their understandings by his unswerving fidelity to the letter of what he taught. To his knowledge, there was a criminal world permeating all else, corresponding to evil as associated or existing side by side in the same universe with good. This criminal phase of human life would never be eradicated. It had existed through all time, and would remain forever. Some individuals are born predisposed to criminality; they become criminal as a matter of choice, love its requirements, and die thoroughly debased without having felt throughout their whole lives one genial gleam of God's beneficence. This was a part of the philosophy of Hamilton Hitch. These were some of the facts on which he reflected and for whose purposes he became an active chief in the kingdom of thievery.

It will be seen from what has been written heretofore on the subject in these pages that his studies in this peculiar science were of a progressive nature and that the attainments derived from them grew larger in proportion to the increase of his social and political power. In Omaha he did little more than plan and resolve, but here we find his organization in shape and operating with greater promise of success than the Confederacy itself. In accepting the judgeship of the court of exigency, he stipulated for certain privileges. One of those was that he be accorded the power of selecting the men of his own guards. As this seemed a reasonable proposition, it was readily granted him; but mark the result — every man selected was a thief! It was the first time since his escape from the gallows that he had had a good opportunity of striking at righteousness with effect; and, uniting his experience of years with the dark, crafty knowledge of his nature, he delivered it a tremendous blow. The guards here mentioned were two in number — the first, called the outside guard, being composed of fifteen mounted men; the second, the inside guard, made up of a similar number unmounted, or footmen. Each guard had a leader, called a captain through courtesy; for, be it remembered, the members, any or all of them, did not belong to the regular army, but came into existence for the special purposes here mentioned. Their duties consisted in obeying the mandates of the Judge regarding the removal or conveyance of prisoners from a distance to the court. The mounted men attended to this service, while the inside guard did the work of cooks, cooks' assistants, orderlies, gravediggers, and the necessary cleansing of the entire establishment. They received clothing, rations, and pay from the government for their public services, and a guarantee of continuous employment from the Judge for their private ones. Thus circumstances shaped the course suited to the most sanguine hopes of Hamilton Hitch, and puffed him up with the proud reflection that evil was more remunerative than good and therefore more desirable.

It was wonderful how actively he began the business portrayed in his inner life when he held the law in his own hands. He formed a "lodge" with its staff of officers, its oathbound initiation ceremonies, its regular periods of meeting, and its code of by-laws. Whenever a new member was initiated, the members of the lodge wore masks. This was considered a precautionary measure, and had in it the air of mystery suited to the occasion. Every man in both guards was a member of the lodge; indeed, none other would be employed in such capacity. In the beginning, when the right kind of men were not available, the organization was limited to eight or ten, but gradually increased by the application and initiation of new members. It was a curious fact that it was not necessary to be a Southern man in order to gain admission to the organization. The broad lines on which the society had been planned settled that condition. It was intended for the world at large, and therefore must have universal features. Hence Hamilton Hitch readily took strangers into service. They were from almost all parts of the world. Some of them were criminals who had escaped justice by a hair's breadth; yet now that safety gave them a little comfort, they complied strictly with the rules made for their regulation. They felt themselves in the last ditch. They had found in the past the opportunity of evading the civil laws of the country, but here any divergence from the rules made by Hamilton Hitch entailed certain death; therefore they became as obedient as good citizens for the time being. It was seldom the organization reached its full complement of men.   Vacancies were created by sickness and consequent retirement by deaths, and the transfer of members to other parts of the country as civilians for the formation and government of new lodges.   All these operations were, of course, conducted in the most secret manner possible, as were also all acts undertaken professionally — that is, thefts.   Every member of the gang was instructed to note where any chance for a petty theft or robbery became available.   The case was then examined in secret by an inner circle of the lodge, and if found safe and worthy would be attempted by so many of the men as were deemed necessary to perform the work.   Articles of value stolen in one city were invariably sent to a distance, so that they could not be identified when sold ; and very valuable articles were held for a long time before being offered for sale, for a similar reason.   If money were captured — that is, stolen — by the thieves, it was divided among all members of the lodge according to the rank, standing, and efficiency of each.

Hamilton Hitch attained such eminence in the society that, while sharing in its emoluments, he neither took part in the thefts nor feared implication in them if any other members happened to be accused by the law officers before the regular courts.   This immunity from the responsibilities of crime was spread in the by-laws and emphasized with the threat of death in case it was disregarded.

We heard the names of the captains of the guards mentioned in the court when the Judge sentenced Herondine. It may be said in passing that they were Northern men.

Sternbeard was a little man with no special qualification other than that he assumed to know more than his fellows. This assumption of knowledge was a kind of fanaticism due to the smallness of his mind and the operation of a few facts upon it. At home he started as a quack doctor, but, feeling the insignificance of that profession, merged into plagiarism. In other words, he affixed his name to another man's work and claimed to be the author of it. To cover his theft more effectively, he selected a foreign author — a French writer on a scientific subject. What was more extraordinary still, he did not know French, but employed a French-American to make the translation. Nothing but a thoroughly debased mind could sustain such a character as this. This phase of thievery is worse than robbery on the highway, because, while it is a *bona fide* theft, people do not often view it as such, and punishment rarely, if ever, comes to the offender. Sternbeard's adventurous speculations carried him south; and, hearing of the court of exigency, he applied to the Judge for a position. When the two men came to understand each other, Sternbeard was made captain of the outside guard; for Hamilton Hitch, who, as everybody knows, was an ignorant man, believed that it was wise to promote learning with the hope that one day it would turn to craft. This settlement of his worldly affairs gave Sternbeard an unctuous flavor. He wore a sanctimonious air, as of one who had been gifted by the gods or born religious. He had also a little spring in his step while walking, executed so as to attract the notice of the vulgar and cause them to imagine him a great man. In order that his identity should be concealed as far as possible, the name Sternbeard had been given him when he joined the guards of Hamilton Hitch This was suggested by the fact that he appeared to have gone to some trouble to grow a beard without success. Some of the leading men in the guards, seeing it, turned the exhibition into ridicule by calling him Sternbeard. Notwithstanding the fact that he then and there discarded the idea of having a beard, and appeared afterwards with a shaven face, the name was accepted and held by his companions as appropriate, and he was called by no other.

This method of naming men also applied to Greenlaugh, the captain of the inside guard. Of the two officers Greenlaugh was the greater villain. He had been an associate of Sternbeard in the North, and had copied some of his methods. He was larger in stature, but smaller in mind. Everything he attempted was on a small scale, for, to tell the truth, he was the nearest approach to a genuine fool that any ordinary person could meet in a lifetime. As a plagiarist he went the length of stealing an obscure pamphlet on fishhooks and how they wound the fish that bite them. No man ever attempted authorship with a duller comprehension of its requirements and less attainments intellectually than Greenlaugh. He was flatfooted and slightly bowlegged, and walked with a sanctimonious air, as one gifted with the power of divination. When first introduced, Hamilton Hitch gazed at him pleasantly. He recognized by intuition that he had before him a man thoroughly selfish, capable of stealing anything or everything within reach, and devoid of all feeling for his fellowmen. For these traits of character he was promoted to the position where we find him at the trial of Herondine. He acquired his name through the peculiarity of his laugh, or smile. This smile played upon his features most while he contemplated mischief. It was he who visited prisoners in their cells and by false promises of friendship endeavored to obtain from them facts relating to the movement of Northern troops or any information that could be used to advantage in the South or in the lodge. Greenlaugh's features were square and soft, the nose being a broad pug, the forehead low, the eyes a bluish gray, and the mouth large. Those who stood around Hamilton Hitch at the first meeting heard him dub the man "Greenlaugh," and they all approved, because to their minds it was most appropriate.

When an applicant for admission to the society did not choose to be a member of the military organization, he received such instructions as were necessary to carry on the work of thievery in civil life wherever he had determined to organize a new lodge and run it subject to the rules from headquarters. On the night before the time appointed for Herondine's execution such an applicant made his appearance before Judge Hitch. It was after dark, just about the time the Judge had finished supper,— when, with a full stomach, he was seated on the veranda in front of his rooms, where some creeping vines had formed a shade and given to the breath of night a cool and pleasant feeling. The stranger stood behind the woman of the house, who came to introduce him; for it was customary for her to witness the Judge's meeting, when at home, with all visitors, lest some of them should prove objectionable.

"Here, Judge," said the woman, stepping aside, "is one that wants you on business." She seemed to hesitate about saying "man," because the visitor was a little person who looked into every corner of the house with as much caution as if he expected to discover a skeleton in it, and shook his feet at intervals, giving the impression to his companion that he intended to get rid of them before the termination of his journey.

The two men gazed at each other in wonder. There

appeared recognition on both sides, but each man seemed too full of past memories to speak.

Finally the Judge gave the customary sign for the woman to withdraw ; and when the door closed behind her he said to the man :

"What change has been wrought in you, or what has driven you here ? "

The little man smiled, shook his boots alternately, and answered :

"This has wrought the change. It is really so." He held up before the Judge's view a small triangular piece of metal suspended from a strip of ribbon. It was the token which, as the reader may remember, Hamilton Hitch had given Crow Whifton before leaving Omaha immediately before the war. It was the first step towards the initiation of the man into the society which the Judge afterwards formed. It was the sign that the novice had been faithful and was entitled to protection and membership.

"Do you understand anything beyond this token ? " said the Judge.

"I do," replied Whifton confidently — for it was he.

"How did you procure it ? "

"By study."

"What element did you examine ? "

"The criminal element. I examined the darker shades of life and viewed that which has been through all time. I saw the other side of good to be the variety of life which some call evil. I found it a great field, and knew you were a worker in it to advantage. It is really so."

"How did you know my designs ? "

"I read them off the mind of another man. One of the stable men in Omaha and I compared notes once, and we discovered what you were and the kind of business you intended pushing in future. We had inklings enough to teach a dozen men."

"You are smart, Crow Whifton. If you desire military service, I shall appoint you to a place over the heads of my two captains. I can make you major."

Whifton was staggered by the magnificence of this offer. He smiled, bowed his thanks, and answered:

"I must go north. I fought at Bull Run on the other side. With proper instructions I can carry out your plan in my old place at Council Bluffs."

The Judge appeared well satisfied with this proposition. In turn he felt exultant that Whifton should come so near the interpretation of his pet project without the delay incident to the use of an extra word.

"I'll endow you with full powers this very night," he said. "You must appear immediately before the masked lodge."

The Judge arose hastily to give instructions to his men in order that the necessary preparation be made for the initiation of a new member. When he returned, he had the woman in attendance carrying some light refreshment. It could be seen he had been moved to this liberality by some powerful motive — the one that had appealed to the secret working of his inner life; and, besides, every fiber of his person seemed touched to harmonize with his fondest expectations in that his society was multiplying almost beyond belief.

After some minutes spent in social entertainment the Judge conducted Whifton to the anteroom adjoining the masked lodge, where he gave him in charge to the outside doorkeeper, while he, the Judge, disappeared so as to prepare the lodge for Whifton's reception. The outside doorkeeper introduced Whifton to the inside doorkeeper, who in turn presented him to the lodge; and thus he found himself in one of the strangest situations of his life. The apartment was well lighted and commodious. Military accouterments hung on the walls. The officers of the lodge wore badges, each having been also provided with a writing desk, while the man who presided had his seat on a platform in the east end of the room. Although no coward, Whifton was shocked on beholding all the members present behind black masks. This feeling was aggravated when they began to move and speak. After a number of ceremonies had been performed and a series of admonitions delivered to Whifton regarding his future conduct, the presiding officer asked what testimony was there to show that this man was worthy to receive the first degree of the lodge. Immediately a door opened near the platform of the president and some one in a superior lodge dress appeared and said:

"I, the unknown and the gifted one, say the man is worthy."

On hearing this, all the members rose to their feet and remained standing, as they understood this to be the oracle and master.

It was the Judge.

Then the president continued:

"Crow Whifton, the highest testimony known to us has been given in your behalf. We consider you henceforth endowed with the first degree of this institution, a worthy brother and colaborer in the field defined by our great chief, — and may your enemies perish wherever they appear."

At the conclusion of this speech the Judge retired and the lodge resumed its normal appearance. The president again said :

" Vice-president, conduct our newly made brother to the inner circle, where he will make his request and receive the evidence of the power in the keeping of our chief."

Whifton was led through the door where the Judge had recently appeared, and instructed by his guide to make any request he wished as a memento, or remembrance, of his initiation.

" What is it you desire?" asked the Judge, who, as a kind of high priest of the proceedings, remained masked and clothed as he had appeared recently before the lodge.

Whifton felt dazed for an instant, like some poor wight who had suddenly come into the possession of a large fortune. It seemed incredible that the possibility of what he wished to ask was within his reach. In a voice that trembled with emotion he said :

" I demand the release of Herondine ! "

As if a thunderclap had struck the house the Judge gave an exclamation of surprise. It resembled the groan of a man robbed of his money.

" Herondine belongs to the Confederacy," said the Judge.

" This is why the exercise of your power will be made more conspicuous," returned Whifton.

" But I never reprieve. They call him who sentenced Herondine ' Judge Neverfail.' What you ask is too immense."

" You will not attempt to obstruct what you have worked so hard to establish?" said Whifton, growing more confident in the belief of his ultimate success. " The rules and

conditions laid down for our guidance in the society must
be observed to the letter by you as well as by us; otherwise
your commission ain't worth smoke.   What is the Confederate government to you compared with the beauty and
glory of your darling project?"

Here again the Judge moved uneasily in his seat and
whimpered as if his soul was held in some mysterious iron
grasp.

"Have it out," continued Whifton.   "Let your pet
scheme mature to the full extent; then it will mean something.   The men who lead, as well as those who follow,
will understand it is no half measure, but the ideal of the
thief made reality.   We care not for life or death.   It is
the sunshine of the heart that makes existence endurable.
This sunshine in some is darkness — which is a paradox,—
while with others it may be the instinct of committing
crime.   Herondine is a mere point that must not be held
to retard the business of the society for an instant of time.
You have power to release him.   The demand is made
under the most secret as well as the most sacred of seals —
that of united brotherhood — and you know it cannot be
denied."

Whifton ceased, and the Judge became absorbed in profound reflection.   Good and evil stood face to face.   It
was a passage at arms with the life of Herondine as the
stake.   Whatever power was claimed by the one, or self-
confidence by the other, they were here for a battle to a
finish.   Evil, as represented by Hamilton Hitch, appeared
to have the upper hand; yet when the difficulty between
the two came to be examined logically, the pleasant light
of good began to appear to the discomfiture of its opponent, like the dawn above the mountain top in the face of

night. The little man Whifton made a simple motion in behalf of good, and the whole institution of the other side trembled to its center. All the security of composure calculated on by the chief availed not when a plea for rectitude came up for consideration. He found his position untenable, his reasons flimsy pretenses, and a coil of anxiety winding round his affairs, threatening disastrous consequences.

"There is a difficulty impossible to surmount," resumed the Judge, "in Herondine's case. I pledged my word to the detective bureau that I would witness the lowering of his coffin into the grave tomorrow morning, and I cannot withdraw my promise."

"That can be easily met," returned Whifton. "The coffin intended for Herondine can be carried to the grave and buried, but he need not be in it — don't you see?"

"Ah, Whifton, you should be major here," said the Judge, with a long-drawn sigh. "You have defeated me on my own ground, but I admire you all the same."

After the adjournment of the lodge, Whifton's plan for Herondine's release became known to the members of it, and preparations were made by the outside guard to escort him through the Confederate lines.

CHAPTER XXIV.

A PECULIAR NIGHT BIRD.

IT was late in the night when Aunt Frill and her companions lost hope of Herondine gaining his liberty. As intimated in a previous chapter, they had settled down to the indulgence of extreme grief when it became understood that no one to whom application had been made was willing to undertake the pleading of so complicated a çase as his lest the intercessor should invoke unforeseen trouble on himself. To avoid attracting undue attention while mourning for the fate of their dear relative, the lights were extinguished in the sitting room and the ladies congregated in the recess of a large bay window overlooking one of the streets of the city. Aunt Frill, although imbued with as deep sorrow as Grace Herondine or Aunt Funton, yet out of curiosity peered into the night and listened to its combination of sounds.

From the distance deep-toned noises came to the ears, varied and startling, as if heavy cannon were jolted against the earth and great wagons laden with material were rolled over the macadamized roads. At intervals there were heard lesser sounds — the tread of troops of horse, the hammering of workmen on wooden structures, or the accidental jar of two substances in collision. Aunt Frill knew what these meant — the building of fortifications around Richmond. On the street in their immediate vicinity, the stream of pedestrians had grown gradually less as the night advanced, like the thinning out of leaves from the trees by the first blasts of autumn winds. It was singular how this decreasing of individuals on the sidewalks seemed to follow a universal law. At the midnight hour the moving mass had disappeared, but, strange to say, a new phase of human life was just beginning to exhibit itself. Here and there could be detected a listless wanderer whose direction and aim seemed purposeless. Some of these strollers had been ejected from saloons in such a maudlin condition as to be unable to determine where they were going; others seemed intent on seeking an open hostelry as a substitute for the

place just left, in the hope of meeting some boon companion and continuing their carousal; while a third class found
comfort or heart solace in the shadow of the tall buildings
of obscure streets where narrow lanes and alleys abounded,
dyed black in the darkness of night, in the absence of their
fellow-men, in the silence and irresponsibility of their surroundings, and in the reflection, ignorantly foolish in
itself, that God was not there. Aunt Frill also knew that
these unfortunates had been called "night birds," and that
they were not inhabitants of any one particular city, but
could be detected everywhere on the face of the earth where
large congregations of people resided with or without civilization.

While cogitating on this curious fact, Aunt Frill saw two
horsemen ride suddenly into view. They appeared to be
bearers of important news, and to follow the custom of
army men by their fearless demeanor, quick movements,
and nonchalant air, for their faces were turned towards
each other as if they were engaged in conversation. These
minute details had no more than taken possession of her
mind when she experienced a genuine surprise. The
horsemen pulled up in front of the house! One of the
men, dismounting, threw his bridle reins to his companion
and proceeded to pull off his gloves, or gauntlets, such as
troopers wear. Aunt Frill could perceive that he was
quite a small man, and muffled so as to conceal his features.
Irresistibly the sentence flashed through her thoughts,
"This is a peculiar night bird"; but she arose in much
agitation, telling her companions that messengers were
before the front door, possibly carrying some news of
Herondine. This revelation caused a general disturbance
among the ladies, for it was the last incident they expected

to occur of all probable or possible. Hearing a knocking on the street door, Aunt Frill threw up the window and inquired the purport of the visit and the purpose of the visitor.

"Is there a lady here with two aunts?" said the man.

"Yes," answered Aunt Frill, "Mrs. Grace Herondine."

The trooper raised his hand as a signal of silence, saying as he did so:

"Please, madam, don't mention names. However, it will save further questioning. It is really so. Tell the lady to step forward.'

Aunt Frill retired and Grace Herondine appeared at the window. The little trooper held some papers in his hand, but with the other he drew the muffling closer around his neck and seemed to hesitate before he began to speak. No doubt the form of the beautiful lady drove him into a surprise from which he could not instantaneously recover. His voice, too, trembled as he said in low tones:

"A friend of your husband, and, I may say, of yours, has appeared here within the last few hours and taken a great interest in his case."

"Oh, it is the President in Washington that has sent one!" said Grace Herondine hastily; but as the man shook his head to indicate his dissent from the truth of that proposition, she continued, "or, perhaps, the commanding general of the Northern army or some of the men whom my aunt has seen today."

The little visitor seemed distressed by this speech. He muttered some incoherent words that none of the listeners understood. He spoke to his own heart thus: "Oh, why did I come so near to her and have a part of my beautiful dream dispelled!" Then he resumed his conversation.

"The person is a stranger to you, madam, and probably ever will be. Our time is limited : listen to what I have to say. Your husband's release is assured; the why and the wherefore may be determined hereafter. It is not that he will be aided in making his escape, but that he will be given unconditional liberty and an escort to convey him beyond the lines of the Confederate army around Richmond. Notwithstanding all this, madam, the utmost caution is necessary so that this generous act may not miscarry or be diverted from its first purpose. Therefore procure a conveyance at once to carry you and your friends to the point indicated in this note written by your husband."

Grace seized the note, and, stepping backward to a light which had just been procured by Aunt Frill, recognized Herondine's writing. In this communication she was requested to repair without delay to a certain village, where he would join her and from which they could travel homeward in safety. As Grace returned to the window to thank the messenger, she was handed another paper.

"It is a pass," said the little man. "I understand," he continued, "that the owner of this house where you are rooming has a rig that will carry you and your people through the lines. This seems all there is to do."

He hesitated an instant as if about to add something more ; and Grace, on her part, was going to make further inquiry regarding the generous liberator of her husband, but said to herself, "Alton B. will know." She merely repeated aloud to the trooper :

"Thank you."

In an instant the little man regained his saddle, turned his horse's head in the direction whence he had come, and rode off in a lope accompanied by his companion.

Then there began hurried preparations for departure in the apartments occupied by Herondine's friends. They were so overwhelmed with joy that they spoke and acted like crazy folks. They giggled, laughed hysterically, and screamed in suppressed voices. Aunt Frill, who at intervals enjoined caution, was affected as much as Grace Herondine or Aunt Funton, but, notwithstanding, she attended carefully to every detail essential to the important occasion. In half an hour the party was ready and started under the guidance of the Southern man with the Northern wife, who had acquired full assurance that the movement was in every way legitimate.

It will be readily understood by the intelligent reader that the little trooper who carried the important message to Grace Herondine was no other than Crow Whifton. Through his interference the two guards under the command of Hamilton Hitch were ordered to perform extra duty that night so as to effect the liberation of Herondine before daybreak. The undertaking was difficult and tedious; but Whifton, the hero of the hour, worked with uncommon energy, infusing his spirit also into his companions for the same purpose. To secure the faith of the ladies in the plan he saw it would be necessary to have a note in Herondine's handwriting, and hence he deputized Greenlaugh to procure it for him. Greenlaugh waited on Herondine with the air of one who had been a special friend all his lifetime.

"My dear sir," he said on entering the cell where the prisoner was confined, "we would never permit you to suffer. The Judge has the reputation of being cruel, but you will now understand how liberal he is. He has just ordered your release. On the request of a friend, he readily consented to let you go. We are all glad of it, and propose to escort you beyond the city tonight. Write, therefore, a few lines to your wife, giving the necessary information where to meet you, and we shall deliver the note to her without delay. Of course, you understand we all must do things very quietly, on account of the unfortunate condition of the country."

Herondine could scarcely believe the tidings true. He wrote the lines asked for, however, knowing there was no compromise in so doing, and prepared for departure when his keepers deemed the time propitious.

"To whom am I indebted for this generous act?" he inquired; for he felt, no matter what his character, he would reward without stint the man instrumental in delivering him from death.

Greenlaugh smiled, but did not answer directly. In addition to his other accomplishments, he was a great liar —a fault which no amount of exposure was ever able to amend.

"It is not known who the friend was," he replied. "We all had a hand in it, because we hated to see you pass in your checks so soon."

"What a generous crowd you are!" said Herondine in a burst of enthusiasm. "Now that you remind me of the fact, I have remarked the orderly and good-natured behavior of the men in this establishment. They are all grayhaired, too, showing benevolence and sanctity above the average military man."

"Oh, my dear sir!" returned Greenlaugh, bubbling with suppressed laughter, "you have no idea of their virtues. I could easily spend hours at a time recounting instances of the goodness of heart existing among them.

It is a thing worth remembering — they even go the length of sharing each other's gains.''

At the conclusion of this significant eulogy Greenlaugh bowed himself out of the cell, leaving Herondine under the impression that the captain of the inside guard was one of the most pleasant and honorable men on either side of Dixie's line.   It was then that Whifton, accompanied by Greenlaugh, visited Grace Herondine and arranged for her transit through the city.   This done, as already recounted, he summoned the detail of mounted men designed to accompany Herondine.

In order to prevent officious questions from detaining them on suspicion of the real intent of their march, Whifton had a blouse and hat of one of the guards conveyed to Herondine with instructions to wear them and appear as if he belonged to the troop, as Whifton himself had done.   Greenlaugh was selected to command; and, the Judge having furnished the necessary papers which authorized this body of local cavalry to travel wherever their commanding officer pleased, Herondine, mounted on a spirited animal, started with them through the darkness on his way to liberty.   On the march the men rode two abreast, Greenlaugh being on the left of the front file, where Herondine had been placed, while Whifton made up the single file in the rear, closely muffled so as to conceal his identity.   Thus Herondine and Greenlaugh had ample opportunity of conversing on leading questions of the times, leaving Whifton to commune with his own thoughts on the past and future.   All these features of the journey had been prearranged, Whifton desiring on his part absolute immunity from recognition.   Herondine, therefore, did not know of him whether he had been long with the troop or a mere stranger, or that such a man as Crow Whifton existed, although, doubtless, he observed the strange appearance of the single file in the rear.

This singular reticence and love of being apart from social intercourse with his fellow-men made Whifton's thoughts valuable, because he reasoned not for opinion's sake but for the purpose of discovering the whole truth. This method, trifling as it appeared, gave him immense power. When, in Washington, he had heard of Herondine's capture, he compared the fact with some information he had obtained from the stable man of Omaha, now wounded in the hospital, concerning Hamilton Hitch. This man, the hostler, was a novice in thievery (for he had been approached by Hitch), and understood that Whifton was serving a similar term under the tutelage of the man just named, because he had seen them together during the balmy days before the war. Through this source Whifton discovered that Herondine would be tried as a spy by the very man from whom no mercy could be expected. It was then he became meditative, as seen in the hospital at Washington, and in due time came to the conclusion that he could rescue Herondine single-handed if such jurisdiction as reported secretly to him had been given Hamilton Hitch. During this period he clutched the triangular badge as a thing of value. It was the symbol of mysterious brotherhood existing between them, and would prove itself at the proper moment. If it had been given him as a sign of membership in a gang such as Hamilton Hitch loved all his lifetime, was it likely that the Judge would turn aside now from his ruling passion just on account of his position and surroundings? Oh, no, no! Whifton knew better, even though he had been but a dealer in trifles.

Therefore, reasoning up to this point, he determined on going to Richmond, satisfied he could save Herondine.

There was another question to be considered — indeed, the most important of all. Whifton was really an honest man : how, then, could he become an organized thief and be still honest? He would sacrifice himself, he said mentally, for her sake — his secret love. If she were happy, of what consequence was it whether he was within or without the ban of the law? Whatever transpired, the retention of his ideal love was a certainty. Besides, there was no other method possible by which Herondine could be saved; and, what was also singular, with none other than a thoroughly corrupt judge, villainous in the extreme, could this be done. Thus, although committed to evil through the force of circumstances, he would achieve an immense amount of good; that is, he espoused evil to win good, inadvertently stumbling on the far-famed theory that ''The end justifies the means.'' He did not question whether the good gained would be sufficient in the estimation of the Supreme Power to cancel the evil and leave a balance of good to the credit of the operator, because he knew not how the Supreme Power would judge him ; but his heart and his spirit urged him to the performance of the noble deed at any price or at any cost. His method would doubtless be condemned by his fellow-men. He was more or less, on his own part, terrorized by the easy transition from theory such as came to him in Council Bluffs to the reality of the first degree in crime in the lodge at Richmond, with its secret purposes, its brotherhood sworn to be faithful to each other at the expense of the people at large, and its stamp of eternal exclusion from that liberty of soul which every good man loves to possess;

yet, when he turned to the secret motive that guided him, all appeared well. Having secured the main facts — or essential truths, as they might be called — regarding the case of Herondine and his judge, the remaining details were easy of accomplishment. He procured a settlement of his account from the War Department; the good President Lincoln gave him a pass through the Northern lines; and as a civilian at large he made his way to Richmond. With his peddling propensities and knowledge of human nature, he soon found where Herondine was confined and the outward character of Judge Neverfail. We know what followed.

Whifton now felt like the hero of a great battle; his designs were coming to a close crowned with unexampled success. From the moment he stood in the doorway of Judge Hitch's chambers everything went his own way. There were opposition and contention, but for him there resulted no failure. Like what may be written of Michael, he had the power of good to assist him at the same time that he knew the vulnerable parts of his archenemy. It will not be difficult to understand this condition of success when we reflect that what Whifton had assumed to be true was really so, and hence when he came to conclusions he found them correct. The exultation of spirit which forced itself upon him as he rode on this eventful night in Herondine's escort was something awful. He was like one entranced by a celestial vision which erased everything from the memory but joy. Instinctively he recognized the beings in front of him, but his inner self was the custodian of his thoughts and the only witness of his happiness. How he chuckled behind the mask of his high coat collar and the deep darkness of night, free from the obtrusive gaze of the heartless boor and the sneer of the idiot!

The escort was challenged several times while en route to its destination; but the smiling countenance of Green-laugh, backed by the authority vested in him, removed every barrier and silenced the clatter of every questioning tongue.   It was the last hour of the night when the troop came to the appointed place of meeting.   The darkness had become deeper than before, as if it had concentrated itself for the purpose of holding further sway over the domain of space then in its possession, irrespective of the claims of any disputant.   Greenlaugh, having been posted in regard to the identity of the house where Herondine's friends were waiting, halted his men before a handsome residence which, notwithstanding the unseasonable hour, had a light in each of the front windows.   The captain, dis-mounting, advanced and tapped lightly on the door, which was immediately opened, revealing the forms of three ladies in the hall light within.   Greenlaugh, after a few words of introduction, wheeled round, and, drawing his sword, which is customary when an officer gives a command, said:

"Le Count Herondine, dismount, advance."

Then the soldierly figure of Herondine was seen issuing from the gloom into the light.   The captain stepped aside; and Grace Herondine, coming from the hall of the domi-cile, received her husband in her arms.   There was a wild and passionate ecstasy exhibited by these two people which the good only are destined to enjoy.   The cup of their happiness was full to overflowing.   Having tasted the bitterness of adversity, they had come to the understanding of the nature of true bliss.

Every one present, even the restless Greenlaugh, feared to move lest the joy of these two loving hearts should be disturbed by the slightest interruption.   Whifton's dimin-

utive form, as it appeared in the darkness, resembled that
of a minor god. There was a majestic air connected with
it, due to internal light, as if the mind had become possessed of some golden achievement unseen by human eye,
but far-reaching in its power to entrance with acute glad-
ness the sensibilities of man. Notwithstanding the gravity
of his demeanor, the curves bounding the outline of his
person showed one in deep sympathy with the principal
actors of the scene. Every movement made by the husband and wife was scrutinized by him with the keenest
earnestness; but when he witnessed their embrace and unbounded gratification, great tears rolled down his cheeks,
which the obscurity of the situation fortunately hid from
view. He, Whifton, had won for his love that which she
desired most. Therefore he had made her most happy.
The price paid for his own sacrifice was here given up.
His reward was on hand — that consciousness of magnanimity which in life nothing can destroy. The terms of the
contract with his heart on the one side and his conscience
on the other were ratified, and the greatest act of his life
was finished. Henceforth reflection would multiply his
joy until he became like a divine person, happy in a world
of unhappiness. Even the gloom which at that moment
encompassed him seemed fringed with purple and azure
associated with bursts of brilliant light more fascinating to
the vision than day. He imagined he discerned long
avenues of picturesque scenery, with glimpses of pale luster
beyond, and bright colors lining the hillsides and highways
to perfect a view that none but the great of soul can ever
behold.

Herondine, after entering the house, returned immediately, and, addressing Greenlaugh, thanked him and

through him the men in a neat speech. He then handed
the captain a purse of money as a souvenir of his good
will, to be distributed among them ; and added, if Greenlaugh ever desired service in the North, he, Herondine,
would most certainly secure it for him.

Shortly after he had ceased speaking, a vehicle resembling a stagecoach came up to the front door, into which
Herondine, his wife, and his aunts were handed. Then
the driver, seizing the reins, cracked his whip, which was
the signal for departure, called alternately the names of his
horses; and springing into the road in response to the
appeal, the spirited animals moved away at a gallop.

Whifton returned to Richmond with the troop so as to
obtain full instructions in regard to his new duties at
Council Bluffs ; for he had determined on engaging again
in business at that thriving point, being fully satisfied also
that a three-months' campaign ending in a great battle,
of which he had been a participant, was sufficient warfare
for a little man of his physical capabilities.

The sun had not yet risen when Greenlaugh's command
returned to quarters. Shortly afterwards a bell was heard
tolling a funeral knell   Whifton knew this was designed
to represent the burial of Herondine. From a convenient
place he witnessed the mock procession, and, looking up,
saw Hamilton Hitch in a morning gown gazing from a
window as Herondine's coffin was lowered into the grave.

Before noon of the same day Whifton received his final
instructions regarding the organization of a lodge of
thieves in the vicinity of Council Bluffs. As a mark of
distinction, Whifton need not personally participate in the
acts performed by the other members, but judge and direct
them like the chief at Richmond. Then the little trooper,

resigning his horse and uniform for the less gaudy habiliments of a civilian, journeyed homeward, verifying Aunt Frill's idea that, either from a good or a bad standpoint, he was "a peculiar night bird."

CHAPTER XXV.

A SPIRIT THAT RESPONDED.

IT was singular Furflew's adventures were as exciting and dangerous in his new field of operations as those of Herondine just related. Ordered to Saint Louis from Washington with the reputation of being an experienced and reliable spy, he was assigned to a hazardous duty connected with the military operations then in progress in Missouri. While he had Herondine as a guide and ventriloquism as a stock in trade, Furflew had been comparatively safe in the past; but now, when thrown wholly on his own resources, where the employment of sound judgment was an absolute necessity, he became restive under the self-consciousness of insecurity which his surroundings entailed. Besides, the detective force on the side of the South had gained a description of him through the sharp practice of Danderton Hitch. On this account he feared to renew the demonstrations of his favorite arts, but, instead, dressed to represent a traveling agent, easily seen to be spurious. On the third day after passing through the Confederate lines he was captured and his true character ascertained. The position of the Confederates being uncertain in Missouri at that time, it was determined to settle all trivial cases like Furflew's with the utmost dispatch; therefore he was led out to be hung to the nearest tree in the vicinity of the cantonment. On this occasion there was some show of merriment at his expense, one of the men asking him in a jeering way why he had not selected a profession less liable to elevate a body. To this and other questions of a similar kind Furflew made no reply. He had made up his mind that his last hour on earth had come, and hence it seemed immaterial to him whether his captors took exception to his silence or otherwise. As a solace to his mind he began reviewing his own life and calculating what he might have been if he had followed some other course. This gave him a little comfort, for the ideal carried with it atoms of consolation for distress far beyond the power of the real to produce. He thought of Herondine, of his cleverness, his patriotism, and the loss his death would bring to the ranks of the detective forces of the North. These reflections accompanied the preparations going on for his execution. It is possible his peculiar thoughts were evoked through that means. He saw the rope with a noose, the barrel upon which he was to stand, and the tree from whose stout limb he would end his career on earth. Nay, he mounted the barrel; the rope was placed around his neck; his hands were tied behind his back; and the executioner was about to secure the other end of the rope to the tree, judging the proper distance, when a man in the crowd made a movement demanding a little delay, as if he had not been fully satisfied of the guilt of the accused. The question was then propounded for Furflew:

"Have you any friend that would volunteer to say a word in your behalf?"

Furflew started as if awakened from a dream. His mind flew to several persons in succession, but as quickly did he turn away from them, concluding that the mention of their names could not serve him in the present emergency. He thought of his wife, from whom he had divorced himself. Perhaps she had come west and would influence the persons concerned in his present difficulties so as to induce them to set him at liberty; but when he fixed his thoughts on her as a possible companion in the future, he raised his eyes to heaven and prayed, ' O God, if she is coming, let me go out by way of the rope!" He thought also of Saracen Gay and Flappins; but he remembered when he quitted Washington these Southern friends of his were in that city, and he was afraid to mention them lest on investigation his captors might become acquainted with his real character. Seeing the quandary in which Furflew was involved, the executioner shook the rope, thinking that additional fear might possibly aid him in finding an answer. This rude method of calculation seemed to produce good results, for presently Furflew raised his head and replied:

" The one man on earth who ever gave me an insight into human power was Rob Riddleton. If he were here, he would speak for me, you bet."

Immediately on hearing these words every countenance changed expression, and, for the matter of that, every tongue repeated the words, "Rob Riddleton!" with the utmost surprise. These were trivial incidents, however, compared with what then transpired, as if the spirit of Rob Riddleton had responded to the call There was seen coming into camp a horseman dashing along at full gallop. Furflew had seen that horseman once before, coursing between the lines on the morning of the battle of Bull Run, and his mouth opened in wonder, and his heart palpitated with expectation far beyond that exercised by the knowledge of the approach of death. Every head turned to behold the newcomer, for he was a gallant-looking man on the back of as fine a horse as could be seen among ten thousand. There was a brilliant luster in his eyes and a bloom upon his cheeks that a drawing-room beauty might envy. Some of the men, taking off their caps, shouted, "Welcome, Rob Riddleton!" It appears he was well known to them as a Confederate scout; and on this occasion there was nothing to make them doubt it, for he was dressed in the full uniform of one.

"What have we here, Captain," he said, after pulling up in front of the condemned man; and without waiting for an answer continued: "Why, bless my soul! it is Furflew, one of my men. How near you came, Captain, to the commission of a grave mistake! I heard of this little affair a short time since, and came prepared."

Here Rob Riddleton pulled a document from his breast and handed it to the man in charge. It was an order for the release of Furflew signed by the Southern general commanding in Missouri. The captain of the detachment, feeling himself actually in error, was not slow in setting his prisoner at liberty, with many excuses to the scout lest he should make an unfavorable report of him to the general. Riddleton assured him there would be no further words on the subject by him, and, pleasantly bidding the men goodbye, leisurely rode out of camp accompanied by Furflew. When a short distance from view the man was invited to a seat behind his new chief, and in this manner was conveyed to the nearest hamlet, where a horse was procured for him and the journey resumed. All these movements were made with the utmost caution and expedition.

As will be remembered, Rob Riddleton was playing a dual part. He was one of the chiefs of the secret service in

Saint Louis in the interests of the North, as Herondine was at Washington; but, unlike Herondine, he took extraordinary chances and boldly assumed the garb of a Confederate scout when it suited his purpose. On the occasion here related, he was absent when Furflew was assigned to duty. On being informed of the detail, however, when he returned, he saw in an instant that the man would lose his life on account of the nature of the duty if he did not send him aid at once. He concluded in this manner because he knew Furflew's capacity; and in his judgment his mission would be a failure with the loss of a man. The wonderful intrepidity of Riddleton, however, would not permit him to acknowledge the defeat of his bureau. He took the case in hand regardless of danger to his own life, and traveled in true scout fashion until he actually carried Furflew off from the gallows. The general's order was bogus. Notwithstanding his success, Rob knew instinctively that he could practice acts of this kind only at long intervals, and even then with considerable risk; for the detectives of the Confederacy were active, efficient, and painstaking. It was true many regiments of the Southern army knew him as a Confederate scout, but the most trivial circumstance might at any time reveal his true character and deliver him into the hands of his enemies. It was well that he took the precaution of beating a hasty retreat from the cantonment above mentioned, else he would have been captured in camp. What led up to this contingency will be seen presently.

The secret service bureau of the South entertained doubts as to the genuine character of Rob Riddleton. Indeed, there were reasons and reports offered to show that, notwithstanding the fact that some Confederate generals con-

sidered him "safe" and "true," he was an emissary of
the enemy. Hence he had long been marked among the
suspects, and strict orders had been given several men of
the department to dog his footsteps with the ulterior purpose of arriving at the truth in his case.

When Danderton Hitch reported the capture of Herondine, it was seen he was an adept in detective work. It
was conjectured also that his services as a whole had been
so valuable he would undoubtedly be promoted to the line
of the army with the rank of brigadier general. As an
inducement to hasten this desirable end, it was thought
wise to commit into his hands the management of the
Riddleton problem. With this understanding, he was
hastily ordered to change station and look out for his supposed Northern rival.

In the field of his new duties the first news that reached
Danderton was the secret report of the capture of Furflew,
to which had been added a description of the man. The
mention of Furflew's broken nose brought to Danderton's
mind all the train of incidents connected with his own
detective service in which the spy had figured, and his
gratification and curiosity became so intense that he determined on seeing him dead or alive. With this idea in
view, he mounted his horse and rode direct for the cantonment where Furflew was detained, on the same day that
Rob Riddleton directed a similar journey. Thus by a
series of curious circumstances two of the foremost scouts
connected with the civil war were brought together as if
it had been designed to test their strength and capacity by
a hand-to-hand struggle. It was not more than an hour
after the disappearance of Riddleton and Furflew until
Danderton came into camp. He was accompanied by a

posse of three men well mounted and therefore prepared to carry out his design without asking for further aid. On hearing that Riddleton had carried Furflew off he grew joyous beyond description. He made no comment on the action of the captain in charge, but merely asked to see the order on which the late prisoner had been released. Satisfied with his inspection, and learning the direction taken by the fugitives, he at once spurred his horse into full pursuit, directing his men at the same time to follow with equal speed. At the village where Rob Riddleton had procured a horse for Furflew Danderton received further information of those for whom he was in quest. They were only twenty minutes ahead. This fact showed he had gained on the party on account of the delay, or slow motion, made by it from the camp to the hamlet. Danderton was further informed, however, that the men were well mounted and had left in haste as if aware of the pursuit. Inspired by his success, Danderton grew wild with enthusiasm. He laughed hysterically while tightening his saddle girths, spoke in a hurried manner to his companions, instructing them meantime in regard to their conduct in the anticipated conflict; "for," said he, while springing into his saddle, "the game is located." Then he let the reins rest on his horse's neck and urged him to full speed. The clatter of hoofs on the road accompanied by a cloud of dust told conclusively that his assistants understood what was required of them and were fully equal to the occasion.

Returning again to Rob Riddleton and Furflew, we find, after leaving the village, the chief admonishing the man of the necessity of steadiness in the saddle and swiftness of pace. There were fully twenty miles to be covered before reaching anything affording safety, and it was possible Rob's bold achievement might be discovered in the meantime and proceedings be instituted looking towards his arrest.

As for Furflew, he no longer possessed any sense of fear. His idol was by his side, and therefore it would be profanation to doubt his power in any extremity. Was he not the spirit that responded so promptly to his call when on eternity's brink? No other than Rob Riddleton could have performed such a wonderful act. It seemed like romance or impossibility. The glamour which encompassed Furflew's soul while witnessing this last achievement promised to remain with him forever. First, it made him dream in ecstasy, then voluble and high-spirited as if he had become the proud possessor of half the world. He raved about Rob, told him of Herondine's capture, of Saracen Gay, and what splendid success that invariably followed the exercise of ventriloquism, hypnotism, and trick of the loop.

While laughing at Furflew's quaint humor, Riddleton looked over his shoulder along a curve of the road on which they had just passed, and behold! at the extremity of it, distant about two miles, he saw a dark mass coming his way. Suddenly he became grave, gazing more intently at this suspicious object. Gradually its true nature was revealed. It consisted of a small body of horsemen riding at full gallop, evidently charged with some important mission. "Ah!" said Riddleton, half aloud, "they are pursuers, and we're the pursued!" Then he glanced at his horse, patted him on the neck lovingly, gathered up the slack parts of the bridle reins, and, saying to Furflew, "Come," bent to the distance before him like a streak of lightning. In vain Furflew attempted to keep in his company. After riding half a mile Rob came to the conclusion he must either abandon the man or drop into the slow movement of his horse and share his fate. This was a very unfortunate predicament. Rob's own swift steed could easily distance any animal on the road and carry him safely to his destination; but if he took advantage of these noble traits of his horse, the object of his expedition would end in failure and for the first time in this war he would be obliged to acknowledge defeat. Riddleton could not brook such disastrous conditions. He would, he thought, carry his designs through to successful completion or die in the attempt. Arriving at this conclusion, he wheeled his horse to the right-about, galloped towards his pursuers, and urged Furflew to greater expedition.

In order to make the man understand the situation, he said, "The Rebs are on our track"; and, pointing in the direction of the approaching horsemen, he continued, "They are right here!"

Furflew whipped his horse into greater speed. While he grew troubled as a consequence of hearing such unfavorable news, yet he did not lose faith in the power of his guide. Smiling through his excitement, he answered:

"You're worth a score of 'em. You can lay 'em out by the dozen, and don't you forget it."

It was at this time they approached a crisis. A short distance ahead was a house whose appearance indicated that it was devoted to the business of refreshing travelers. All parties viewed it with eager eyes. Danderton had gradually lessened the distance between him and the Riddleton party. He could behold the situation as his enemy reached the vicinity of the house; and fearing lest aid might be furnished

him — for Missouri was not then known to belong to either
North or South — he raised a rifle which had been secured
to the pommel of his saddle, aimed, and fired. Although
fully half a mile away, Riddleton's horse was seen to fall,
and his rider roll in the dust.

"We've got him," shouted Danderton, as he slackened
the pace of his horse so as to receive the congratulations of
his companions, who, besides according him well-merited
praise, cheered lustily.

When Rob Riddleton's horse fell he was within a hundred feet of the house above mentioned. Rob was unhurt,
and, after a brief acquaintance with the soft dust of the
public highway, arose and ran forward vigorously. He did
this so as to direct Furflew how to act without the delay of
an instant, for he saw something that might probably render
them assistance. It was a two-horse team standing in front
of the hotel, harnessed to a light ambulance, and owned,
no doubt, by a person refreshing himself in the wayside
caravansary. Without a moment's hesitation he motioned
Furflew to take the team. This order was promptly obeyed,
Furflew jumping on to the box seat while Rob took possession of the center of the conveyance. What was their
astonishment and dismay on finding, while attempting to
drive, that the horses would not move. They were a pair
of balky animals just abandoned so as to give them time to
get rid of their irritability. At the door of the hostelry
stood the owner of the vehicle smiling at the discomfiture
of the men, and in no way angry at their conduct, for he
was well aware they could not drive off. Furflew whipped
the animals to no purpose; but Rob, turning to the man at
the door, said, "I'll settle for this rig hereafter"; and the
person addressed, still holding to his first opinion, that the

aforesaid rig could not be moved, nodded an assent. Then
Rob seized the reins and began the whistling of a melodi-
ous tune that attracted every ear and soothed every living
individuality within its range. It was loud without harsh-
ness, exceedingly rich in tone like the exquisite note of the
blackbird, and rolled into symphonies one after the other
until the listeners were charmed even into laughter. The
time, place, and the danger threatening them seemed only
to add to its fascination. The musical sounds rose and fell
on the atmosphere with a sweet cadence never heard previously in that neighborhood; and if it were not known to
a certainty that Riddleton was the operator, the men who
listened would have imagined the music had emanated from
the clear sky above them through some unaccountable
agency. As for Furflew's private opinions in the case, he
regarded this act of his chief as the greatest exhibition of
human skill in an emergency ever witnessed, and, moreover, that it was far ahead of ventriloquism. The effects of
it on the horses were marvelous and instantaneous. From
the time the first notes struck their ears, the nervous attack
which afflicted them began to subside, and in twenty
seconds afterwards, at an encouraging word from Rob,
they bounded into the center of the highway and galloped
off.

The cheers that accompanied this wonderful feat had
scarcely died away when those of the pursuers were heard
with equal force and enthusiasm. It was seen that a conflict now was inevitable. Rob had no idea he could escape
by means of the ambulance ; he merely wanted to keep his
party together, as much under cover as possible, and to be
in motion while the battle raged. He knew how to calculate chances and estimate the value of smallness whether

it related to time, space, or incident. No sooner had he
gained success with the horses than he began to prepare for
battle.   He secured the reins to the front of the wagon,
ordered Furflew to lie down in the deepest part of it, and
unloosed his pistols.   Furflew pleaded to be permitted to
assist him; but Rob felt he would perform more efficient
work single-handed, and replied that he wished to have his
orders obeyed.   A glance at the back of the ambulance
revealed the temporary character of the covering — some
thick glazed canvas, buttoned to the sides and capable of
being taken off in an instant.   He undid the under fasten-
ings, placed his hand upon the upper ones, and was in the
act of detaching them also when an order from without
commanded him to halt.   With a quick motion of his
hand he swept the canvas away and stood an instant facing
his enemies.   Even in that short time he was not idle.
His hands sought his trusty weapons.   There was a fierce
fire blazing in his eyes, and his brow became dark like an
angry sky at the coming of a storm.   Danderton, who
was in front of his party, attempted to draw his pistol;
but like a flash two bullets whizzed through the air from
Riddleton, one of which passed through Danderton's
body and the other through one of his men.   Both fell
like saplings in the forest before the ax of the woodsman.
The two men left of Danderton's party bravely returned
the fire and seemed intent on continuing the pursuit.

"Go home!" shouted Rob, discharging his pistols a
second time with that unerring certainty for which he was
remarkable; and the men in question slid from their horses
into the highway dead or wounded.

"Furflew," said Rob, while he rearranged his weapons,
"we shall have cold chicken and a bottle of claret at the

next station. Get up, old man; what are you lingering there for? One would imagine you wanted to go to sleep.''

" I could worship you," said Furflew as he scrambled from his retreat and resumed his seat on the box.

Strange as it may appear, the balky horses traveled in admirable style during the remaining part of that day, carrying the party in the ambulance to the end of the journey contemplated.

The report sent to the Southern authorities of this little affair gave the loss at two killed and two wounded, Danderton being among the killed. Riddleton was not hurt. The property abandoned by him was taken charge of by the hotel keeper and accounted for. On arriving at headquarters, the men were highly commended for their conduct and given a complimentary dinner, at which Rob made a speech and Furflew exhibited his powers of ventriloquism.

In regard to future service, Furflew considered he had performed enough for one man. Besides, the department was engaging a large number of new men, and the first year's campaign was practically at an end. He therefore informed Rob Riddleton he wished to retire from active duty so as to recuperate and enjoy the ease and security of civil life. Rob considered the proposition favorably, and, when he sent in his official report, recommended Furflew to be accorded the privilege requested and a bounty for his valuable services. These were accordingly given him, and thus Furflew became possessor of a handsome sum of money, which, when added to the savings from his pay, would enable him to engage in commercial pursuits or purchase a small country home.

As Riddleton was on his part going to take a month's vacation, and the time had come to part company with his trusty follower, he asked Furflew what he was going to do as a civilian.

" Now that you remind me of it, Chief," said the man, placing the right-hand forefinger against the side of his head as if the touch implied the calling forth of great wisdom, " I'm going into the circus business. I can go through half the performance myself, and I only need a few more hands to fill the bill. Money? Why, there's barrels of money in it ;— and let me tell you, Chief, I'll get Saracen Gay and Flappins to join hands with me. We'll have the best show you ever saw. Saracen Gay is rich. He could be master of the horse — ringmaster — while Flappins was acting the bareback rider. They'll tumble to it, you bet, when I meet 'em. Why, sir, I love a circus. I'd have had one long ago if I'd had half a chance; but now I'll catch on for all that's out."

Riddleton smiled at Furflew's idea of happiness in civil life ; and with pleasant thoughts on both sides the friends parted.

CHAPTER XXVI.

SHOWING THE DARK HAND.

WHIFTON'S return to Council Bluffs was hailed with delight by the inhabitants. Short as had been the time since his departure, a large number of people were added to the population and several substantial improvements made. Railroad men and speculators were giving brisk prices for land. The town was remapped ; and without intentional irreverence it may be said also that it was mobbed. Those who did not know Whifton personally heard glowing accounts of his patriotism and knowledge. When encountered on the main street he was called "Colonel," and it was understood he had been wounded so severely at Bull Run as to be incapacitated for further service, although, to all appearances, he was stronger and healthier than before.

From past experience in Western towns Whifton had learned much of speculation, and he was satisfied the best way of saving money was to invest it in city property. As the amount to his credit was considerable, he took a hand in the purchase of real estate, and thus became at once identified with the progress and prosperity of Council Bluffs. This settlement of his financial affairs, however, was only the beginning of his good fortune. The citizens recognized in him a representative man, one worthy of any position in their gift, and at the first opportunity elected him justice of the peace, which carried with it the title of "judge." What he had dreamed of in early days reached him in reality, and with it honor and fame and wealth.

It was seen by those who knew Whifton best, that, notwithstanding his easy circumstances, he was beset by some mental trouble, either a burden on his conscience or a secret that could not be told. His abstraction was very marked. He meditated deeply, hummed love songs occasionally, and was heard to sigh like one in actual distress; but, as he never mentioned the causes of these peculiarities, it became the general belief that his troubles were due to his "wound," if not to the depth of his learning. To himself there was no mystery in these strange visitations. His burden was twofold — the sustenance of his ideal love and the prose-

cution of the commission given him by Hamilton Hitch.
There was no doubt his magnanimous conduct displayed in
the interests of Herondine brought him immense satisfaction and chastened his spirit to such extent that he could
feel the presence of some divine principle moisten his eyelids before he slept at night; but behold! his feelings of
love increased until they became almost insupportable.
When he told Furflew that he had found love "salubrious,"
he accounted only for the condition of his mind at that
time. Of the future he knew nothing, nor of the character of love that is fostered and fed for years beyond the
period prescribed by nature in which its functions are legitimate and necessary. He did not calculate on the love
that consumes body and soul as if encompassed by mysterious fires, that strikes the heart with as sure an aim as if
directed by fate, and gradually lessens the vital forces of
the victim until relieved by insanity and death; yet something akin to this fearful visitant seemed to confront him.
When he first began to study its true intent he was a prosperous citizen, but it made him tremble as if the shadow
of death had come to him knowingly. He made no
attempt to escape from it, but, like a true votary, clung
with reverence and adoration to its peculiar sensations,
whose intensity was certain to bring his life to a premature
close.

If the good, the grand, and the beautiful created such a
menace to the life of Whifton on the one hand, oh, what
must have been the threatening aspect of the conditions
imposed by Hamilton Hitch on the other, which would
bring all that was virtuous in him to degradation and make
him hate the hour he was born! Again he accused himself
of lack of wisdom, adding these words: "If we misuse

goodness, it is as bad as anything else. It is really so. The powers that surround love keep guard over it, and will strike if you come too close. That's what's the matter with me." He stood between two colossal difficulties, like one in a dark canyon with little to aid his escape and fully conscious of his predicament. It might be thought possible to evade compliance with the terms of the contract with Hamilton Hitch now that Whifton was among friends; but he knew that to trifle with the secret conclave of the masked lodge was to trifle with his own life: besides, the Confederacy was growing in strength and power, and who could tell what the end would be? Whifton was full of resources, for, as is well known, he possessed a far-reaching imagination. He began work on the contract problem. He would, he thought, perform something, however unsatisfactory it might prove to be, and take risks on the balance. As it was with his love, so would it be with his lodge. He would look upon it in a mental panorama and decorate its several departments with a full measure of the ideal. In other words, he would institute a mock lodge and call it a real one. With this end in view he arranged one of his rooms to represent a hall, placed books upon the seats as officers, and went through all the forms prescribed in the by-laws for a genuine meeting. In the inner chamber he presided personally over the destinies of the novitiate, heard imaginary requests, and bestowed the customary favors. After every detail had been attended to, he made his report to the chief at Richmond. His statement was explicit, yet so guarded in the phraseology as to be understood only by the party for whom it was intended. This account of Whifton's proved satisfactory to Hamilton Hitch, and, it may be added, to Whifton himself. It was as real as the burial of Herondine, having everything in it with the exception of the most essential factor.   Indeed it may be remarked in passing that such is the character of many an enterprise whose projectors never, perhaps, fully understand the causes of failure.

With the return mail came newspapers from Richmond announcing the commission of a great robbery.   Whifton trembled on seeing the heading, for he concluded the masked lodge was beginning to exhibit the "dark hand," as the nefarious practice of thieving might appropriately be called.

The robbery mentioned was a most daring one, executed in broad daylight, having scores of people as witnesses; yet not only did the robbers escape, but no trace whatever could be found of their place of concealment.   The general public where the criminal act had taken place were astounded at the boldness of its character.   Nothing like it was ever known to occur in that neighborhood at any previous time, and some conjectured that it must have been executed by the enemy.   The detectives engaged on the case followed up two or three clews without success; and after the expenditure of a great amount of conjecture, fuss, and movement, the daring deed had to be reckoned among the crimes of the unknown.   Whifton received an account of the principal incidents in cipher from Hamilton Hitch, but, of course, was obliged to keep it secret as he valued his life, and long afterwards learned its entire history.

Sternbeard, captain of the outside guard, drew up the plan, and Greenlaugh selected two men to execute it, besides giving substantial aid on his own part.   The person from whom the money was stolen was a contractor who had been engaged to furnish a portion of the army with supplies, the amount involved being thirty thousand dollars. Greenlaugh had ascertained the time when payment would be made, and was actually present when the robbers got off with the booty. The contractor was his "friend," a member of the social set into which Greenlaugh had insinuated himself at an early date on the representation that his Northern relatives were rich and in sympathy with the Confederacy. Some of the other arrangements of the deeply laid plot were as follows. The wife of one of the gang was sent into the city to rent a house. She was to pay in advance a month's rent, get in a few articles of furniture, and begin housekeeping after the manner of other wives. The first week's washing to be hung out was to consist of two towels, a dishcloth, a nightcap, a check apron, and a pocket handkerchief, not to speak of larger and more pretentious articles. She was to inform the inquisitive neighbors that her husband and her brother were blacksmiths by trade soon to arrive in the city, and expected government work. Care should be observed that the house be situated in a locality inhabited by business men, for, as is well known, such places are generally deserted the most part of each working day, the men being engaged at their business houses, while their wives are visiting or shopping. After this part had been carefully attended to, a couple of men were detailed for the principal work. They were, of course, properly disguised, having been dressed in workingmen's clothing. Some artificial abrasions were placed on their faces and they carried masks to be used at the last moment. One of these men hired a horse and an express wagon at a livery stable, the nearest that could be found to the rented house; and started for the scene of action at the appointed time.

After receiving the money, which was in Confederate notes, the contractor and his friend Greenlaugh stepped into a street car for the purpose of depositing the treasure in bank. The highwaymen were prompt in following. The masks were on. The men drew their pistols and demanded the money. The contractor, who loved his life much better than war, became stupefied at the presentation, but Greenlaugh protested loudly against the action of the robbers. For this interference he was felled to the floor of the car by a blow; but, of course, the scene had been prearranged for effect, and he was not hurt. When he scrambled to his feet the road agents had decamped with the money. Still Greenlaugh acted with consummate pretension to rectitude. Standing an instant at the door, he cried out, "Stop them! stop them!" and fired two shots from his revolver. At this juncture a great crowd surrounded the car. Policemen and newspaper reporters came up in dozens and got the facts from the parties concerned. The passengers were so much frightened that they slunk away through the crowd sooner than relate what they had witnessed.

In the meantime no one followed the robbers. They drove off in the express wagon as if they had come out on a picnic. They were actually out of sight, having doubled a corner, when Greenlaugh fired. In any case they would not have been hit, because there was nothing in the pistol at the time of discharge but blank cartridges. After half a dozen windings through the streets the robbers were safe. During the following ten minutes they left the wagon in front of the livery stable, having previously paid for it, and dropped quietly into the house where the woman had the first week's washing on the clotheslines and was ex-

pecting the arrival of her husband and her brother, the
blacksmiths. As a matter of fact, no one saw them enter
the house, and they were therefore as safe from arrest as if
buried under a mountain. They left no trace, suspicion,
or clew by which the officers of the law could reach them
in their hiding place. Besides, they were domiciled in a
"high-toned" neighborhood. A policeman searching for
criminals there, instead of finding anything of the kind
would probably lose his star for his pains. Where the
robbers were not, however, there was great activity in
searching for them. For miles beyond the city limits the
country was "scoured," and several arrests were made.
Tramps found loitering around saloons in the city were
critically scrutinized, and if the least doubt existed in the
mind of the guardian of the law regarding their honesty
they were "run" into headquarters in order to show the
efficiency of the work then in progress. Nothing was left
undone to capture the robbers excepting their actual capture, which to some of those engaged in the pursuit would
be the most deplorable thing of all.

One noticeable feature of the case was the eulogy printed
in the newspapers on the conduct of Greenlaugh. He was
described as "fighting the highwaymen single-handed for
fully twenty minutes, lodging three bullets in one of them
and two in the other, and would have brought them both
down if it had not been for the crowd." All the journalistic notices of the robbery agreed in asserting that if the
destinies of the South were in the hands of such able men
as Captain Greenlaugh success would unquestionably follow. Such is the judgment of the world.

The robbers remained for three days in the house secured
for them, feasting on the best the markets afforded, reading

thrilling accounts of the robbery in the daily press, and playing cards in the intervals. The supplies necessary for the occasion were ordered by the woman and delivered at the door in the usual manner. She was a cash customer, with a smile of happy innocence on her face, and therefore could command all the services available in the make-up of six delivery wagons, including horses, drivers, and assistants. Nothing in the appearance of the house indicated disturbance or criminality. The blinds were up; the glass of the windows clean; the woman appeared frequently on the front porch, ostensibly to sweep the dust off its surface, but in reality to establish the idea in the public mind that everything under her jurisdiction was legal or businesslike; the smoke from the chimney curled upward in as graceful-looking wreaths as if they emanated from the most aristocratic smokestack in the neighborhood; and the odor of beefsteak frying through a heavy margin of chopped onions often made the passer-by turn with delight towards the place and linger longingly a few moments in its shade. When public excitement began to subside, the transfer of the two men from the hiding place to their quarters was safely made. When it was dark the woman ran them over in a dogcart. Next morning she summoned a secondhand furniture dealer to apprize and carry off the household goods, and delivered the key to the owner of the house with the information that her calculations had miscarried and she was obliged to move. The landlord did not seem the least disturbed by such a trifle, it had occurred so often before; and as he had pocketed one month's rent in advance, therefore she was free to return to her original home without further tax or question of any kind.

When the members of the outside and inside guard assembled thereafter in secret session under the observant eye of Hamilton Hitch, great indeed was the rejoicing. There was a jollification such as is rarely enjoyed either by civilians or soldiers. In the technical phraseology of epicures there was a " spread "— a supper consisting of the choicest viands procurable and old wines whose flavor seemed to indicate that they had been fortified in some lone paradise near the setting sun amid rose-tinted light, perfume, and flowers. Excitement ran high. It could be seen that the glare in the men's eyes resembled that of savages, modified, however, by the presentation of good cheer and the further prospect of sharing a division of the spoils. Some of them ground their teeth from excess of pleasure.

The spirit of the occasion, however, was exhibited in Hamilton Hitch. He resembled a god, and with the addition of a few extra touches could easily represent the archfiend. He wore over his shoulders a cape of black cloth trimmed with fur and secured at the neck by a golden clasp. A star on each breast made of polished gold glittered at every movement and commanded attention through the fascination of a deep, rich glow which touched the heart of the beholder. Every look of the man, his movements, manner, and language, spoke eloquently of his triumph over good society, and pointed towards his individual cleverness. He fairly reveled in fame. Nothing transpired throughout the whole proceedings of the robbery to interfere in the least degree with its success — a circumstance heretofore unknown in connection with such cases — and, as a matter of course, the credit of it was due to him first and to Sternbeard next for attending to the correct mapping of the details. Nor was Greenlaugh left unnoticed. Hamilton Hitch took occasion to speak of him in glowing terms, pointing out specially the cleverness displayed by him throughout the very difficult part he had to perform, and every man present cheered lustily to show his appreciation of his merits.

Sternbeard and Greenlaugh sat side by side at the supper table. While they appeared interested occasionally in the remarks of others, the drift of their own conversation lay between themselves. Greenlaugh was a great talker, while, on the other hand, Sternbeard excelled in listening. Greenlaugh magnified small things, showing the light character of his intelligence, and hence he clattered for hours on a subject that an ordinary conversationalist could sum up in ten minutes. He appeared to possess the rare gift also of conducting two processes of the mind at the same time — listening to the conversation of another and speaking on his own account, although it might be doubted if the first of these was really anything but pretense. He possessed a restless soul, like one stung into activity by hereditary meanness or acquired evil whose virulence kept it eternally in motion. As an instance of this, it may be pointed out that while all his companions had resigned themselves to the pleasures of the hour Greenlaugh was whispering into the ear of Sternbeard the terms of a new plot. This was no other than the introduction of a bunko game among the men so as to win their money. Sternbeard listened to the proposition with much gravity, as if the solution of an intricate problem had quenched the fire of his mirth, but his cold heart nevertheless quickened its pulsations on reflecting how easily and without offense the treasure could be secured in the manner described. As a further inducement favorable to the scheme, Greenlaugh represented that they could employ two of the men to conduct the game at a fair rate of compensation, and divide the great bulk of the gains among themselves. He said there were a couple of poker players in his guard on whom they could depend for secrecy and to whom he had already spoken on the subject. These men had been notorious sharps in civil life, as well as being pals; and if there was anything more than another for which they were distinguished, it was that they sold out, deceived, and robbed their associates whenever a favorable opportunity presented itself — a trait of character seldom found even among thieves. On this account they were reckoned the most dangerous men in the whole crowd. Furthermore they acted as spies on the conduct of their companions, often giving secret information to the captains concerning some of the men that was actually false, so as to promote prejudice and enmity that might possibly be turned to future use against them. Of these two underlings the man named Lorraf was Greenlaugh's favorite. He was diminutive in size, but offset this deficiency by being a most despicable criminal. The last act he performed before quitting home was to rob his mother — an incident so heartless that ordinary mortals who read of it wondered why he was not stricken dead by lightning. Still he was the confidential man of Greenlaugh, and the person who stood first in his esteem, if the estimate of the fellow could be called such. Rinz, the other man, was tamer in his iniquity. In conversing with people, he made an attempt to reason, and ordinarily he was polite; but theft in any shape or under any circumstances was congenial to him. Both men were gray; furthermore they possessed the bulldog characteristic features of thugs, and hated with all the strength in their possession the appearance or presence of a good man. Sternbeard having favored the scheme sketched by Greenlaugh, it was further agreed to obtain the permission of the chief, so as to legalize the transaction. In making the formal application, Greenlaugh represented that the men desired the privilege of playing their favorite games, to which Hamilton Hitch made no objection, as he saw there would be no infringement on any of his rules; besides, gambling bore so close a relationship to theft that he was rather inclined to encourage its practice.

When the sumptuous repast ended there was a division made of the money. Three of the men with musical instruments played favorite airs during the distribution, making the occasion one to be long remembered. Hamilton Hitch retired early. His share of the booty amounted to one fifth of the whole, and it was his wish to gloat over this new acquisition alone, where he might chuckle or laugh to his heart's content. The captains withdrew to the sitting room of Greenlaugh after giving all the necessary instructions, and the men engaged in play.

At midnight Greenlaugh looked into the common hall where the men were congregated, and found that the poker players had piles of the bills in their possession. Stealing back to his apartment, for he feared to tread heavily on the floor lest the noise should disturb the conditions of success then fully apparent, he stated the facts to Sternbeard, when both retired to rest.

The men played until the gray light of morning began to appear at the windows, then whatever remained unfinished was postponed until the next evening. Lorraf arose from one table and Rinz from another, winners of all the money gambled during the night, amounting in the aggregate to about ten thousand dollars. The losers dropped off one by one and went to sleep without a murmur. Some would have been content with the supper without money, while a few suspected that one or more of the men in authority was at the bottom of the game as an instigator. These soreheaded fellows determined to keep close watch. If there was to be any crookedness, they too would take a hand, and woe betide their opponents when they came to play the new game.

———

CHAPTER XXVII.

A STRANGE COMPROMISE.

THERE is a striking similarity between a great military campaign and mankind in general : at every rounded period or skirmish some one drops out for aye. Besides Whifton and Furflew, whose retirement to civil life has been already noted, Herondine found it necessary to sever connection with the secret service and return home. The strain upon his nervous system during his incarceration in prison and subsequent trial, where even the semblance of justice did not appear, went far towards paralyzing his energies, and demanded a long period of rest. His wife, the beautiful Grace Herondine, had also suffered severely. It was evident if anxiety for her husband's welfare continued she would probably contract some nervous disease, and therefore another reason presented itself urging Herondine to accompany her into the seclusion of private life. The authorities in Washington, fully alive to the importance of the services rendered by Herondine, readily agreed to his wishes, and furthermore conferred on him the title of brevet brigadier general.

This settlement of the career of a great character enables us to invite the attention of the reader to the continuation of the history of Whifton. Notwithstanding his physical disability, he studied law while a justice of the peace and was admitted to the bar. Still the two great troubles of his life weighed mercilessly upon him, threatening total extinction. The physicians consulted in the case were in a quandary regarding his ailment, for they did not agree with the opinion of his friends that it was due to the effects of his former wounds. In obscure cases of this kind it is safe to prescribe change of air; so Whifton was recommended to go east. This advice was agreeable to him, for he imagined, after considerable reflection, he could do a great deal on his own account to settle the difficulty. His plan was to consult Furflew. If learned men like the doctors, he thought, did not know how to stop his "decline," as he termed his illness, perhaps nonprofessionals would have better success. Who knew so much of the world, for instance, as Furflew? None that he was acquainted with. He had heard Saracen Gay call him "Professor." Did not that indicate that he knew almost everything. Furflew also was the only person to whom was communicated the facts regarding his, Whifton's, ideal love, and on such premises, no doubt, the man might possibly be able to prescribe a remedy. Besides, Furflew had been the companion of Herondine, the man of all others who had won the heart of Grace Finnestare by nothing short of the supremacy of knowledge. Therefore he had laid down the lines on which he would travel in quest of relief.

Traveling to Washington leisurely, he found on his arrival the city filled with strangers, and vast preparations in progress for continuing the war. The most astonishing circumstance, however, that occurred during his first perambulation through the national capitol was the ease with which he discovered the man he sought. On every available space designed for the display of placards could be seen the important announcement, "Bannister Furflew's Great Circus Is Here." "Great circus!" reiterated Whifton in surprise. "What wonderful luck that man was born to! It is really so. I suppose he has a heart as light as a bird." While in this mood Whifton soon found where the circus was located, and there, near the front entrance, he met his friend.

Furflew was dressed in flashy clothes. He exhibited also a golden chain and locket, several rings on his fingers, and a diamond stud in the breast of his shirt. At a distance he appeared superb, especially in view of his assumed air of superiority; but on a closer inspection his swarthy countenance brought him down to the original level. Besides this, the deep lines on his neck, the lusterless gleam of the eye, the lank gray hair and the partly shrunken frame gave evidence that other battles besides those of war had come to him and left him a loser.

Knowing there were several hours available before the commencement of the afternoon performance at the circus, the friends adjourned to Furflew's box office, which stood at the right of the main entrance, so as to compare notes on their respective situations. In reply to an inquiry as to how he liked the circus business, Furflew replied:

"There's money in it. As for liking, I'm never tired in the circus ring. I do the juggling and the best part of

the farce where ventriloquism is shown off. The people
laugh a great deal, and I enjoy it. I have your friend Saracen Gay, and Flappins also. Gay appears in the farce in
a fantastic dress, that pleases him, and his man is my bareback rider. In a year I calculate on stowing away about
fifty thousand dollars as my share. You see how it is :
people are coming in here every day, either as volunteers
for the army or on one pretext or another, and they all
want a little amusement. I saw the chance and took it.
That's all there's to it."

Whifton referring to the character of his patrons, Furflew answered :

"All kinds come ; and, by the bye, I had a lady here
a short time ago who was well known to our friend Herondine. In fact, it was at her house he roomed when in
Charleston. She was a widow known then as Mrs. Whirlston, but is just married a second time and on her wedding
tour. I forgot to ask the name of her husband. Then she
told me about her daughter Cynthia. Instead of marrying
Tuppins, a man that waited on her for years, she goes to
work and runs off with a painter who struck the town only
about two weeks before. They got married, of course ;—
but look at the ingenuity of the thing ! Tuppins is still
working with a farmer as if nothing had happened to
bother him."

Suddenly the two men turned to the subject of Herondine's escape. Furflew, who was vain enough to imagine
he knew everything pertaining to the war since secession,
pleaded want of knowledge in the present case, while
Whifton, rapidly reviewing the incidents in his mind, felt
he must keep them secret. Hence when Furflew said of
Herondine, "He could never have got away if he hadn't

had powerful backing," Whifton promptly answered, "It is really so."

"And now about yourself," continued Furflew. "You're looking somewhat under the weather, old man. What did you run against? or were you so badly hurt that you cannot get over it?"

Whifton, pausing before making reply, answered:

"My wound dates back before the war. Don't you remember what I told you about the ideal and the tangible, the lady I loved in secret and the good I imagined it brought me?"

"Why, yes, I often tried to recall the word that you said suited me, but could not to save my life. How did you get hit?"

"The feeling increased until it rests like a great weight on my heart."

Furflew, with a gleam of humor in his eye, remarked:

"How odd that the two of us should come out about equal — you struck in the heart and I in the ribs and on the head! The ideal brought you a dead weight just as the what-you-may-call-'em brought it to me."

"What made me come here," resumed Whifton seriously, "was actually to consult you in the case. Your knowledge of the world is so wonderful, I thought perhaps you could not miss knowing what would relieve me."

Furflew seemed flattered by this language. He coughed, while looking into the distance, with an air of self-importance, as if he meditated consulting some mysterious oracle suspended in the atmosphere or otherwise.

"What did the doctors do for you?" he asked.

"The first told me quinine was necessary; the second recommended salts for fifteen consecutive mornings; the third, blisters; the fourth, that I should go to the springs; the fifth, to stay at home; the sixth, powdered pumpkin seed; and so on until I came to the last, the change-of-air man.''

" Now that I think of it,'' said Furflew wisely, "you can join our company and get cured right away by having a good laugh once in a while. We can make a place for you if you have no objection. Start in to lead the big elephant ! ''

" Why,'' responded Whifton, " I'm a lawyer, and you know it would never do to be found in such company.''

" Oh ! '' resumed Furflew laughing, " that alters the case; for if the elephant knew of it, he'd back out for sure.''

However — to come down to the bed rock of the thing — if I can't do anything for you myself, I know who can. I always found him handy when I was in trouble; and he'll be the same to you, because he loves to do good.''

" Ain't he a doctor ? '' inquired Whifton, for the philanthropic character given the man rather confused his thoughts on the subject.

" Naw,'' returned Furflew contemptuously, " but he ain't the worse on that account. He read above 'em, all round 'em, and crosswise; so you can see how much he knows.''

After further discourse concerning the extraordinary ability of his benefactor, Furflew gradually approached his identity.

" First and last, he was my best friend,'' he resumed. " Twice he saved my life, and between times I learned more from him than I ever could from a dictionary or an almanac. After losing Herondine I joined him — but you must have heard before of Rob Riddleton. Now, Whif,

I tell you the best thing on the cards. We'll just take a run up to him and settle the matter in half an hour. Fortune favors us; for he came to the city yesterday, and I know exactly where to find him."

Whifton had heard of the celebrated scout, but was at a loss to understand why this fame should make him skilled in the diagnosis of obscure complaints and the application of remedies suited to their requirements. Noting this apparent inconsistency, Furflew replied:

" He'll tell you of the thing on common-sense grounds. That's all we want. I could go the length myself and hope to make a purty fair job; but you must be sure before making any change. Riddleton is our man."

After rendering this decision with as much emphasis as if he were addressing the big elephant in the circus ring, Furflew descended the steps of the box office and repaired to his dogcart and piebald horse, hitched to a post in the vicinity of the circus for his convenience, and into which he invited Whifton. Driving uptown, Furflew found he had risen to the importance of a celebrity; for a number of small boys accompanied by dogs followed his rig, and some of the urchins speculated quite audibly as to the position likely to be assigned the new man, Whifton, whose diminutive form had not been previously noticed in the circus establishment.

At the hotel Furflew had little difficulty in reaching the presence of Riddleton. The noted scout received his former assistant with cordial expressions of friendship, and assured him he was ready to render him any service in his power. Without making any reply to this kind invitation, Furflew placed before his former chief two complimentary tickets for reserved seats in the circus, and " hoped," as he said, "of proving in front of him the value of jugglery and ventriloquism," to which Rob pleasantly replied that he would probably look into his crib, the circus, before leaving town.   Then with a great show of mystery Furflew introduced Whifton, and the preliminary statement of his peculiar case.   Rob was amused, as well as flattered, by Furflew's great faith in his judgment, and listened with grave attention to the details so as to get at the essential points, the better to render a just decision.   He also questioned Whifton, who answered promptly and without reservation on all subjects excepting the name and position of the lady of his love.   These he would ever keep secret.   When all the information was in, Rob spoke as one who had been inspired with a full knowledge of the truth.   He began by saying:

"You must compromise."

Furflew, who was seated near Whifton in front of the speaker, said blandly:

"I knew it.   You must compromise."

Riddleton continued:

"Should you adhere to the original design of loving the ideal without reservation, you shall die a premature death. People sometimes call it death by means of a broken heart. The reason of this is obvious: you invade the line of the law as laid down in the universe for the regulation of love, all its requirements not being fulfilled, and hence the counterpoise contemplated by them never appears.   It is not recommended that you turn away wholly from your ideal, but merely adopt such means as may remove your physical suffering, with the chances in your favor of restoring you again to good health.   This remedy is found in marriage.   It constitutes what I have called the 'compromise.' While it is not a union with your love, it is, never-theless, a step further than where you are now in the direc-tion demanded by nature."

At the word "marriage" Furflew and Whifton exchanged glances, and groaned audibly. Furflew especially seemed rattled, for he remembered having given Whifton the result of his experience with the dreaded condition as a warning, so as to induce him to continue a single life.

"I am giving you the cure," continued Rob, "not my individual opinion. Prepare to carry it into execution, because it will prolong your life."

The silence following this speech reminded the visitors it was time to leave; so, after offering their patron profuse thanks for his valuable advice, they departed. When they reached the street and regained the cart, Furflew seemed very much dissatisfied.

"How I'm disappointed in that man!" he said gravely.

"For my part," returned Whifton, "I consider him very wise and very learned. It is really so. I feel it in my bones he has told the truth."

"It is not what I expected," resumed his companion curtly. "Why should he at this time of day tell you to get married, after all my experience before your eyes and when I calculated curing you myself through the dint of good times with the circus." ·

Whifton was inclined to smile at this reasoning, but re-frained from showing any signs of amusement lest it should offend his friend. He remarked, however:

"I would travel the same journey again for the same in-formation. It is really so."

This emphatic affirmation convinced Furflew that Whif-ton had been juggled into the unholy belief of which he

was then possessed. "Now, this is what I call real hypnotism," he said mentally—"a man to be brought over in
an instant from the side he was standing on before for
years." Then he added aloud:

"Well, I am glad, old boy, I put you on the right track.
If ever you regret the new change,—if ever you have to
skip, as I did, remember the elephant job is open to you!"

Soon after this conversation the men parted, with many
expressions of friendship that would endure and hopes of a
future meeting when everybody had become happy.

Whifton returned home deeply impressed with a belief
in the efficacy of the compromise. It was remarked when
he reappeared on the street that he held his head high,
stepped briskly over the street crossings, and tittered at
every silly expression within hearing distance as if he were
in full accord with its deficiencies and significance. These
signs made people shake their heads in a mysterious manner, many asserting there was "something in the wind,"
while deeper thinkers were ready to guarantee that a turning
point in Whifton's life was approaching. When, however,
it transpired that he intimated his intention of occupying
one of his own houses and buying furniture, he advanced
immediately from being the subject of innuendo to that of
table talk and finally became the talk of the town. He did
not disguise his intentions regarding matrimony; and the
publicity given them, therefore, harmonized with his
wishes. One of the vagaries of society, however, coming
under his observation at this time caused him no little surprise, as well as that it created a difficulty in his way never
anticipated. When the truth became fully established that
he was no longer in the field, but on the market, where his
individual liberty was to be exchanged for the blessings

showered on the life of a married man, he was assailed by a vast quantity of mail matter from the four principal sections of the city, in which could be enumerated almost every class of human beings rich and poor. Among these missives were invitations to dinners, luncheons, lawn parties, tea parties, suppers, socials, hops, and private theatricals by the dozen. Nor were these the only evidences of his progressive situation. The street where he resided was also an object of interest to the public, with such favorable results that it became a fashionable promenade. Of course, it would never be insinuated here that this selection had been stimulated by the desire of any one particular class to view Whifton's property, or remotely Whifton himself; but his own experience appeared to be that he counted on one occasion among the promenaders fourteen eligible widows, nine grass widows, twenty-one old maids of retiring aspect, thirty-seven new women, and scores of others married and single.

Whimpering to himself, Whifton remarked: "It is decidedly evident the 'compromise' is full of attractions, when one meets all this at the very door. I had no idea the market was so well stocked. Look at me — with one foot a'most in the grave, diminutive, ill-looking, prone to oddities and special diet, and thought by some Eastern people fit only to lead the big elephant in a circus. Notwithstanding all this, I can select a wife from the ranks of beauty, worth, and even wealth to my heart's content. Oh! it is a beautiful provision, no matter who gives it or how it comes."

Whifton went to visit at the residence of a rich farmer whose place lay on the suburbs of the city and who kept a hog ranch. The only daughter, who doted on title or fame of any kind, encouraged the judge's visits and always agreed with whatever view of a subject he chose to take. This species of flattery, or, as some uncharitable persons would call it, "soft soap," soon had its effect on Whifton. How he reasoned on the case it is not now necessary to mention, but he saw enough to convince him he would not be rejected; so he made the important proposition, which resulted favorably, and was married. Strange as it may appear, Whifton's physical ailments, and through them the mental ones, gradually improved, and in a short time it was apparent to everybody he would fully recover his health.

The war went on without him.

While the thunders of great battles were heard beyond the horizon, he wrestled with the difficulties of law on the one hand and family cares on the other.

Children were born to him as if, like European princes, the government were ready and willing to appropriate immense sums of money for their support. The Whiftons grew in numbers, importance, and respectability. They lived well in magnificent quarters, and were accounted valuable members of society. Did he ever think of his ideal love? Oh, yes! It was yet in his inner heart, but obscured and growing less, like the sun when he sinks to his rest, leaving in the western sky traces of the glory which surrounded him here — a beautiful memento, brilliant enough to be a companion of, and to mingle with, the stars.

CHAPTER XXVIII.

SEEKING THE OLD LAIR.

THE Pottawattamie County hospital, located in the suburbs of Council Bluffs, received into one of its wards, about the close of the war, a patient whom none of the attendants could recognize as belonging to the city. A farmer carrying some produce to market found him in a helpless condition on the roadside, and charitably carried him in where he would receive proper attention. The incident in itself was commonplace, for, unfortunately, such scenes occur with unremitting frequency in public institutions of this kind; but beneath the exterior forms of it, in the present instance, there lurked a hideous tale of one who had fought the world for mastery in the character of a criminal and had suffered woeful defeat. The patient, unconscious at the time of admission, revived under judicious appliances and careful nursing. It was found by the attending physician that the man had been shot in the left arm, that in consequence he had suffered from debility aggravated by exposure, and that it was as likely as not he would die. When his speech became audible, for he muttered a good deal, mentioning the name of Judge Whifton, it was concluded that he wished to obtain the services of a justice of the peace so as to make an ante-mortem statement. Hence a message sent to the Judge with the facts brought him in due time to the hospital.

Whifton walked up the center of the sick ward with a lofty air, as one weighted with the wisdom of the bench and the responsibility of protecting society from every species of attack known or imagined. The attendant who guided him, stopping near the foot of a bed at the extremity of the ward, made a motion with his hand towards the occupant of it, saying, " This is the man," and then withdrew. For a moment Whifton saw nothing other than a wretched countenance shrunken almost to death, but immediately thereafter, when the stranger turned his languid eyes upon him, he began to tremble as if seized by an ague fit. This was due more to surprise than fear, for he recognized in the sick man one above all others never expected to be seen in such condition; namely, Hamilton Hitch.

As if drawn by magnetism, Whifton approached the man and took a seat available near him, gazing rapidly round the apartment so as to ascertain if their conversation could be conducted without the presence of listeners. Fortunately there were no other patients in this ward, which appears to have been reserved for such cases as the one now in it. Whifton did not speak ; he only gazed wonderingly at his companion, while his heart fluttered and his brain became confused with the pressure of multifarious ideas within it. He breathed with difficulty—almost gasped— and the pallor overspreading his face was even more deathly than that on the features of Hamilton Hitch. The sick man, observing Whifton's condition, said in a strange piping voice, " You are surprised." Then, as one who had important information to impart and desired to give it regardless of the absence of comment or reply, he continued :

" When everything else failed, I thought of coming to you. I knew I would receive protection, not only because I favored your application for the release of Herondine, but because I felt you were always good. In the depths of the extremity to which I was reduced, a strange longing came over me to return even into the neighborhood of my old home in Omaha, where I had lived so many quiet years. This desire urged me still further with a hope that after a little time spent here I might escape into the wildest part of the plains and burrow in it like a wild beast. For once, per-haps, I would receive the full measure of my expectations.

"Before it is too late, let me tell you what happened in the South. Soon after that first affair of ours—the thirty thousand dollar job—it was discovered by the men that Sternbeard and Greenlaugh had plotted to win their money. This fact divided the lodge into little bickering parties as much opposed to each other as the contending armies in the field. In about a year after this we had another robbery, when we realized about ten thousand dollars. It was an open day affair conducted after the plan formerly pursued, and was quite successful. The person robbed was a banker's messenger returning with his day's collections and intercepted before reaching the bank. After the division of the money, the men began to play poker as usual, Lorraf and Rinz being the principal dealers. When it was found that the sharpers were raking in all the money, there was a row. Men drew pistols, and, after the use of some fiery language, fired. The two captains, about coming on the scene, were warned to keep away until the storm subsided or they would be shot. There was great uproar, and I was called down to restore order. I suc-ceeded with much difficulty. Some of the men threatened myself. It was found that Lorraf and Rinz had received injuries from which they soon after died. My report of the unfortunate affair stated that the men were shot by their comrades for mutiny. That covered it. I then gave orders to stop gambling altogether, but they were not obeyed. The captains found through private information that the men had formed self-preservation societies, so as to maintain what they called their rights, and oppose us during future critical periods of trouble. I knew that this kind of independence would ruin everything. It was anarchy within anarchy, and must end in destroying itself.

" It is singular how logical conclusions may be made ineffectual by circumstances. My plans were well conceived and calculated to be successful; but when tested by the ways of the world and law, they failed. This was because some item in the plan proved unsound, bringing disaster on the others. It was straight enough for a few fearless men to surprise and threaten and rob an individual; but to keep these fellows afterwards in line, bound down by rule to secrecy and forgetfulness, was the greatest part of the work. When employing the men, I did not take into consideration their liability to mental weakness, drunkenness, treachery, and other evil propensities associated with persons who have set the law at defiance. I have now learned that if you call forth evil it will strike yourself. Should you design it for the injury of others, it will turn in its path and wound you even to death, so merciless is it. Here you see the difference between a good and evil design and good and evil agents. The results in the one case will be beneficial, but in the other disastrous and death-dealing. My life was a delusion. I hated society; but this only made my own mind a torment, while the people enjoyed themselves as heretofore. Surely this was no advantage to me. Experience taught me more than anything else.

" I received frequent reports of the dissatisfaction of the men, due to the most trivial causes, and it was hinted that both Sternbeard and Greenlaugh were not above plotting mischief to myself. Thus it became apparent that nothing would arise to me out of my creation, my lifelong study of the masked lodge, but dissensions, threats, heart-aches, and mortal fear of assassination. There was another potent cause of trouble amongst us; namely, disagreement on account of variation in our opinions. It was curious to watch the way this seemed to be produced. While the men were busy with ordinary duty, there was some little peace; but when dressed in new clothes and filled with a good dinner, they ventilated the most extravagant ideas. The most ignorant men stood on their feet the longest in debate, and asserted positively that they would not believe anything but their own opinions, no matter what happened. About the time of these discussions it was suggested to me to permit individual members of the guards to go into the city at night for the purpose of 'holding up' belated business men or others who should have been at home with their families instead of in the street. At first the permit was not given or sanctioned; but the party pleaded so persistently that, suppressing my better judgment, I let them go. This break into my original plans proved ruinous. In a period of one month from the time referred to, three of my men were admitted to hospital on account of wounds received in their midnight raids, and six captured as outlaws and held to answer for robbery in the superior court. As they had been dressed in civilian clothing at the time of their oper-ations, they were not known to belong to my company of troops; but we entertained grave fears that some of them might peach.

"There never came a day that did not reveal some ter-rible possibility hanging over us of imprisonment or death. The war news proved a great source of uneasiness. From

having been confident of the success of the Confederacy, I
grew doubtful and finally lost all hope. The withdrawal of
the army from Richmond was the signal for breaking up
the lodge. The men seemed crazed with the prospect of
release from the restraints of the lodge, and actually howled
like half-famished wolves. Many had old scores to settle,
and they adjusted them with a vengeance. Sternbeard and
Greenlaugh were shot at several times by their own men,
but managed to escape unhurt, although their hats and
outer garments must have been perforated by bullets. They
went north. For my part, I was obliged to abandon
everything and take to flight to save my life. Even as I
fled precipitately, one of the men, seizing a carbine, fired
at me. The ball struck my left arm, fracturing the bone.
I fell as if dead, which prevented further assault; but I
revived soon afterwards and made my escape as far as the
Federal lines, where one of the doctors bound up my arm.
The balance of the lodge scattered so thoroughly as to
leave no evidence that the institution had ever existed.
It pulverized itself. The members were terrorized at sight
of each other after my control had been suppressed, and
slunk away singly so as to begin a new career among
strangers planned according to their individual ideas.

"Nothing in my whole life brought me such a severe
lesson as this castigation which I received at the hands of
my own set, fellows that I elevated to the distinction of
being my friends and brothers. Herein, of course, was my
error—that such selection and classification should ever be
laid on evil lines with the expectation of achieving success.
I felt I had been whipped at my best trade. Uncompromising defeat came to me at my own door. I could overcome
my enemies by the force of concentrated evil in my inward

nature, but when my friends plotted for my destruction I became helpless. Besides, mark my condition: I had grown old; I was alone; Danderton was dead; all my money, placed at the disposal of the Confederate government, was lost, without even the chance of recovering a cent on the dollar; the personal property in my apartments was valueless, owing to the disturbed condition of the times; and my life stood in imminent danger from friends on the one hand and foes on the other. On the broad surface of the earth everything viewed through my mental vision was black and threatening. Strange that at such a moment I looked into the sky, and the balmy influence which instantly reached my spirit turned my thoughts to other and better subjects,—back along the crooked road of my poor life,—back to the days spent with my early innocent companions,—back to my mother! Oh God! I wept like a child at such memory when held side by side with my own willful career, that had carried me to the edge of the pit and was about to throw me in. Necessity then forced me to consider if I had performed even one act that might be accounted good, and I remembered that you had persuaded me to liberate Herondine.''

Whifton, who had recovered equanimity of mind, interrupted the speaker by saying:

"It is really so; and furthermore, let me tell you, if you manage to live I might get you something. Herondine is a noble man, and powerful. We dare not now even imagine what he might do in the future if asked.''

A peculiar light gleamed in the eyes of the prostrate man, which seemed to be some phase of geniality created by the hope held up by Whifton. The semblance of a smile flitted across his features like the sheen of the moon coming an instant through the clouds over the dark surface of a pool.

"I thought of you," he continued. "Among other things, I imagined if we had been companions in the lodge, I chief and you major, you would have gradually brought me over to your way of thinking."

"How much better it would have been," said Whifton, "if we had been companions in civil life, living according to law and in full possession of the privilege of legitimate freedom, fearing no charge, envying no person his success, proud of our native home, and happy in the possession of plenty!"

The sick man made no direct reply. He mused as if seeking a reason to justify his criminal life. Then he answered:

"Teaching was too weak for my trouble. I never attempted to resist the infatuation which stealing held out for me. If I ever considered for a moment whether or not I possessed power sufficient to overcome this infatuation, when I came to examine it there was none. You must remember there are roses without perfume and oranges without seeds. Therefore something more than mere words was necessary to turn me aside from my evil course—some radical chastisement, which eventually came. When I had determined on my destination, I arose, and, catching a horse, for there were many of them in the place, mounted and proceeded on my journey. Passing through the scenes of recent battles, I encountered many difficulties. Feeling my strength giving out, I feared I would never see you again. A few persons assisted me upon my representing to them that I was a wounded soldier returning home. A short distance from town my horse fell unable to travel further; and believing that my time had also come, for I felt the weakness of death at my heart, I sank by the roadside and became unconscious. When I recovered I found myself here. Then I asked to see you."

"How am I to steer through the danger?" inquired Whifton in a low voice.

"Give them a card with this piece of information on it," returned Hamilton Hitch: "John Chiselton, en route to the Black Hills; wounded; paid off in full; accounts checked and settled."

Whifton, taking a notebook from his pocket, wrote as directed on a fly leaf, which he held for presentation to the superintendent of the hospital. Then his companion resumed impressively:

"I release you from all bonds, promises, contracts, or obligations involved in your connection with our society. I leave you absolutely free, and hope you may be happy."

Whifton rose to depart, saying he would look in next day.

Before he left the hospital, Whifton handed to the superintendent the fly leaf with its inscription, and remarked in an official manner:

"The sick man desired me to hand you this note, and requests you would accept it as his record, to which the superintendent replied, with a good-natured bow and a smile, "Certainly. Thank you," but, as if to relieve himself, and his honor the Judge, from the unpleasant memories of the case, inquired lightly:

"Do you think it will rain, Judge?"

"Ah! well, now that you give me the cue," said Whifton, "I believe we have had or will have a fall, but probably may be obliged to wait until it comes. It is really so."

The superintendent laughed at what he considered a well-turned witticism, while Whifton thought he had had a narrow escape from becoming ridiculous, on account of two subjects pressing his brain at the same moment—the fall of Judge Hitch and the coming of a storm.

Next morning Whifton received a message from the hospital that "Chiselton" died at midnight. Notwithstanding the career of the man, the petty judge was shocked, on receipt of the news of his death, by a combination of fear, friendliness, sorrow, and joy. The last chain that had bound him to a condition of mental depression fell broken at his feet, and he stood in the light of day a free man.

In reviewing incidents of his past life, Whifton saw clearly and forcibly how he had been rewarded even by circumstances for the act of rescuing Herondine. The trivial offense originally and innocently committed by which he promised to keep secret for twenty dollars the crime of another, dragged him forward little by little until he actually touched heinous iniquity, without, however, incriminating himself; but this was due to the fact that the peculiarity of his love directed him into a channel that ultimately saved him from ruin and premature death.

As to the fate of Hamilton Hitch in escaping the gallows, it may be considered by some persons a misfortune that he did not receive his just dues. To his own mind, there is no doubt that during the last days of his life, hanging would have been a relief to him as tending to cut off the mental torture by which he was assailed. In whatever direction he turned his thoughts, he met nothing but visions of crime, treachery, and debasement below the level of the brute. There was no beauty on the earth or in the heavens to administer solace to his soul, because he had schooled himself to live without it during the long years of his existence; and even now, while life flickered within him, he loved to brood over dark phases of human nature, wretchedness, and iniquity. His bodily sufferings, also, must have been excruciating; and the fear of pursuit or detection by some of his own gang made him feel like a wild beast hunted by bloodhounds! He died in the night —a time, too, when good men die—but with him there was no hope or consoling word or kind adieu or prayer for a place in the blissful state beyond the grave. The remains were buried in the potter's field in a grave without a head-stone or any exterior sign to indicate that the place was occupied save certain measurements marked in the records of the cemetery. The world went on in the usual manner, and the criminal was at rest.

CHAPTER XXIX.

THE RESULT OF FINAL REPARATION.

AS Whifton's mind grew stronger under the impetus of good health and freedom from terror such as had afflicted it in the days of Hamilton Hitch, he resolved on making final reparation for his offense, if such it could be called, in having had any association whatever with the thieves of the masked lodge. To do this effectively he believed it essential to consult Herondine, as well as that he would reveal to him the whole proceedings and get his advice. As on former occasions, there would be one secret reserved from exposure—his love for Grace Herondine, which was now so far mollified as to permit him discussing kindred subjects without pain.

At that time Herondine was a member of the United States Senate, having been selected for that exalted position in accordance with the wishes of the people of New York in consideration of his services during the war. Hence Whifton's journey east would carry him again to Washington—a contingency quite agreeable to him, as he delighted in perambulating through the wide streets of the national capital with the fascinating prospect of meeting war veterans by the score on every corner. It was a sight long to be remembered when Whifton, dressed like a country judge in striped pantaloons, diagonal cutaway coat, and piqué vest, stood at the doorway of Herondine's office in the Capitol and waited an introduction to the distinguished New York senator. The western man was a trifle pale, his face being also elongated on account of the weight and importance of his thoughts; but at intervals he would proudly protrude his breast forward, look upward as if critically examining the workmanship of the ceiling, and shake his little boots alternately the better to adjust the covering of his nether limbs.

Herondine's reception of Whifton was cordial. When he became aware that his visitor could supply what may be called the "missing link" in his own history, which heretofore was wanting and referred to the person or cause responsible for his liberation, he became at once deeply interested and invited a repetition of the whole story. Whifton's narrative of what came under his observation from the time he quitted Washington to the death of Hamilton Hitch proved astounding to Herondine. The accuracy of the details, backed by authentic documents in Whifton's possession, dates, descriptions of individuals, and collateral information obtained from Furflew and Rob Riddleton, made the whole statement very reliable and complete.

"You remember," continued Whifton, "the single-file man in rear of your escort when leaving Richmond, muffled beyond recognition? I was that man."

"Such heroism as this I have never seen equaled," returned Herondine. "I recollect the person well," he continued, "for I invited the captain's attention to him. Greenlaugh replied you had recently joined the troop but they had not yet given you any distinguishing name. However, I watched the outline of your figure before parting, and can readily recognize it now."

With renewed interest in the information obtainable, Herondine questioned Whifton on special points.

"How did you hope to influence Hamilton Hitch, in the first place?" he said.

"From my former acquaintance with him. I knew he was bound to have some villainous business on hand as a side issue, which if concurred in would gain his favor. Besides, I heard about his secret work before starting. I had a token left me by him at the time of quitting Omaha for the South."

Here Whifton related how he first met Hamilton Hitch as already known to the reader. Then in turn he questioned Herondine:

"How do I now stand in the eye of the law?"

"To begin with, I exonerate you," returned Herondine. "The means you employed to save my life, if free from any motive, would undoubtedly be criminal; but the whole history of the case shows the absence of criminal intent, with the saving of my life the only object in view, and therefore your action was not merely commendable but deserving a rich reward. Now, tell me further: why did you select me in preference to many other men then in the hands of the Confederates? Was there any secret motive moving you to this course? I was a stranger, residing even in a different state from yours, and had not the advantage of knowing you."

Whifton knew this question would come, and was prepared for it. He replied:

"I had no power with the parties holding other prisoners, and you were the only one under the jurisdiction of my man. When informed by Furflew of your capture, I knew by the description he gave of the party that the leader was Danderton Hitch. This meant to me that you would be carried to Richmond, and all the rest that was to follow came plainly to view. I admit no other man could judge as I did at that time, but this was because he had not the same amount of information. Your rescue appeared so easy that I would even hold myself a criminal if I did not go forward and procure it. It is really so."

This forcible exposition of Whifton's motives proved satisfactory to Herondine. It appeared wonderful, and yet the results as achieved by Whifton were so plainly derived from causes such as those that would sway the action of a thief like Hamilton Hitch that they could not be denied. Herondine was profuse in his thanks, and invited Whifton to spend a month with him in New York during recess.

"Many changes have occurred in my establishment since the first year of the war," he said. "My father-in-law, Judge Finnestare, is dead some years. My two aunts also died. Madam Gloriana left to join some of her relatives, and Felice went south at the close of the war. Mrs. Herondine is well, and we have three children — two boys and a girl."

Whifton apologized on account of inability to accept his friend's invitation, pleading family cares and official duty; "but," said he, "I wish very much to know the fate of some of the characters who figured with us in the years just passed."

Herondine, understanding the purport of the question, replied:

"Rob Riddleton remained connected with the secret service during the war. His career was distinguished by wonderful exploits, and truly his services were exceedingly valuable. Furflew made a fortune at the circus business, from which he retired after two years' experience. In New York he purchased a fine residence on a fashionable street, and joined a club where he enjoyed himself to the full extent of his desires. I was told that he died recently, some said on account of having eaten fourteen lamb chops one night before retiring to rest and during the progress of the club's high jinks. Saracen Gay, having seen the world in many of its everyday aspects, including the elephant of Furflew's circus, returned to his estate in the South contented and determined to remain there the balance of his life. His chief delight now appears to be the holding of dialogues with Flappins on all the scenes witnessed by them during their travels, thus living their lives over again, to their own great amusement as well as that of their listeners."

At the introduction of the names of Sternbeard and Greenlaugh there was a long pause, after which a lively discussion ensued as to what further action, if any, would be taken in respect to them by Herondine and Whifton.

"Unfortunately, I have recommended them for permanent positions," remarked Herondine, "not knowing their real character; But as their associates are all honorable men, they may not in future swerve from the paths of duty and rectitude. Now," he continued impressively, "we come to you. Your action in my behalf has made you great. The consciousness of it must be a source of gratification to you during your life and a kind of ideal heirloom in the history of your family for ages in the future. Moreover, it is only proper that you be suitably rewarded for deeds that few men would undertake to perform. Through my influence with the President, and in acknowledgment of your valuable services, I shall have you appointed United States district judge in the district in which you are now a justice of the peace. This will be a permanent position, and enable you to live comfortably, enjoying at the same time honor and renown."

Whifton turned pale with delight at the announcement. To him it was the unexpected. What he had sought in these latter days—namely, health and peace—he had found as soon as he understood how to comply with natural law, thus reconciling him to the belief that the practice of good deeds will surely bring an earthly reward. Now, however, a great source of emolument as well as a great dignity was going to be thrust upon him as if to elevate his mind beyond the limits assigned to those of men, to charm his soul with the emotion of fame and his heart with the liberality of wealth. He was amazed at fate—if this approaching prosperity was any sign of its existence—or that peculiar train of circumstances which followed his actions and finally laid such immense treasures at his feet. What had he done? he asked himself. Simply played a

straight game, never reneging once. That was all. And
for this heaven and earth seemed moved simultaneously,
impelled by a common desire to offer him the rarest gifts
in their possession. Oh, how blind are those who espouse
the methods of a villain in the expectation of gaining
anything, whereas by a little wisdom exercised in one's
own behalf, a little perseverance in the pursuit of right as
required by law, and a little patience, everything in the
hand of nature suitable to human life may be obtained, with
the power of enjoyment given gratis. High as was the
esteem, however, into which Whifton had been elevated,
great as were the gifts bestowed on him, yet he sighed for
the unattainable, verifying the supposition that, owing to
the varying incidents associated with human life by which
it is disturbed like the restless tides of the sea, complete happiness is an impossibility. In the plenitude of his joy he
turned back to the time when he first loved Grace Finnestare. How beautiful it would have been, he thought, if
these favors had come to him then. He might have gone
forward encouraged by the judge, her father, and heard her
sweet voice make music for his soul; perhaps have felt the
tips of her fingers on his brow, like the touch of an angel;
and — who knows? — he might have won her.

For three days Whifton remained in Washington the
guest of Herondine. He was introduced to the President,
saw the great public buildings of the city, and wandered
through the Capitol as if it were a fairy castle whose dome
on the interior had been beautified by a celebrated designer
named Jack Robinson. As indicated by Herondine, Whifton was appointed district judge. When the time for parting came, each of the friends seemed very much distressed
— Whifton because he venerated Herondine, and Heron-

dine because he felt gratitude for Whifton. So is it with the parting of all good men.

Whatever others may have to write or speak of American men in public office, it can be asserted positively that the two here mentioned, with whose history we have been more or less concerned, were honorable and just, faithful and true, and preserved their integrity pure and unsullied to the end. Whifton's record went through all the western country, and some lawyers ventured even to quote his opinions on the grounds that they were clearly logical. Whifton, however, died a short time ago, leaving a fortune to his widow and children, besides a good reputation.

Great was the surprise in the Herondine household when Grace heard the true history of her husband's rescue.

"I was almost positive," she said to Herondine when discussing the subject "that the President or the Secretary of War moved the authorities in Richmond to save you."

"And I," responded the husband, "believed it must have been derived from my friends in the Senate, or an individual friend residing in the South in touch with the executive."

"It seems almost incredible," resumed the lady, "that one of the people—that is, of the class devoid of wealth, influence, and political power—should be willing and capable of achieving such an extraordinary deed."

"It proves to us, my dear," replied the husband, "that even a single person, when directed by sound knowledge into the pursuit of justice and right, may gain more substantial benefits than a thousand men led by false principles and ignorant demagogues."

The description of Whifton given by Herondine reminded Grace that she saw him when he delivered to her a note from her husband and also a card of instructions on the night of their departure from Richmond.

"I remember him," she said, "and wondered at the time that a person apparently so frail should be in the military service without some special cause. It seemed to me he had been pondering deeply over a far-off subject, for he muttered incoherent sentences and once shivered as if chilled with cold. It was probably his strangeness that made him implicate himself in such fearful danger."

"Strangeness be it," said Herondine. "His action may deserve that appellation too, perhaps, but it is not the less meritorious on that account. I imagined the Secret Service had most power to reach me when in trouble, but had I staked my hopes upon it I were lost. It seems to me," he continued, "that Judge Whifton's achievement points towards an important lesson in human affairs. Men and women in all classes of society can render the highest service to themselves, to their country, and to the world at large, if they study and perform what is really right, just, and true to the requirements of law."

Herondine lived a long and happy life; and when he and his wife died, a great concourse of people followed their remains to the grave, which was situated amid blooming flowers, green shrubs, and grasses charged with rich fragrance, and where the gentle west wind afterwards came betimes to sing a pæan to their memory.

THE END.